# THE SCALES OF JUSTICE

## VOLUME II

EDITED BY
GEORGE JONAS

INTRODUCTION BY
EDWARD L. GREENSPAN, Q.C.

A Lester & Orpen Dennys/CBC Enterprises Co-publication

FIRST EDITION
SECOND PRINTING, SEPTEMBER, 1986

**Canadian Cataloguing in Publication Data**
Main entry under title:
The Scales of justice

Based on the CBC radio drama series The Scales of justice.
ISBN 0-88794-124-9 (v. 1, bound). — ISBN 0-88794-120-6 (v. 1, pbk.). — ISBN 0-886190-117-3 (v. 2).

1. Trials (Murder) — Canada — Radio scripts.
I. Jonas, George, 1935- II. Greenspan, Edward L.
III. Scales of justice (Radio program)

KE9304.S32 1983 345.71′02523 C83-098805-X

Design by David Shaw/Bookends East
Typeset in 11 pt. Baskerville by
Fleet Typographers Limited

Printed and bound in Canada by
Imprimerie Gagné Ltée for
Lester & Orpen Dennys Limited
78 Sullivan Street
Toronto, Canada M5T 1C1

# Contents

# Introduction

## *Edward L. Greenspan, Q.C.*

There is no better symbol of our judicial system than the scales of justice for it is these scales that represent impartiality and total objectivity. The use of scales to symbolize justice has been traced back as far as 2200 B.C. when, in Egyptian tomb writings, they were depicted as the instrument for determining truth. The significance of the symbol is always clear: The ideal of justice is often-times difficult to attain.

In this the second volume of criminal cases recounted in "The Scales of Justice" radio series George Jonas has selected ten cases which raise profound questions about the operation of the criminal justice system. Some cases raise basic issues of guilt and innocence; others raise questions concerning the fairness of the judicial procedure itself, both in Court and during the investigatory stage.

As I said in my introduction to the first volume, one standard by which a legal system may be assessed is whether it convicts only the truly guilty. Perhaps no case has raised that issue more starkly before the eyes of the Canadian public than the conviction for murder of Steven Truscott. The Truscott conviction, which was based wholly on circumstantial evidence, has continued to be a source of debate not only in legal circles but also among the public. It is the first and only case in which the Minister of Justice directed a Reference to the Supreme Court of Canada as to the propriety of a conviction, and in which that Court heard live testimony. With one Justice dissenting, the Supreme Court of Canada affirmed the conviction, but doubts remain. Much of the prosecution's case turned on the validity of findings made by experts. Evidence called before the Supreme Court of Canada by Truscott's counsel tended to cast doubt on the reliability of this evidence. In this age of increasingly sophisticated technology, where more and more reliance is placed on scientific opinion, where trial by experts and even machines is a spectre, the Truscott case may still give us reason to pause and evaluate the direction the law is taking in the areas of opinion evidence and expert evidence.

However, whatever criticisms may be levelled at the Anglo-Canadian system of justice, the Belshaw case puts in high relief the problem of the alternatives to that system. The Canadian system of justice is an adversary system in which the state and the accused are represented by counsel, and the judge and jury stand as impartial arbiters. Since each side of the case has an advocate acting in its own interest, the prosecution and defence place before the independent trier of fact the relevant evidence derived through the examination and, most important, the cross-examination of witnesses. With certain rules intervening to prevent some pieces of evidence from being introduced to avoid unfairness to the accused or to protect the integrity of the system, it is my belief that the adversary system, with all its flaws, is the best system ever designed. Further, by placing the burden on the prosecution to prove the guilt of the accused beyond a reasonable doubt and absolutely protecting the accused's right to remain silent, the Canadian system attempts to even up the scales of justice when the massive machinery of the state brings an accusation of crime against one of its citizens. After reading "By Reason of Doubt", the story of the Belshaw case, in which a Canadian citizen was tried in Switzerland, under the inquisitorial system, consider which system you would like to be tried by if you were charged with a serious criminal offence.

"I'm Not Living Like This Anymore" is the story of the Stafford prosecution in Nova Scotia. This case attracted Canada-wide publicity and raises disturbing questions about the defence of self-defence and the role of prosecutorial discretion. Mrs. Stafford had been physically abused and her family and friends victimized by her common-law husband, Billy Stafford, for years. Finally, she killed him while he lay unconscious in the family truck. One of the defences raised was that of self-defence, not only of herself but of her relatives. Notwithstanding the brutality with which the deceased had treated Mrs. Stafford, the Crown had chosen to proceed on a charge of murder, a charge which carries a minimum penalty of life imprisonment. Moreover, when Mrs. Stafford was acquitted by the jury the Crown appealed on the basis that Mrs. Stafford was not entitled to the defence of self-defence. The Crown argued, and the Court of Appeal agreed, that since at the moment of the killing Billy Stafford was passed out in the truck, Jane Stafford had no immediate need to defend herself or other persons under her protection and she was therefore not entitled to the plea of self-defence. The Court of Appeal observed that "the remark of Jane Stafford, after having fired the lethal shot, to the effect that it's all over, I ain't going to have to put up with it no more, was not in reference to any need to protect her son, but that she had brought to an end the problems which she had continually faced from her association with Billy Stafford".

The criminal law attempts to recognize the frailties of human beings and to take into account that, in some cases, circumstances combine to deprive ordinary people of their ability to act independently and make rational choices. The law of self-defence in particular is founded in this principle. As the Court of Appeal held that self-defence was unavailable to Mrs. Stafford, one way in which the unusual circumstances could have been recognized would have been through the exercise of discretion by the Crown in its choice of charges — by laying a lesser charge such as manslaughter, for which there was no minimum punishment.

Finally, after the decision of the Court of Appeal the Crown agreed to accept a plea of guilty to manslaughter and the result which should have been obtained originally was actually achieved.

The Scopelliti case is another self-defence case which settled an important point of law. Prior to the Scopelliti finding, an accused who relied on self-defence could lead evidence of the violent character of the deceased only if the accused was aware of it at the time of the incident. In the Scopelliti case, the accused, a shopkeeper, testified that he was attacked by two teenagers and was forced to shoot them in order to defend himself. However, he was the only witness to the incident and some of the evidence seemed inconsistent with the deceased's being the attackers. Fortunately, however, the trial judge permitted the defence to lead evidence that on prior occasions the two deceased had attacked other persons for no apparent reason and this lent credibility to Mr. Scopelliti's version of events as to who was the aggressor. Mr. Scopelliti was acquitted and on a Crown appeal the trial judge's decision was upheld. The acquittal of Mr. Scopelliti was not greeted with universal approval. It figures prominently in Jerry Amernic's book, *Victims*, the story of the Victims of Violence group. The question raised is whether it was fair to place before the jury the propensity of the deceased for violence. However, as the Court of Appeal noted, it would have been open to the Crown to lead evidence of Mr. Scopelliti's disposition for violence, if there was any. The Crown led no such evidence and in fact the testimony at the trial indicated that Mr. Scopelliti was a quiet, peaceful shopkeeper.

While I indicated earlier that in the Anglo-Canadian system of justice the judge stands as the independent arbiter deciding the case on the basis of the evidence presented by the parties, the justice system cannot always turn a blind eye to the manner in which evidence is obtained. In particular the courts should not countenance police activity which goes beyond the investigation of crime and actually creates crime. The existing judicial response to this problem is demonstrated in "Snow Job", the story of the Amato case, where the accused alleged that he had been entrapped by the police into trafficking in narcotics. The entrapment "defence" does not merely raise issues as to how the police should allocate resources — that they should be detecting crime rather than creating it — but calls into question the role which Anglo-Canadian judges have assigned themselves of *not* attempting to supervise the investigation of crime. To recognize an entrapment defence would be to recognize that the courts must intervene when the very process of the Court is being abused because it will be perceived as condoning activity which is unfair. In the result Amato was convicted but a divided Supreme Court of Canada, in upholding the conviction, left open the question whether in a proper case the entrapment defence would be recognized.

It seems likely that the courts will finally recognize that defence in light of the guarantee to fundamental justice in the Charter of Rights and Freedoms. In a recent decision the Supreme Court of Canada determined that a trial judge *does* have power to stay proceedings where "compelling an accused to stand trial would violate those fundamental principles of justice which underlie the community's sense of fair play and decency and to prevent the abuse of a Court's process through oppressive or vexatious proceedings". A stay of proceedings is not the equivalent of an acquittal but rather a recognition that although the accused may have committed an offence there are certain values which transcend the question of legal liability — values that require the Court to stop the prosecution, lest it be perceived as lending its support to unconscionable prosecutorial or investigatory activity.

The Charter of Rights figured prominently in the case of Cathy Smith. While the attempt by the State of California to extradite Cathy Smith for the murder of John Belushi attracted world-wide attention because of the high profile of the deceased and the sordid circumstances of his death, the legal proceedings in Canada raised an important issue concerning procedure in extradition cases. In any case tried in Canada the accused, except in very limited circumstances, has the right to confront the witnesses against him and cross-examine those witnesses. However, in extradition proceedings the prosecution may prove its entire case by way of affidavit evidence thus depriving the accused of the right to cross-examine witnesses. With the proclamation of the Charter of Rights, and the guarantee of fundamental justice, Cathy Smith's lawyer sought to challenge this procedure. Her lawyer felt that had he the right to cross-examine the witnesses he could demonstrate fatal weaknesses in the case. It has been said that cross-examination is the most powerful tool for exposing the truth. It would be unthinkable for a person to be convicted in Canada on evidence which could not be tested by cross-examination, and cross-examination is rightly held to be a fundamental protection and a fundamental principle of justice. Yet the Extradition Act authorizes the extradition of Canadian citizens to another jurisdiction to face charges of the most serious of crimes on a mere paper record. The extradition judge, however, ruled against Smith and his decision was upheld by the Ontario Court of Appeal. In the end Cathy Smith was extradited on the basis of this documentary evidence and now faces a charge of murder in California. Only time will tell whether the Canadian justice system failed Cathy Smith.

"John Down's Body" is the story of the controversial trial of Katie and Sandy Harper in 1982, for the murder of Mrs. Harper's first husband in 1959. Aside from the extraordinary time element, the case addresses one of the most difficult problems in criminal trial procedure: the issue of when accused persons should be tried together, as opposed to when the circumstances demand severance, or separate trials.

The general principle is that persons accused of committing a crime jointly should be tried jointly. On the other hand, when, as in the Harper case, the two persons involved raise antagonistic defences — each denying guilt and blaming the other for the crime — serious problems can arise in a joint trial. Whichever defence lawyer goes first in cross-examining Crown witnesses may be "caught in the middle" in a highly unfair way. All of his efforts to undermine witnesses damaging to his client may be negated by the other defence lawyer who can, in the guise of further cross-examination, re-establish the Crown witness's evidence against the first lawyer's client.

Beyond this procedural difficulty, there is the even larger problem of evidence admissable against one accused that would not be admitted in a separate trial of the other accused person. Although judges are always careful to admonish the jury as to the limited use of such evidence, there can be little doubt that real prejudice is possible in such a case. The courts do have a remedy for problems of this sort — severance of trials. It is a procedure often resisted by Crown attorneys on the basis of the additional time and costs incurred thereby. In my view, such considerations should *never* be determinative when the fairness of our justice system is at stake.

"The Thirty-Three-Thousand-Pound-Trap" is another entrapment case and, like the Amato case, raises issues as to the role of the authorities in the instigation of crime. Unlike the Amato case, however, in the Sexton case the conspirators were not enticed into committing a criminal offence which they had no intention to commit — it was more a matter of the authorities giving the accused a chance to commit an offence. This case does, however, raise the issue of the ethics of police assistance to and condonation of crime and, most of all, the allocation of resources for that assistance. While Gary Sexton and his co-accused were convicted of conspiracy to import and traffic in marijuana this conviction was secured at enormous expense to both the U.S. Drug Enforcement Agency and the Canadian authorities, and this expense was not merely the result of a complex investigation. Rather, a large amount of money was spent simply to assist the eager conspirators to complete the offence. The U.S. authorities not only arranged for the ship to import the narcotics but helped out when the ship needed repairs. While there is probably little doubt that the conspirators wanted to commit the offence, equally there can be no doubt that they could never have carried it off without the financial and other aid of the authorities. The question remains at the end of the case — was it worth it? Is the drug-importation problem not serious enough in Canada without the authorities wasting time and money to assist incompetent smugglers?

When racial prejudice raises its ugly head decent members of society turn against it and take steps to change the circumstances from which it arose. Sometimes, however, the victims of prejudice cannot wait, cannot turn the other cheek, and they fight back. "Game Misconduct", the story of the Smithers case, shows the tragic consequences. The victim, a teenage member of an amateur hockey team, and a good and decent boy, in the heat of the game hurled racial slurs at Smithers, a black member of the other team. Smithers, too, was a good and decent boy. The dispute between the boys continued after the game and Smithers kicked his tormentor. Unfortunately, the victim had a rare physical defect and this kick caused the boy to choke to death. Smithers was charged with manslaughter. Because of the racial overtones the case attracted the attention of certain pressure groups who attempted to influence the outcome. While the Smithers case raised legal issues as to causation of death in homicide cases, issues which were ultimately determined by the Supreme Court of Canada, the real lesson of the case may well be that one of the great strengths of our judicial system is its ability to stand above the fray and not bow to improper influence or the rule of the mob. In the Smithers case the trial judge recognized the intense emotions which the prosecution had generated and, in a sensitive judgement and sentencing, placed in proper perspective the role of the criminal law. The fact was that an assault had taken place and a boy had died. As the Supreme Court of Canada agreed, the crime was manslaughter even though a blow which would have only caused minor discomfort for most persons was, in this case, fatal to the victim. As much as words may hurt, when a person turns from words to action and assaults another he must take his victim as he finds him and be held accountable for the results, even though unintended, of that assault.

"Second Time Around", the trial of Gary Staples for the murder of cab driver Gerald Burke, demonstrates the flexibility of our legal system and its ability to correct itself. The appeal procedures in our criminal laws are a long way from being impediments to the resolution of a case or havens for trivial technicalities — though the media may all too often view them as such. In fact, it is the provincial courts of appeal, and ultimately the Supreme Court of Canada, that offer us the careful, dispassionate scrutiny of trials that our system needs to prevent miscarriages of justice at the lower-court level. In the Staples case the Ontario Court of Appeal took the unusual step of ordering a new trial for the accused based on affidavit evidence presented before them — evidence they decided could not have been reasonably available to the defence at the time of the original trial. When the new trial was ordered this fresh evidence was tendered and partly because of it the accused man was acquitted.

On another level, the acquittal in that second trial offers a testimonial to the brilliance and compassion of the late Arthur Maloney, one of the finest courtroom advocates this country has ever known. As I indicated in my commentary during that episode of "The Scales of Justice", excellence in criminal law is much more than a matter of flashy, aggressive cross-examinations or rhetorical appeals to the jury, and Arthur Maloney's masterful defence in the Staples case provides an object lesson in the difficult art of criminal defence.

# Truscott: The Children's Hour

*Guy Gavriel Kay*

## The Cast

Commentary by Edward L. Greenspan, Q.C.

| | |
|---|---|
| **STEVEN TRUSCOTT** | Eric Peterson |
| **MR. DONNELLY** for the defence | Frank Perry |
| **MR. HAYS** for the Crown | Harvey Atkin |
| **DOUGLAS OATS** | Torquil Campbell |
| **JOCELYNE GODDETTE** | Terri Hawkes |
| **LYNNE HARPER** | Reena Schellenberg |
| **PIERRE BERTON** | as himself |

With the support of (in alphabetical order): Diana Belshaw, Zoe Carter, Roger Dunn, Alan Fawcett, David Ferry, Thomas Hauff, Dawn McNeil, James Morris, Michael J. Reynolds, Simon Reynolds, Don Saunders, John Scott, Paul Soles, John Stocker, Sean Sullivan, Sandy Webster, and Murray Westgate

## Scene 1 / Summer Evening in a Small Town

*Truscott rides up on a bicycle and stops.*

**LYNNE:** Steven. Hey, Steven.
**STEVEN:** 'Lo, Harper.
**LYNNE:** Hi. Watcha doin'?
**STEVEN:** Just riding.
**LYNNE:** Hot, eh? Must be ninety degrees.
**STEVEN:** Yeah.
**LYNNE:** I wanted to go swimming in the pool, but you gotta have an adult with you, and my parents wouldn't take me. They drive me crazy.
**STEVEN** (*not too interested*): Umm.
**LYNNE:** Hey...if you're not doing anything, could you give me a ride up to the highway?
**STEVEN:** How come?
**LYNNE:** There's this man in a white house east of the junction and he's got some ponies he lets me see. Couldja give me a ride, huh? Please?
**STEVEN:** Sure. Okay. Hop on.

**GREENSPAN:** ***A summer evening in the country. And the children at the RCAF base near Clinton in southwestern Ontario were doing what children have always done on hot summer evenings: playing in the schoolyard, fishing in the stream, diving into the water at the old swimming hole, or just lazily cycling about. But on that evening of June 9, 1959, something was to happen that would violently shatter the peaceful mood of the Air Force base and eventually trouble the conscience of an entire country to this day. When twelve-year-old Lynne Harper jumped onto the crossbar of fourteen-year-old Steven Truscott's bike, the two of them rode off together into Canadian history. My name is Edward Greenspan, and in this episode of "The Scales of Justice" we begin a special two-part examination of what is possibly the most famous case in Canadian criminal law — the trial of Steven Truscott.***

***Lynne Harper did not come home on the night of June 9. For whatever reason, no real alarm was raised. The following morning, though, her father began making enquiries around the base, and at about 7:45 he came to the home of Warrant Officer Dan Truscott...***

## Scene 2 / At the Truscott House

**DORIS TRUSCOTT** (*answering the door*): Yes, hello?

**HARPER:** Hello, Mrs. Truscott. I'm Leslie Harper. I don't think we've met, though I know your husband, of course.

**DORIS:** Oh. Well, Dan's not here just now, but can I...

**HARPER:** Actually I was hoping to catch your boys before they left for school... You see, my daughter, Lynne, didn't come home last night, and I was wondering...

**DORIS:** Oh dear. Ah, Kenneth, do you know...

**KEN:** Nope. I know her, but I didn't see her at all yesterday. She's in Steve's class isn't she? Hey, Steven?

**STEVEN:** Yeah?

**DORIS:** This is Flying Officer Harper.

**STEVEN:** Hello, sir.

**HARPER:** Hello, Steven. I wonder if you might have seen Lynne yesterday at some point.

**STEVEN:** Yes, I did, sir. I gave her a ride on my bike up to the highway.

**HARPER:** When was this?

**STEVEN:** About 7:30. She hitched a ride east. I saw her get in a car as I was on the bridge.

**HARPER:** She hitched a ride!

**STEVEN:** Yeah.

**HARPER:** Oh my God!

**DORIS:** Oh dear.

**HARPER:** She hitched a ride!

**GREENSPAN:** ***With this information, the situation changed to emergency footing, and Officer Harper alerted the police. The first policeman to arrive was a Constable Hobbs from Goderich, fifteen miles away...***

## Scene 3/Inside a Police Car

**HOBBS:** Now, Steven, we need your help here. Exactly what did Lynne say to you when you rode her up the road?

**STEVEN** (*not really concerned yet*): Just that...ah, she wanted to go to this white house on the highway where there were some ponies.

**HOBBS:** What else?

**STEVEN:** Well, she said she was mad at her folks because they wouldn't take her swimming at the pool and...ah, she said she had to be home at 8:30.

**HOBBS:** Now what did you see when you dropped her off?

**STEVEN:** Well, on the way back I stopped at the bridge, watching who was at the swimming hole, you know. And I looked back, and I saw Lynne with her arm out...hitching a ride, you know. And then a car stopped for her, and she got in, and they went off east.

**HOBBS:** What kind of car was this? Could you tell?

**STEVEN:** 'Fifty-nine Chev, I think. It was grey, and it had a yellow licence plate.

**HOBBS:** You could tell the make?

**STEVEN:** Yes, sir. I know cars pretty well.

**GREENSPAN:** ***A Constable Tremblay was the next policeman to arrive, and he too interviewed Steven in the presence of his father that afternoon. The interview was basically a recap of the earlier one with Hobbs. But then, at 5:00, Tremblay returned to the Truscott house. Dan Harper was away, so this time Steven's mother joined him with the policeman. Tremblay took Steven to the bridge where he said he'd been when he saw Lynne get into the grey Chevrolet...***

## Scene 4/The Bridge

**TREMBLAY** (*dubious*): You sure you could see the car from here?

**STEVEN:** Yes, sir. This is where I was.

**TREMBLAY:** Well, I'm watching those cars go by and I can't tell what make they are, and there ain't nothing wrong with my eyes, son.

**STEVEN:** This one was stopped, sir. It stopped to pick her up.

**TREMBLAY:** Still, it's a pretty fair distance. You sure it was a Chev?

**STEVEN:** 'Fifty-nine Chev, sir, yes. It was grey. And it had a yellow or maybe an orange licence, or maybe it was a bumper sticker.

**DORIS:** It could have been a yellow bumper sticker. We have one on our own car. From Storybook Gardens. In London, you know...

**GREENSPAN:** ***The next morning, Thursday, Steven was again called out of school by the police. This time he was asked for the names of any children who might have seen him cycling up the road with Lynne...***

## Scene 5 / Inside a Police Car

**STEVEN:** Well...ah, Arnold George — we call him Butch — was swimming in the river...I waved to him. And, ah...oh yeah, Douglas Oats was on the bridge when we rode across. And Richard Gellatly saw us on the road.

**HOBBS** (*making notes*): Richard Gellatly, okay.

**GREENSPAN:** ***Meanwhile, at 1:00 on June 11, two days after Lynne had disappeared, the search began. At the schoolyard, 250 men gathered and set out, 125 on each side of the County Road. The plan was to cover the County Road and Highway 8 all the way west to Clinton and east to Seaforth. It didn't take that long though...***

## Scene 6 / In the Bush

**MAN:** God, I'm dying of the heat!
**HOBBS:** We just started, for God's sake.
**MAN:** I know, but it's gonna take forever to cover all this ground.
**HOBBS:** Quit bitching. How would you feel if it was your daughter missing?
**MAN:** I don't have a daughter. And besides — oh no, oh Jesus, no...(*Shouts*) Here she is! Here she is!
**CAST:** Over there. Over there. Found her over there...
**HOBBS** (*flatly*): Yeah, here she is.

# Scene 7/At the Crime Scene

**HOBBS:** Here's the pathologist... Dr. Penistan, thank you for coming. This is Dr. Brooks, the station medical officer.

**PENISTAN:** Hello.

**BROOKS:** Hello, Doctor. I'm afraid it isn't too pleasant here. I've already identified the body... We're keeping the parents away for... well, for obvious reasons.

**PENISTAN:** All right... let me make some observations here, then we'll move her and get going on the autopsy. Will someone take notes for me?

**HOBBS:** I will, sir.

**PENISTAN:** Very well. We have the body here of a young girl — how old was she, Dr. Brooks?

**BROOKS** (*grimly*): Twelve.

**PENISTAN:** Of a twelve-year-old girl. She is dead. Subject to later confirmation it seems clear that she has been raped. She is lying on her back in a wooded area — what is this place called, Officer?

**HOBBS:** Lawson's Bush, sir. Would you say she was killed by strangulation?

**PENISTAN:** It looks that way. We have here a sleeveless blouse that has been torn and tied about her neck. I would say that is how she was killed. For the rest, gentlemen, you'll have to wait for the autopsy.

**HOBBS:** When, sir?

**PENISTAN:** I'll do it in Clinton this evening. Dr. Brooks, will you assist?

**BROOKS:** Yes, of course.

**HOBBS:** What we really need, Doctor, is a time of death.

**PENISTAN:** I know that. I'll do what I can.

**GREENSPAN:** ***Dr. Penistan was as good as his word. Later that night he made what was to be the most important medical finding of the case: he declared that, based primarily on an examination of Lynne's stomach contents, he could put the time of her death at between 7:00 and 7:45 p.m. on June 9. This forty-five-minute time period pointed a finger of guilt directly at Steven Truscott.***

***Inspector Harold Graham, later to become Ontario's Commissioner of Police, arrived from Toronto to take charge of what was now a murder case. And Steven was taken to the Goderich police station...***

## Scene 8/In a Guardroom

**GRAHAM:** All right, Steven...do you know what these papers are?

**STEVEN** (*frightened now*): No.

**GRAHAM:** These are all the statements you've given us over the last three days. And do you know what I think?

**STEVEN:** No.

**GRAHAM:** I think they're lies. A pack of lies, Steven. You've been lying from the start. You never took her to the highway. She never hitched a lift. You never even reached the bridge. You took Lynne Harper into Lawson's Bush and you raped her and you killed her.

**STEVEN:** No! I didn't!

**GRAHAM:** Oh yes, you did. And do you know how I know?

**STEVEN:** I didn't kill her!

**GRAHAM:** Yes you did, Steven. Because the autopsy report is in. And it says that Lynne died between 7:00 and 7:45 that night. And that's when you were with her, Steven. Nobody else. What time did you get home?

**STEVEN:** I was home by 8:30. My mom saw me. I had to be home to babysit. I was at the school before that — by 8:00, lots of kids saw me. I was at the school by 8:00!

**GRAHAM:** You killed her before 8:00 then. She didn't get in any grey Chevrolet on Highway 8, Steven. She never got to Highway 8. You killed her in Lawson's Bush.

**STEVEN:** I didn't kill her!

**GRAHAM:** I don't believe you, Steven. I don't believe anything you ——

**STEVEN:** I didn't kill her!

**GREENSPAN:** ***At 9:30, Steven was transferred from the Goderich Police Station to the guardhouse on the* RCAF *base. Inspector Graham wanted a medical examination done and Dr. Brooks telephoned a Dr. Addison of Clinton, a general practitioner. Brooks and Addison performed the examination in the presence of Steven's father. The doctors found the usual assortment of scratches and scabs one might expect on a fourteen-year-old, but then they found something else...***

**BROOKS:** Look at this!

**ADDISON:** Oh, yes, yes. We have here, yes, two severe lesions on either side of the shaft of the penis...

**BROOKS:** These are raw sores! The size of a quarter, both of them. Like a brush burn!

**ADDISON:** Yes, a brush burn, yes. Steven, how on earth did you get such a sore penis? Have you been masturbating?

**STEVEN:** No.

**BROOKS:** This is important... This is very important...

**GREENSPAN:** ***Dr. Brooks was right — these lesions on Steven's penis were to be extremely important, though not perhaps in the way the doctor thought. At any rate, according to Dr. Addison, after the physical examination was over, he had a further exchange with Steven, when no one else was in the room...***

**ADDISON** (*in a fatherly tone*): Now, Steven, if you have done this thing I want you to tell me now, because the police are going to find out later anyway. Why don't you get it off your chest? These scrapes on your penis look pretty bad, Steven, they really do.

**STEVEN:** It's been like that for four or five weeks.

**ADDISON:** Four or five weeks?

**STEVEN:** Yeah, like, not really sore, not hurting, but sort of looking like that.

**ADDISON:** But you've got a raw scrape there, Steven.

**STEVEN** (*acutely embarrassed*): Yeah, well... yeah, I was masturbating 'bout a week ago and I ripped... I ripped off some of the skin...

**GREENSPAN:** ***Dr. Addison would later testify to this exchange with the jury out of the room at Steven's trial. The judge ruled that all of Steven's conversations with Dr. Addison — of which this one was only a part — were inadmissible, a ruling designed to benefit the accused. But on this particular issue, it might well have had the opposite effect... At any rate, the police now considered the crime solved. At 3:00 a.m. Steven was taken back to the Goderich police station and there he was charged with the murder of Lynne Harper.***

***Because Steven was only fourteen, the Crown had to make an application before a judge of the juvenile court to have the trial held in adult court. Despite the opposition of Steven's lawyer, J. Frank Donnelly,*** Q.C.***, the application was granted. The next stage was the preliminary hearing. The following scene is speculative, but it illustrates some of the acute difficulties facing Donnelly and the Truscotts in 1959...***

## Scene 9 / In Donnelly's Office

**DAN TRUSCOTT:** Frank, this is insane! The press are going crazy. They're reporting every single word that the Crown witnesses are saying...

**DORIS:** And because we aren't calling witnesses nobody knows anything about Steven's story.

**DONNELLY:** I know, I know. It's very unfair... There's talk in Ottawa now about amending the Criminal Code to ban publicity during preliminary hearings. It's long overdue.

**DAN** (*bitterly*): Much good that'll do Steven. How are we going to find a fair jury here?

**DORIS:** Can't we have the trial somewhere else?

**DONNELLY:** A change of venue? Yes, well, ah,... Mrs. Truscott, I've discussed that with Dan. You see, we could apply for one, but if we do move the trial, well, we have to pay the cost of putting up all our witnesses wherever we move it to, and as you know there are going to be a lot of witnesses, and well, ah...

**DAN** (*angrily*): And what that all means is that we aren't rich enough to make sure Steven gets a fair trial. I don't make enough money to defend my own son!

**GREENSPAN:** ***There is absolutely no doubt, whatever one may ultimately conclude with respect to the Truscott case, that the publicity given to the preliminary enquiry was gravely prejudicial to the defence. Subsequently the Criminal Code was indeed altered to provide, quite properly, for non-publication of evidence at the preliminary stage. And later, as well, the introduction of legal-aid assistance would help to remedy the financial constraints that hampered Donnelly in conducting his defence. All of this though would happen well after the trial of Steven Truscott in Goderich in the fall of 1959...***

## Scene 10 / In Court

**JUDGE:** Gentlemen of the jury, I don't suppose it is possible to have lived in Huron County in the last two or three months without hearing something about this case. Please dismiss it from your minds now because you try this case according to the evidence heard in this courtroom, not on newspaper comments or gossip we hear in the community... Now, at this stage of the case, Crown counsel will tell you what the Crown's case is all about. What he tells you is not evidence, of course, but what he tells you the evidence is going to be, that is what it is going to be.

**GREENSPAN:** ***Second-guessing is easy, and probably inevitable in a case as notorious as this one was, but one comment may be worth making. It seems fair to say, looking back, that the Crown attorney in the Truscott case acted with a zealousness that deviated somewhat from the ideal. And the first difficulty surfaced during his opening remarks — something very rare...***

**CROWN:** ... in addition, gentlemen, you will hear evidence that on that Friday night when the accused was interrogated a statement was taken from the accused by Inspector Graham and the other police, a statement signed that night by the accused and ——

**JUDGE** (*strongly*): Mr. Hays!

**CROWN:** I don't intend to say anything about it.

**JUDGE:** You shouldn't have said anything about it at all.

**CROWN:** Even the fact that it was taken at all?

**JUDGE** (*angrily*): I may have to discharge this jury and start all over again. You shouldn't do that, you know. I will have to consider that.

**CROWN:** I felt, My Lord, that the reference...

**JUDGE:** Never mind what you felt. Nothing, nothing, nothing about it.

**DONNELLY:** Is Your Lordship going to consider the remark made by my friend? I submit it was a most serious statement.

**JUDGE:** Just a minute... Will the jury retire for a minute please?

*The jury files out of the courtroom.*

**JUDGE:** You see, if the statement goes in, no harm is done, but if the statement goes out, you have made a mistrial right now. If it isn't admitted you have made a mistrial.

**GREENSPAN:** ***Two days later the matter of the statement came up. The police were heard with the jury out of the room and the trial judge ruled that the circumstances of the taking of the statement were***

*completely unfair. He refused to admit it as evidence. Was a mistrial declared? Well, somehow, somewhere along the line, the judge seemed to have forgotten his original ruling, and the defence, for some reason, never reminded him — the trial continued, and there can be no doubt that a gravely prejudicial remark by the Crown attorney was allowed to pass. The jury may well have concluded that the statement was a confession that for some technical reason was being kept out. It wasn't — but they didn't know that. Since the statement did not become evidence, the jury should never have heard a word about it. At any rate, after that controversial opening, the Crown began putting in his case. What was that case? Well, there were sixty-one Crown witnesses called in this complex case, but generally speaking the evidence fell into three broad categories: the doctors, the police...and the children.*

**CROWN:** Call Richard Gellatly.

*Gellatly walks to the stand.*

**JUDGE:** How old are you, Richard?
**RICHARD:** Twelve.
**JUDGE:** You're twelve. What grade are you in at school?
**RICHARD:** Grade eight.
**JUDGE:** Yes, shout good and loud. Don't be afraid of speaking too loud here. Do you know what it means to take an oath?
**RICHARD:** You hold a Bible in your right hand and you swear to tell the truth.
**JUDGE:** Yes, are you prepared to do that today?
**RICHARD:** Yes.
**JUDGE:** To tell the truth?
**RICHARD:** Yes.
**JUDGE:** I think we can swear this boy.
**CLERK:** Take the Bible in your right hand. Do you swear that the evidence you are about to give...

**GREENSPAN:** *This was to be a process repeated over and over again with a steady parade of child witnesses. Most were sworn, but some were not. The difference is that the unsworn evidence of a child requires corroboration before the jury can consider it in its deliberations.*

**CROWN:** Richard, do you live down at the RCAF station with your father and mother?
**RICHARD:** Yes.
**CROWN:** And on the evening of June 9 were you down at the river?
**RICHARD:** Yes.
**CROWN:** What time did you go down there, Richard?
**RICHARD:** About 6:30, somewhere around there.
**CROWN:** How long did you stay there?
**RICHARD:** Oh, I stayed for half an hour or so.
**CROWN:** Then what did you do?
**RICHARD:** I came home to get my swimming trunks.
**CROWN:** Were you on foot or on bicycle?
**RICHARD:** Bicycle.
**CROWN:** I see. Did you know Lynne Harper?
**RICHARD:** Yes.
**CROWN:** Do you know Steven Truscott?
**RICHARD:** Yes.
**CROWN:** Did you see either of them on your way home to get your trunks?
**RICHARD:** I seen both of them.
**CROWN:** What were they doing, Richard?
**RICHARD:** Steve was riding Lynne down towards the bridge.
**CROWN:** And what time would this be?
**RICHARD:** Around 7:25. I could be a few minutes out.
**CROWN:** Now you went home and got your swimming trunks and then what did you do...?

**GREENSPAN:** ***What the Crown was trying to do was complex but very important. He wanted to place a number of children on the County Road between seven and eight o'clock that evening who could collectively give evidence to support his theory. That theory was that Steven and Lynne never reached the bridge, let alone Highway 8. The Crown's contention was that after passing Richard Gellatly — who* had *seen them, and who Steven said he had also seen — Steven and Lynne went off the County Road into Lawson's Bush, the bike was hidden, and Lynne was raped and killed...***

**CROWN:** Call Philip Burns.

**GREENSPAN:** ***Eleven-year-old Philip, in Grade six, was heard as an unsworn witness.***

**CROWN:** Now Philip, on June 9 were you down at the river on the County Road?
**PHILIP:** Yes.
**CROWN:** And where were you?
**PHILIP:** At the swimming hole.
**CROWN:** And what time did you leave to go home?
**PHILIP:** Around seven.
**CROWN:** Why do you think it was seven, Philip?
**PHILIP:** Because I asked Mrs. Geiger the time, and she didn't know but Mr. McCafferty said it was around five to seven.
**CROWN:** Did you see anyone on your way home?
**PHILIP:** Yes. Jocelyne Goddette came down and she asked me ——
**CROWN:** No, no, no. I think, Philip, what Jocelyne said to you isn't the kind of thing we talk about here. Ah, where was this, though?
**PHILIP:** On the closest side of Lawson's Bush to the station, to home.
**CROWN:** Do you know Steven Truscott?
**PHILIP:** Yes.
**CROWN:** Did you see him at all on your way home?
**PHILIP:** No.
**CROWN:** Do you know Lynne Harper? Did you see her on your way home?
**PHILIP:** No.

**GREENSPAN:** ***The Crown called Mrs. Geiger, the woman Philip had asked the time of, and she testified to seeing Richard Gellatly cycle south and Philip Burns begin to walk south at about the same time — 7:15. So Richard, older and on a bike, is placed ahead of Philip. He saw Steven and Lynne. But little Philip walking along the County Road behind him never saw them on their supposed trip across the bridge and up to the highway. The Crown's theory for this was simple: Steven and Lynne weren't on the road. They were in Lawson's Bush. But what about the other child, the one Philip said he talked to? What did Jocelyne Goddette have to say?***

**CROWN:** How old are you, Jocelyne?
**JOCELYNE:** Thirteen.
**CROWN:** And last spring were you in the same class at school as Steven Truscott and Lynne Harper?
**JOCELYNE:** Yes, sir.

**CROWN:** And on Monday, June 8, the day before Lynne disappeared, did you have a conversation with Steven at school?

**JOCELYNE:** Yes, sir.

**CROWN:** And will you tell the court what the conversation was, please?

## Scene 11 / In the Schoolyard

**JOCELYNE:** Hey, Steve, guess what I did yesterday?

**STEVEN:** How would I know?

**JOCELYNE:** I went over to Bob Lawson's barn and I saw a newborn calf there. It was so cute.

**STEVEN:** Yeah? I know where there are two more if you want to see them.

**JOCELYNE:** Sure!

**STEVEN:** Want to go this evening?

**JOCELYNE:** Aw, I can't. I gotta go to Guides after dinner.

**STEVEN:** Can you make it tomorrow?

**JOCELYNE:** I'm not sure...but I'll try.

## Scene 12 / In Court

**CROWN:** Where were you to go with him?

**JOCELYNE:** Well, he didn't tell me on Monday.

**CROWN:** Well, go ahead.

**JOCELYNE:** And then on Tuesday he asked me if I could go, and I said I didn't know, and he said if I could go, to meet him on the right-hand side of the County Road outside the fence by the bush and — Oh, he kept telling me not to tell anyone because Bob Lawson didn't like a whole bunch of kids on his property.

**CROWN:** And this is on Tuesday, June 9. When were you to go?

**JOCELYNE:** Well, at 6:00.

**CROWN:** And did you see Steven after school?

**JOCELYNE:** Yes, sir. He came to my house at ten before six and I told him I didn't think I'd be able to make it because we were just starting supper but I would try.

**CROWN:** And what did you do?

**JOCELYNE:** Well, I got out of the house about 6:20 or 6:30 and I went to Bob Lawson's barn and I asked him if he had seen Steven —
**CROWN:** No! What did you go to the barn for?
**JOCELYNE:** To see if Steven was there.
**CROWN:** And after you left, where did you go?
**JOCELYNE:** Well, I went to see if Steven was at the meeting place.
**CROWN:** And was he there?
**JOCELYNE:** No, sir.
**CROWN:** Mr. Donnelly? Your witness.

**GREENSPAN:** ***Jocelyne's evidence was important. First of all it established a connection between Steven and Lawson's Bush that evening — the bush where Lynne Harper was found dead. Second, it placed another child on the road who didn't see Steven or Lynne, even though she was looking specifically to find him. There were other elements to the evidence — dangerous inferences that would later be drawn — but for the moment, defence counsel had a few cross-examination points to make...***

**DONNELLY:** You've been in the same school as Steven for three years, haven't you.
**JOCELYNE:** Yes, sir.
**DONNELLY:** And I suggest in all that time you've never been out with Steven.
**JOCELYNE:** No, sir.
**DONNELLY** (*more stern now*): No, eh? All right. Now, Jocelyne, do you know a boy named Gary Gilks?
**JOCELYNE:** Yes, sir.
**DONNELLY:** He's in your class at school, isn't he?
**JOCELYNE:** Yes, sir.
**DONNELLY:** I suggest to you that two or three weeks before June 9, that Gary Gilks' brother had found a calf in Lawson's Bush and you asked Gary Gilks about going in to Lawson's. Is that possible?
**JOCELYNE:** I guess it is.
**DONNELLY:** Pardon?
**JOCELYNE:** I guess it is.
**DONNELLY:** And I suggest to you that then you said, quote, "Next time you go I would like to go with you," end quote. I suggest you said that to him.
**JOCELYNE:** I could have.

**DONNELLY:** You could have. Yes. And I suggest that you went on and said, quote, "Maybe we can find some calves," end quote. You could have said that too, couldn't you?
**JOCELYNE:** Yes, sir.

**GREENSPAN:** ***Donnelly had scored a couple of points. He had established Jocelyne as talking about calves in Lawson's Bush, not with Steven but with another boy. This was important, because Steven had always denied having had any such conversation with her. He even denied going to her house at ten to six on June 9.***

***There were twenty-one children called by the Crown, but of those testimonies, the most critical was Arnold "Butch" George's. According to Arnold, who was a good friend of Steven's, he too was looking for him along the County Road around 7:30 on June 9. He saw Jocelyne, and he also saw little Philip Burns walking home, but he never saw Steven until he went to the Truscott house around 9:00 at which point, he testified, the following conversation occurred...***

## Scene 13 / Outdoors

**BUTCH** (*calling*): Hey, Steve!

*Steven comes out onto the verandah.*

**STEVEN:** Hi, Butch.
**BUTCH:** Watcha doin'?
**STEVEN:** Babysitting. I gotta stick around here.
**BUTCH:** Where were ya before? I was lookin' for ya.
**STEVEN:** Down at the river.
**BUTCH:** I heard you gave Lynne a ride to the river.
**STEVEN:** Yeah, she wanted a lift up to Highway 8.
**BUTCH:** I heard you were in the bush with her.
**STEVEN:** No, we were on the side of the bush looking for a cow and a calf... Why do you want to know for?
**BUTCH:** Ahh... skip it. Let's play catch.

**GREENSPAN:** ***"On the side of the bush looking for a cow and a calf" — very damaging evidence. But Butch George had another conversation to***

***report. This one he said took place the next day, Wednesday, also by the Truscott house, and it was even more damaging to Steven Truscott...***

*The boys are playing catch.*

**STEVEN:** Butch, I need a favour.
**BUTCH:** What?
**STEVEN:** Let's stop a sec... Well, like, the police were asking me questions today, you know, about Lynne being missing, and... ah, I told them that when I was riding her to the highway I saw you. Except it wasn't you, it was Gordie Logan I saw and I thought he was you, you know, down by the swimming hole. But I told the police it was you I saw and... ah, I think they're gonna go to your house and ask you, so... you know...
**BUTCH:** Well, okay, I'll tell them I saw you two riding down at the river.

**GREENSPAN:** ***And* that *sounds like someone preparing a false alibi. According to Butch, he started out ready to help Steven in this way, but changed his mind when Lynne's body was found. Now again, despite what Truscott supporters have since said, there does not appear to have been a reason for Butch George to have lied. On the other hand, on cross-examination by Frank Donnelly it emerged that Butch had said nothing about the cows and calves when questioned by the Crown Attorney at the preliminary inquiry. It was a brand-new story. With respect to the Wednesday conversation, the one that seemed to imply that Steven was cooking up an alibi, Donnelly elicited from Butch that, at the preliminary, his version of the dialogue was much less incriminating...***

*The boys are playing catch.*

**BUTCH:** Good catch.
**STEVEN:** The police been to see you yet about Lynne?
**BUTCH:** Not yet.
**STEVEN:** They probably will be... Did you see me at the river?
**BUTCH:** No.
**STEVEN:** You know, it's going to look bad for me.
**BUTCH:** Ah... I might as well tell them I did see you.

**GREENSPAN:** *Two major differences. First, there is nothing about Steven's having told the police he saw Butch, and second, there is no request on Steven's part for an alibi — there is an offer from Butch that Steven accepts. Once more, no reason is apparent for Butch George to have lied at trial, but Donnelly established that Butch had made three different, contradictory statements to the police and that he had read over the last one ten times before going into court. Why? Donnelly asked, and Butch George answered: "I was trying to make sure what I said, what I was going to say."*

*Then came the doctors. Dr. Penistan, the pathologist, placed the time of death at not later than 7:45. He also gave his opinion that Lynne Harper had died where her body had been discovered. Dr. Addison and Dr. Brooks gave their testimony about the lesions on Steven's penis, and both told the jury that such lesions were the sort that could be incurred during rape — in psychological terms, quite possibly the most damaging single piece of evidence at the trial. The police witnesses testified as to their conversations with Steven — and through them his account of the events of June 9 emerged: the ride over the bridge to the highway and Lynne's hitchhiking a ride eastward. Constable Tremblay gave evidence designed to cast doubt on Steven's story...*

## Scene 14 / In Court

**TREMBLAY:** Yes, sir. I went down to the bridge and I observed traffic proceeding up and down Number 8 Highway and I couldn't distinguish any licence numbers on this traffic.

**GREENSPAN:** *Aside from the fact that this was moving traffic, it is important to remember that Steven never said he'd seen* **numbers** *on the plate of the car that supposedly picked up Lynne — only that the plate was yellow or orange. The Crown also filed through the police officers a photograph taken from the bridge designed to show that Steven could not have seen what he claimed... And that, in essence, was the Crown case.*

*As he got up to present the case for Steven Truscott, Frank Donnelly knew that the Crown's medical evidence was going to have an enormous impact on the jury, but he had an expert of his own...*

**DONNELLY:** Dr. Brown, I understand you were a physician with the Canadian Army in Europe for five years?

**BROWN:** I was.

**DONNELLY:** And after that you did four years of postgraduate work?

**BROWN:** Yes.

**DONNELLY:** In what specialty?

**BROWN:** I specialized in what we call internal medicine with emphasis on diseases of the digestive system.

**DONNELLY:** Ah, in your study and work in connection with the digestive system, do you have any experience as to the length of time it takes the stomach to empty after an ordinary meal?

**BROWN:** Yes, I've had considerable experience in that line and after a mixed meal the normal emptying time of the stomach would average somewhere between three and a half and four hours.

**DONNELLY:** I show you Exhibit 26 which a witness told us are the contents of the stomach of the victim in this case. Have you any comment to make?

**BROWN:** Well, I would anticipate that we are seeing this material nearer the time when it is getting ready to leave the stomach. That is, some time after three or four hours.

**GREENSPAN:** ***So the battle lines of the experts were clearly drawn on this issue. On Dr. Berkeley Brown's evidence, Lynne Harper would have been alive until nine or ten o'clock that night. If this evidence raised a reasonable doubt for the jury, it would have to acquit Steven Truscott, because, of course, he was home babysitting by 8:30. But Dr. Brown, the one medical expert that the defence could afford, had more to say in response to the Crown doctors...***

**DONNELLY:** Well then, doctor, you said you spent five years in the army?

**BROWN:** That's correct.

**DONNELLY:** Did you spend it as a medical doctor?

**BROWN:** Yes, I served in Canada, England, Italy, and Northwest Europe.

**JUDGE:** Ah, in a hospital or in the field?

**BROWN:** I was with a regiment.

**DONNELLY:** Yes, and in this time would you have had occasion to do medical examinations of many penises?

**BROWN:** Thousands, I would say.

**DONNELLY:** Pardon?

**BROWN:** Many thousands, I would say.

**DONNELLY:** Many thousands. Now the evidence before this court from Dr. Addison was that on examining the penis of the boy, he found two sores, one on each side of the shaft, each about the size of a twenty-five-cent piece, and that they looked like a brush burn with serum oozing from the sores. Now, what is your opinion as to whether or not such a lesion could be caused by the insertion of the organ into the private parts of a young, small girl?

**BROWN:** I would think it would be highly unlikely that penetration would produce a lesion of this sort. It's interesting that the penis is rarely injured in rape, and when it is, it is usually a tearing injury confined to the head of the penis.

**DONNELLY:** So, in your opinion ——

**BROWN:** I would say it is improbable that the lesion was caused by insertion into the small opening of a girl.

**DONNELLY:** Doctor, what is your opinion as to whether or not these lesions could be caused by masturbation?

**BROWN:** It is consistent with masturbation.

**GREENSPAN:** ***So, on both medical issues the defence had offered a rebuttal to the Crown case. But now it was time for the children again. The heart of the defence lay in the evidence of the boy Frank Donnelly called next...***

**DONNELLY:** All right now, your name is Douglas Oats?

**DOUGLAS:** Yes, sir.

**DONNELLY:** And you're twelve years old and live at the RCAF Station?

**DOUGLAS:** Yes.

**DONNELLY:** Did you know Lynne Harper?

**DOUGLAS:** Yes, sir.

**DONNELLY:** And Steven Truscott?

**DOUGLAS:** Yes, sir.

**DONNELLY:** All right, I want you to think about last June 9. What did you do after supper that evening?

**DOUGLAS:** I got on my bike and rode down to the river.

**DONNELLY:** What did you do when you got down there?

**DOUGLAS:** Well, I was up on the bridge looking over to see if I could see any turtles.

**DONNELLY:** Was anyone there with you?

**DOUGLAS:** Yes, Ronnie Demeray. He was fishing.

**DONNELLY:** Did you see any turtles?
**DOUGLAS:** Yeah. And I was going to go down and get it, but Ronnie told me to wait, and he snagged it by the leg with his fishing rod and got it for me.
**DONNELLY:** And then what happened?
**DOUGLAS:** Well, after that, I'm not sure how many minutes, Ronnie left and went home.
**DONNELLY:** And what did you do?
**DOUGLAS:** Well, I stayed up on the bridge looking for a couple of more turtles.
**DONNELLY:** At any time did you see Steven Truscott and Lynne Harper?
**DOUGLAS:** Yes, sir.
**DONNELLY:** Where?
**DOUGLAS:** They came by me on the bridge.
**DONNELLY:** What were you doing?
**DOUGLAS:** When they were coming by I turned around and put up my hand and said, "Hi."
**DONNELLY:** So you put up your hand and said "Hi," and what did Lynne do?
**DOUGLAS:** She smiled.
**DONNELLY:** What did Steve do?
**DOUGLAS:** I don't think he saw me because he just kept on riding down.
**DONNELLY:** Which way were they going, Douglas?
**DOUGLAS:** They were going north, towards the highway.

**GREENSPAN:** ***And so the defence had direct eyewitness corroboration of Steven's story of taking Lynne over the bridge to Highway 8. Crown Attorney Hays knew perfectly well that Douglas's story had to be smashed and so he set about trying to do so...***

**CROWN:** Have you talked to Steven since that evening?
**DOUGLAS:** I said "Hi" to him once.
**CROWN:** Have you ever talked to him about seeing him that evening?
**DOUGLAS:** No, sir.
**CROWN:** I see. Well now, other witnesses have testified to seeing Steven down at the bridge by himself at 6:30 that evening, Douglas. Is there a chance that's what you saw?
**DOUGLAS:** No, it isn't, sir.

**CROWN:** And then you just added Lynne through the things you heard afterwards?
**DOUGLAS:** No, I saw him and Lynne.
**CROWN:** You did?
**DOUGLAS:** Yes.
**CROWN:** Well, can you assist us as to the time this was?
**DOUGLAS:** No, I can't.
**CROWN:** Well, would you disagree with me that it was about 6:30?
**DOUGLAS:** Yes, I would.
**CROWN:** Well, what time was it?
**DOUGLAS:** I couldn't say. I know it wouldn't be 6:30.
**CROWN:** Well, would it be before 7:00?
**DOUGLAS:** No, sir.
**CROWN:** You are sure it was after 7:00?
**DOUGLAS:** Yes, sir.
**CROWN:** Douglas, do you remember giving the police a statement on Saturday, June 13?
**DOUGLAS:** Yes, sir. That is, I remember giving one, I don't remember the day it was.
**CROWN:** And what did you tell them about the time?
**DOUGLAS:** I don't know. I can't remember.
**CROWN:** Well, I suggest to you that you told them, quote, "I don't know the time but I think half an hour either way from seven o'clock," end quote. Did you tell them that?
**DOUGLAS:** I didn't say it was half an hour either way. I said it could have been half an hour after 7:00.
**CROWN:** You didn't tell them half an hour either way?
**DOUGLAS:** No, I didn't.
**CROWN:** Well, Constable Tremblay read this statement to you but you wouldn't sign it, is that so?
**DOUGLAS:** No. He never read it to me, he gave it to me to read and I never finished it though, and I didn't sign it because mother said not to sign anything unless she read it first.
**CROWN:** Well, why didn't you finish reading it?
**DOUGLAS:** He didn't give me enough time, sir.
**CROWN:** Constable Tremblay didn't give you enough time?
**DOUGLAS:** No, sir.
**CROWN:** And did your mother not let you sign this?
**DOUGLAS:** After she read it I think she would have let me.
**CROWN:** Well, why didn't you then?
**DOUGLAS:** Because the police never came back again to ask me.

**CROWN:** Douglas, have you gone over these times with anyone?

**DOUGLAS:** I didn't go over it with nobody except Mr. Donnelly and he just told me not to put in the times if I wasn't very sure about it.

**CROWN:** Do you remember, Douglas, when you gave your statement to the police that there was a lady writing down in shorthand what you said?

**DOUGLAS:** I remember a lady writing it down.

**CROWN:** But you're saying you did not tell them that it could have been a half hour either way from seven o'clock?

**DOUGLAS:** No. I didn't say it was a half hour either way. I said it was about half an hour after.

**CROWN:** It was what?

**DOUGLAS:** I said it was about half an hour after.

**CROWN:** You said it was ——

**JUDGE** (*angrily*): Half an hour after. That is what he said. It is the third or fourth time he's said it.

**CROWN:** Umm. Ah, yes. Ummm. No further questions, My Lord.

**GREENSPAN:** ***Douglas Oats was unshaken: he saw Steven and Lynne ride over the bridge towards the highway. In order to convict, the jury would have to decide that he was lying or profoundly mistaken, or else they would somehow have to simply ignore his evidence. Then there was another child called for the defence...***

**DONNELLY:** All right now, your name is Gordon Logan and you are thirteen years old, is that right?

**GORDON:** Yes, sir.

**DONNELLY:** And you live on the RCAF base?

**GORDON:** Yes, sir.

**DONNELLY:** Very well, now, Gordon, where were you on the evening of June 9?

**GORDON:** I... I was down at the river swimming and fishing.

**DONNELLY:** And what time did you get down to the river that night?

**GORDON:** A... about seven o'clock.

**DONNELLY:** How did you get there?

**GORDON:** Well, I started walking, but Richard Gellatly saw me and he gave me a lift on his bike.

**DONNELLY:** And what happened when you got to the river?

**GORDON:** I went in swimming and Richard went home to get his bathing suit.

**DONNELLY:** And then what happened?

**GORDON:** Well, I went in swimming for about... ah, until about 7:30 and then I saw Steven and Lynne go by the bridge on Steven's bicycle.

**DONNELLY:** You saw them go by. And which way were they going?

**GORDON:** They were going north towards Number 8 Highway.

**DONNELLY:** Did you see either of them again?

**GORDON:** Yes, sir. I saw Steve ride back to the bridge and I saw him stop at the bridge.

**DONNELLY:** What did he do?

**GORDON:** He just got off his bicycle. I didn't notice what he did from then on.

**DONNELLY:** How long after you saw Steven and Lynne riding north was it you saw Steven alone?

**GORDON:** About five minutes.

**DONNELLY:** Your witness.

**CROWN:** Gordon, where were you standing at this time?

**GORDON:** Ah... just on a big rock that sticks right out on the edge of the water.

**CROWN:** I suggest to you, Gordon, that standing where you say you were standing that you could not tell anyone on the bridge. That you couldn't tell a boy from a man or a girl from a woman. Do you agree or disagree?

**GORDON:** I disagree.

**CROWN:** I see. Well, would you agree that this rock is some six hundred feet east of the bridge? The rock where you were standing.

**GORDON:** I don't think so.

**CROWN:** How far east do you say it is?

**GORDON** (*unsure*): Three hundred, I think.

**JUDGE:** Ah, Gordon, you saw Steve on the bridge as you say when he came back. Are you quite sure that Lynne wasn't with him when he came back?

**GORDON:** Yes, sir.

**JUDGE:** What makes you so sure about that?

**GORDON:** I didn't see her anywhere. She wasn't on the bicycle or anything.

**GREENSPAN:** ***Gordon Logan was possibly the most important defence witness: his account provided a perfect corroboration of Steven's story. Now, it is a fact that the rock at the swimming hole is indeed six-hundred-odd feet from the bridge, not three hundred as Gordon***

*suggested, and it is equally a fact that none of the other boys at the swimming hole — and there were several of them — saw Steven and Lynne ride by, or Steven's return five minutes later. On the other hand, beyond establishing these two points, the Crown certainly didn't shake Gordon's story. However, the trial judge had done something interesting, when he got into the cross-examination himself: by asking if Lynne was with Steven when Steven returned to the bridge he planted a notion he was to pursue by himself when he charged the jury. And the time for that was coming soon.*

*Steven Truscott was not called as a witness, and even though second-guessing on this point will probably never end, it does not seem an unreasonable decision on Donnelly's part, largely because almost everything Steven would have said was already before the jury in the form of the statements he had given the police. The jury knew what he had to say, and Donnelly undoubtedly decided not to risk subjecting his young client to cross-examination by Glenn Hays. Which meant that the time had arrived for the closing addresses of counsel. Each lawyer spoke to the jury for a full day, from 10:00 to 4:30. Donnelly, because the defence had called evidence, was required to go first...*

**DONNELLY:** Now, gentlemen, this County Road was a heavily travelled road. I don't mean by cars, but by people walking and on bicycles, and it was broad daylight — broad daylight — when Steven Truscott returned to the school at eight o'clock. Yet nobody saw Steven Truscott and Lynne Harper go into that bush, and nobody saw Steven Truscott come out. Not a single solitary witness. And then we have Steven Truscott arriving at the swings in the schoolyard at eight o'clock in a perfectly normal manner. I suggest to you he simply could not have done this thing in the time between Gellatly seeing him and Lynne at 7:25, and his arrival at the swings, and further than that, he couldn't have arrived in a normal everyday manner and sat down and talked to these people he knew. The last place he would go if he had done this thing would be to this meeting place at the school where a number of people would see him. His demeanour at that time, I suggest, is consistent only with his innocence... And now I want to conclude by reminding you of certain evidence. You heard Douglas Oats. He said he was looking for turtles from the bridge on June 9 and he saw Steven and Lynne go by towards the highway. My friend cross-examined that boy at length and he didn't shake him one iota.

Not one iota. And then there is Gordon Logan. And what does Gordon Logan say? That he was on a big rock by the swimming hole and he saw Steven Truscott and Lynne Harper ride north across the bridge on Steven Truscott's bicycle, and that five minutes later he saw Steven Truscott come back alone to the bridge and stop and stand there. I suggest to you that the evidence of Gordon Logan and the evidence of Douglas Oats is worthy of belief, and if it is believed it can only lead to one conclusion: and that is that Steven Truscott was telling the truth when he said, quote, "I rode Lynne Harper to the highway and I dropped her off there," end quote. Gentlemen, I know that you will give the same careful attention to weighing the evidence that you have given to hearing the evidence. I am confident that you can come to only one conclusion, and that is a verdict of not guilty for this boy. It is with confidence that I leave the fate of this boy in your hands. Thank you.

**GREENSPAN:** ***Court adjourned for the evening, and the next morning Crown Attorney Hays took the floor. He started quite reasonably, but where he went was somewhere else...***

**CROWN:** Gentlemen, the accused, Truscott, had a fair trial, as fair as anyone can have. You have heard a very eloquent, full, able address by my friend Mr. Donnelly on his behalf. It is not for me to attempt to match that effort. My appeal to you is not on an emotional basis. I appeal to your logic and your reasoning. You heard Dr. John Penistan, a provincial pathologist with highly specialized training and years of experience. He arrived soon after the body was found and attended at the scene in Lawson's Bush. From careful study he gave the opinion that death had taken place where the body was found. And then after an autopsy he gave the time of death as between 7:00 and 7:45 p.m. on June 9. Now who was with her during this time? I suggest that a review of the facts narrows those facts like a vise on Steven Truscott and no one else. Lynne Harper left home at 6:15 that night and...

**GREENSPAN:** ***So far, so good — because it was quite true that Penistan had had the advantage over the defence's Dr. Brown of having viewed the scene and performed the autopsy. But then Hays came to Jocelyne Goddette...***

**CROWN:** Now, what did Jocelyne Goddette say? She says she talked to Steven at school about seeing a calf, and he said he could show her two new-born calves and they were to meet on the County Road by Lawson's Bush. And here is something I suggest is of great importance: He said to her several times, several times, he said, quote, "Don't tell anybody. Don't bring anybody," end quote. Why, gentlemen? What kind of calves were these that had to be surrounded with such secrecy and stealth? What did he have in his mind? And remember, there were no calves. No calves whatsoever. The search party saw no evidence of any calves. I suggest to you that the accused was doing nothing other than fabricating a lure to get Jocelyne Goddette in the bush. She testified that he called at her house at ten to six but she was having her supper, and I suggest to you that if they were late having their supper it was God's blessing to that girl!

**GREENSPAN:** ***No one stopped Mr. Hays at that point, but I want to now. These last remarks — implying that Steven Truscott had rape and murder on his mind that evening — are shocking to the sense of justice. There was, quite simply, nothing in the evidence to support the scenario of a sex-mad adolescent looking for a victim. But Hays didn't stop there, he took it even further...***

**CROWN:** So, she didn't come to the bush. Jocelyne didn't turn up and he gave her up as a prospect and then he went to the school area. And I suggest he saw a substitute in Lynne Harper. I suggest it is a reasonable inference that Steven gave Lynne the same new-born–calf invitation. I don't think, gentlemen, I am asking you to make too much of a deduction but that she would be very likely to fall for the lure of the new-born calves coming from Steven, and that she went with him to the bush and to her doom.

**GREENSPAN:** ***Nowhere was there even a hint of evidence to support this. The remarks were pure and utter speculation. The only witnesses — Crown witnesses — who saw Steven and Lynne together by the schoolyard said that she seemed to be doing all the talking. With these remarks Crown Attorney Hays had deftly woven a sinister, sexually charged web of innuendo — utterly unsupported by the evidence. Later, in fact, the trial judge would point this out to the jury, but the***

***prejudicial impact of this sort of inflammatory address is incalculable, and not to be rectified by an easy, belated caution. Hays had absolutely no right to say what he did, and we will never know the effect it had on the jury. The Crown continued to review the evidence, somewhat more moderately. He reminded the jury of Arnold George's evidence that Steven had asked him for an alibi. He tied this in with the evidence of Douglas Oats and Gordon Logan who said they had seen Steven and Lynne on the bridge...***

**CROWN:** Oats and Logan I submit are part and parcel of the Steven Truscott – Butch George conspiracy. Again I repeat that George was talked by the accused into telling the police a false story. I suggest you can take from the sworn evidence before you that Gordon Logan got in on the same deal, but unlike George, he stuck to it. I urge that he is simply not telling the truth.

**GREENSPAN:** ***The prosecutor ended at 4:30 p.m., and after a short recess the trial judge commenced his long and difficult charge to the jury. It would be possible, but somewhat pointless, to go over this charge with a fine-tooth comb, but one aspect of it was so central that it may well have profoundly shaped the jury verdict...***

**JUDGE:** Now you see, if the accused boy rode Lynne Harper to Number 8 Highway then you must ask yourselves who brought her back, because somebody brought her back. Somebody brought her back. Did he bring her back if he took her? Could he have been coming back, as Logan said, but did he have Lynne with him? As I say, if he was actually at the highway with the girl and brought her back, then it doesn't make any difference that he took her to the highway...

**GREENSPAN:** ***Not surprisingly, Mr. Donnelly objected strenuously to this at the end of the judge's charge, after the jury had gone out...***

**DONNELLY** (*heatedly*): And I do submit, Your Lordship, that your charge to the jury could leave them with no impression except to wipe out the theory of the defence that Douglas Oats and Gordon Logan saw this boy and this girl go north over the bridge. The jury could come to no other conclusion than they should disregard the evidence of Oats and Logan.

**JUDGE:** I don't know where you got that impression.

**DONNELLY:** Your Lordship says "if Truscott took Lynne to the highway and brought her back." There is no evidence to indicate that he brought her back. Any evidence would be that he didn't bring her back. The evidence of Logan.

**JUDGE:** Well, she was back. That is where they may draw the inference he brought her back, if he took her down, because she was back.

**GREENSPAN:** ***The judge recharged the jury on a number of issues, but not on this one. The jury finally retired at 8:38 p.m. Just after 10:00 they returned to the tense courtroom...***

**CLERK:** Gentlemen of the jury, have you agreed on your verdict?

**FOREMAN:** No, My Lord, we have not.

**JUDGE:** You have not?

**FOREMAN:** We want some more information. Can I read this?

**JUDGE:** Yes.

**FOREMAN:** A redirection of evidence, corroborated or otherwise, of Lynne Harper and Steven Truscott being seen together on the bridge on the night of June 9.

**GREENSPAN:** ***The children again. Douglas Oats and Gordon Logan were what the jurors wanted to know about. The very evidence Donnelly claimed the judge had virtually taken away from them by his own unsupported theory that Steven might have taken her to the highway*** **and** ***brought her back. The trial judge carefully reviewed the evidence of Logan and Oats; the foreman thanked him, but as the jury were preparing to withdraw again, His Lordship added something...***

**JUDGE:** So, as I pointed out to you, you must reject the story that the girl got into a car at Number 8 Highway in order to convict. If you find, however, that although he went to Number 8 Highway with the girl, that he brought her back — and she was back, somebody brought her back — you'll have to find that he brought her back and then their going back and forth over the bridge is of very little importance.

**GREENSPAN:** ***Again Donnelly objected, and this time the judge recalled the jury to point out that no eye-witness saw Steven bring Lynne back. The Truscott jury retired after this at 10:45. Ten minutes later, they returned for the last time...***

**CLERK:** Gentlemen, have you agreed upon your verdict?

**FOREMAN:** Yes, My Lord. We find the defendant guilty as charged, with a plea for mercy.

**JUDGE:** Steven Murray Truscott, have you anything to say why the sentence of this court should not be passed upon you according to law?

**TRUSCOTT:** No.

**JUDGE:** Steven Murray Truscott, the sentence of this court upon you is that you be taken from here to the place from whence you came and there be kept in close confinement until Tuesday the 8th day of December, 1959, and upon that day and date you be taken to the place of execution and that you there be hanged by the neck until you are dead, and may the Lord have mercy upon your soul.

**GREENSPAN:** ***His Lordship told the jury that their plea for mercy would be passed on to the authorities, and indeed it was. In the meantime, a fourteen-year-old boy was on death row, and a week after the trial, a well-known Canadian was moved to write a verse about it. Pierre Berton's thoughts on the subject appeared in the*** **Toronto Daily Star...**

**BERTON:** So muffle the drums
And beat them slow
Mute the strings
And play them low
Sing a lament
And sing it well
But not for the boy
In the cold dark cell
Not for the parents
Trembling lipped
Not for the judge
Who followed the script
Save your prayers
For the righteous ghouls
In that higher court
Who write the rules
For judge and jury
And hangman too
The court composed of
Me and you.

GREENSPAN: *Berton was later to say that he had never known a more violent response to any column he had ever written. He was called a "sob sister for a monster" and callers expressed the hope that his own daughter would soon be raped. Early in 1960 the Ontario Court of Appeal unanimously rejected an appeal filed on Steven's behalf, and later in the year the Supreme Court of Canada denied him leave to appeal. Steven Truscott's death sentence was commuted to life imprisonment and, still protesting his innocence, he began serving his sentence.*

*It seemed as if the case was over. It wasn't, however, because the passions associated with the trial of Steven Truscott had only just begun...*

# Truscott: The Darkest Hour

*Guy Gavriel Kay*

**The Cast**

Commentary by Edward L. Greenspan, Q.C.

| | |
|---|---|
| **STEVEN TRUSCOTT** | Eric Peterson |
| **MR. MARTIN** for the defence | Henry Ramer |
| **MR. SCOTT** for the Crown | Michael Tait |
| **DR. CAMPS** | Sean Mulcahy |
| **DR. SIMPSON** | Gillie Fenwick |
| **JAMES BYRNE, M.P.** | Gordon Pinsent |
| **MR. JUSTICE EMMETT HALL** | Mavor Moore |

With the support of (in alphabetical order): Harvey Atkin, Vern Chapman, Max Ferguson, Nonnie Griffin, Tom Harvey, Paul Kligman, Cec Linder, Bill Lynn, Arch McDonell, James Morris, Chuck Shamata, and Ray Stancer

## Scene 1 / House of Commons

**SPEAKER:** The Honourable Member for Kootenay East.

**BYRNE:** Mr. Speaker, the matter which I wish to bring to your attention this evening is based on information I have received from an authoress in Toronto who is preparing a book on the trial of Steven Truscott. Seven years ago, on Tuesday, June 9, 1959, a little twelve-year-old girl in the town of Clinton, Ontario, was brutally raped and murdered. Five months later a fourteen-year-old male child, Steven Truscott, was tried in an adult court by a jury and convicted. From the very outset the cards were stacked against this boy. The entire community had adjudged him guilty because they wanted to believe the murderer had been apprehended. The defence evidence was glossed over in the charge to the jury by the trial judge. The evidence against him was purely circumstantial. Mr. Speaker, I personally am so convinced of this boy's innocence that I am prepared, if necessary, to stake my seat in the House of Commons on the outcome of an inquiry or a royal commission that would examine all the circumstances of the conduct of all the persons involved in: (1) the investigation of the girl's disappearance; (2) the questioning of children at the RCAF station; (3) the interrogation and taking of statements from Steven...

**GREENSPAN:** ***What had happened? When we examined the trial of Steven Truscott, we saw that public opinion following his conviction ran passionately in favour of his guilt. Now, seven years later, for some reason the case was being talked about again, and in no lesser a forum than the House of Commons, but the tide of opinion seemed to have shifted spectacularly. My name is Edward Greenspan, and in this, the second half of a special two-part treatment of the Truscott case, we will be examining why that shift occurred and how Steven***

*:t was brought back, seven years after his trial, to trouble the ıce of a country.*

*In Part One we learned that twelve-year-old Lynne Harper was last seen alive on the evening of June 9, 1959, riding on the crossbar of a bicycle being pedalled by a classmate of hers — fourteen-year-old Steven Truscott. The two children lived on the RCAF base near Clinton, Ontario, and they were seen cycling up a road known as the County Road. Lynne never came home that night, and so the next morning her father began enquiring of other children if they knew where she was. About 7:45 he came to the home of Warrant Officer Dan Truscott...*

## Scene 2 / The Truscott Home

**HARPER:** Hello, Steven. I wonder if you might have seen Lynne yesterday at some point.

**STEVEN:** Yes, I did, sir. I... I gave her a ride on my bike up to the highway.

**HARPER:** When was this?

**STEVEN:** About 7:30. She hitched a ride east. I saw her get in a car as I was on the bridge.

**HARPER:** She hitched a ride?

**STEVEN:** Yeah.

**HARPER:** Oh my God!

**GREENSPAN:** *This was Steven Truscott's story, and he never changed it. The body of Lynne Harper was found in Lawson's Bush, about a kilometre from the schoolyard, just east of the County Road. She had been raped and murdered, strangled with her own blouse. The district pathologist, Dr. Penistan, made two absolutely vital findings. The first was that Lynne had been killed where she was found. The second was that, based on a visual examination of the amount of food in her stomach, she had died within two hours of her last meal — a time estimate that pointed the finger of guilt at Steven Truscott, who on his own story had been with her at that time.*

*On the evening of June 12, Steven was picked up by the police. At 10:30 that night, a Dr. Addison arrived at the RCAF guardhouse to perform a physical examination of Steven. Addison was assisted by the RCAF base doctor, a man named Brooks, and they found something, something that was to be explosive grounds for controversy...*

## Scene 3 / In a Guardhouse Room

**BROOKS:** Look at this!
**ADDISON:** Oh, yes, yes. We have here two severe lesions on either side of the shaft of the penis...
**BROOKS:** These are raw sores! The size of a quarter, both of them. Like a brush burn!

**GREENSPAN:** ***Steven Truscott was charged with murder. His trial saw a parade of children, aged ten to sixteen, called for both the Crown and the defence. The most important of the Crown's young witnesses was a girl named Jocelyne Goddette. She testified that Steven had made a date to go looking for calves at Lawson's Bush with her that evening. She was late. And although she looked all over the area, she never saw Steven. This supported the Crown attorney's theory that Steven and Lynne never made it to the bridge on the County Road, let alone Highway 8. What about the defence case? Steven Truscott did not testify. His account of events was before the jury in the form of his early statements to the police. He had taken Lynne to the highway and seen her hitch a lift.***

***The most important defence evidence was given by two more children. The first was a boy named Douglas Oats, who was on the bridge over the Bayfield River on the evening of June 9...***

## Scene 4 / In Court in 1959

**DONNELLY:** At any time did you see Steven Truscott and Lynne Harper?
**DOUGLAS:** Yes, sir.
**DONNELLY:** Where?
**DOUGLAS:** They came by me on the bridge.
**DONELLY:** What were you doing?
**DOUGLAS:** When they were coming by I turned around and put up my hand and said, "Hi."

**GREENSPAN:** ***This provided direct corroboration of Steven's story, and it refuted the Crown theory that Steven and Lynne had never reached the bridge. Another boy, thirteen-year-old Gordon Logan, testified that he was down at the swimming hole, which is about six hundred feet***

*from the bridge, and he too saw Steven and Lynne cycle across, and he also saw Steven come back alone about five minutes later. The Crown cross-examined both boys severely, but neither was shaken in his story.*

*After the last charge of the judge to the jury though, they were out for only ten minutes before returning to convict Steven Truscott of murder, upon which the judge sentenced him to be hanged.*

*The Ontario Court of Appeal unanimously upheld the trial verdict, and the Supreme Court of Canada refused the leave necessary to appeal the case further. Steven's sentence was commuted by the Diefenbaker government to life imprisonment and he began serving his time. The matter was finished. Except that it wasn't, because of a woman named Isabel Le Bourdais...*

**LE BOURDAIS:** Steven Truscott was a fourteen-year-old boy like yours or mine. He gave a girl a ride on his bicycle. Four boys saw him and two saw him return. Within a few minutes he was back among his friends by the school and chatting with them. He went home to his parents and cared for his younger brother and sister. He went to bed and slept... Some man with a very sick mind raped and strangled the young girl that night. Steven was charged, prosecuted, and convicted. Ever since June 13, 1959, Steven has been in jail. More than six years of his young life, the years when he has grown out of childhood, the years when other Canadian boys went to high school, played baseball, football, hockey, enjoyed parties and dating girls, learned skills and took jobs, grew to maturity: these years have been stolen from him and from his family.

**GREENSPAN:** *Le Bourdais, a Toronto housewife in her fifties, spent several years preparing and writing her book.* **The Trial of Steven Truscott** *was published in March 1966. To say it caused a sensation would be an understatement. The book was a passionate, emotional defence of Steven Truscott and a scathing denunciation of his trial. The doubts it raised and the language in which those doubts were framed struck a nerve deep in the Canadian consciousness. Isabel Le Bourdais had started something, and in the face of the wave of public opinion, the government finally responded...*

# Scene 5 / In Jail

**GUARD:** Truscott. You got company. Look sharp.
**STEVEN** (*flatly*): Yeah, right.

*Isabel Le Bourdais enters Steven's cell.*

**LE BOURDAIS:** Is that the best you can do?
**STEVEN** (*animated now*): Isabel. Hi... I heard you on the radio the other day. Everybody's talking about your book and ——.
**LE BOURDAIS:** Well, they'll have something more to talk about now. I've got something to read you. Sit down and listen. "From His Excellency the Governor General to the Supreme Court of Canada the following question is referred for their Hearing and Consideration: 'Had an appeal by Steven Murray Truscott been made' ——"
**STEVEN:** Isabel, what ——
**LE BOURDAIS:** Hush! Listen! "...'been made to the Supreme Court of Canada what disposition would the court have made of such an appeal on a consideration of the existing record and such further evidence as the court in its discretion may receive and consider?'" And what do you think of that, Mr. Truscott?
**STEVEN** (*stunned*): I...we...They've reopened the case?
**LE BOURDAIS:** They certainly have. A special hearing — a reference they call it.
**STEVEN:** I don't believe it. Seven years after. All because of your book. Isabel, you've done it.
**LE BOURDAIS** (*suddenly awkward*): Oh, well, I...I guess I have.

**GREENSPAN:** ***In 1966 Isabel Le Bourdais was named Woman of the Year by the Canadian Press. There is absolutely no doubt that it was her book that caused the reopening of the Truscott case.***

***In Part One, we pointed out a number of areas where the conduct of the Truscott trial seemed seriously deficient and potentially very unfair to the accused. In the interest of fairness it may well be appropriate now to observe that despite these areas, the Crown case against Steven Truscott was certainly not without its strengths. Here, in a speculative scene, is how the picture might have looked on the days before the reference as Glenn Hays, the Crown at trial, briefed William Bowman and Don Scott, who would be handling the Crown case before the Supreme Court of Canada...***

# Scene 6 / In the Law Office

**BOWMAN** (*responding to a knock on the door*): Glenn, come on in. Don and I have just been finalizing our approach to the reference, how we're going to handle things.

**HAYS:** How's that?

**BOWMAN:** Well, our friend Mr. Scott is a tiger in the courtroom, so I'm going to shelve my own ego and let Don handle all the witnesses.

**HAYS:** Direct and cross?

**SCOTT:** Yes. I'll do those and Bill will make the arguments when the witnesses are finished.

**BOWMAN:** All thirty-three of them, or however many it ends up being. In the meantime, we're sitting here trying to decide what to key in on, how do we focus this reference. So let me pick your brains, Glenn. You were there. What's the strongest thing we've got?

**HAYS** (*confidently*): Dr. Penistan, the coroner.

**SCOTT:** Time of death?

**HAYS:** That's right.

**BOWMAN:** Yeah, you know that's going to be the hottest issue on the reference.

**HAYS:** Look, Penistan's a good pathologist, he did a thorough autopsy, and he gave us a time-of-death before Truscott was even arrested.

**BOWMAN:** True enough. And if she died before 7:45, she wasn't killed by some driver of a grey Chevy with yellow licence plates.

**HAYS:** No way. Hell, once Penistan gave us that time of death we wouldn't have been able to make a charge *stick* against anyone else.

**SCOTT:** Hm... And let's not forget where she was found. Lawson's Bush. A thousand yards from home.

**BOWMAN:** All right, what else have we got?

**HAYS:** Well, all the kids I called. Nobody seeing him on the road.

**SCOTT:** Ah...it helps, but I'm afraid that one might be a stand-off. No, because of the kids who say they *did* see him. Especially Douglas Oats on the bridge, and that boy Logan by the swimming rock. I mean, Oats says he saw Truscott and Harper ride over the bridge together — now, why would he lie?

**HAYS** (*irritated*): Well, why would Butch George lie? And he's our witness and he said Truscott — his best friend, remember — asked him for an alibi and George agreed to give him one.

**BOWMAN:** And then backed down when the body was found. You think Logan and Oats were part of the same thing?

**HAYS:** Could be. I mean if Truscott asked George to cook an alibi, why couldn't he ask someone else?

**BOWMAN:** I don't know. Maybe he did.

**HAYS:** And what about the lesions on his penis?

**SCOTT:** No. I'm not happy about those. Most of the medical evidence now seems to be suggesting that our two doctors were wrong about that. Those lesions just aren't the kind you get from rape.

**HAYS:** Well, the jury sure thought they were. I'll "stake my seat in the House of Commons on it."

*They all laugh.*

**BOWMAN:** I'm sure they did, Glenn. But this is the Supreme Court of Canada.

**SCOTT:** Actually we do have something new. I don't think you've seen this Glenn, listen: [*He searches through his files*.] "Ladies and Gentlemen, I know that five years is not very long for a sentence like mine, but I was very young and ——"

**HAYS:** What the hell?

**BOWMAN:** Hang on. Listen. It's Truscott's application for early parole.

**SCOTT:** "... but I was very young and all I ask is just one chance to prove that I am worthy of being allowed to mix with society... I have paid five years of my life but this has taught me that crime does not pay, so all I ask is please grant me one chance to make a success of my life and prove that one dreadful mistake does not mean I will ever make another one."

**HAYS** (*stunned*): My God. That's a confession.

**SCOTT:** Ah, ha!

**BOWMAN:** "One dreadful mistake" — it sure sounds like one, doesn't it?

**HAYS:** My God. Are you going to file it?

**BOWMAN:** What do you think? Of course I am. Of course I'm going to file it.

**GREENSPAN:** ***The Supreme Court reference in the matter of Steven Murray Truscott began in Ottawa on Wednesday, October 5, 1966, and it was a procedure unique in Canadian history. The Supreme Court does not hear witnesses; it makes rulings on the law. But this time the Justice minister had specifically empowered the court to hear such witnesses as they saw fit and not even the judges were quite sure what their mandate was. The legal talent assembled was exceptional. Bowman and Scott for the Crown were a formidable team, but they were opposed by Arthur Martin, a distinguished lawyer of extraordinary skill and experience who was later to be appointed to the Ontario Court of Appeal.***

***As opposed to a trial where all the Crown witnesses are called, then all the defence witnesses, in the reference, witnesses were called by the two sides in a virtually random manner. The Crown struck the first telling blow, however, and it was, interestingly enough, a direct response to Isabel Le Bourdais. At the trial in 1959, Lynne Harper's blouse, with which she had been strangled, was filed as an exhibit. There was, however, a ten-inch square piece missing from it. Glenn Hays had argued that this piece had been cut loose and lost when the blouse was removed during the autopsy. Le Bourdais wrote that she had done tests with her daughter and that this was impossible. She had another theory...***

**LE BOURDAIS:** The psychotic nature of the killer was not indicated solely by the act of raping and strangling a twelve-year-old girl, but by other factors as well. A piece of the girl's blouse, about ten inches in size, was cut out of the upper left-front section and never found. One concludes that the murderer had scissors with him. Why did he want a piece of blouse at all? Did he have a strange compulsion to keep a piece of the garment which he had tied about her neck?

**GREENSPAN:** ***It is a measure of the seriousness with which the Crown was taking Mrs. Le Bourdais' speculations that one of Don Scott's first witnesses was a man from the Attorney General's laboratory in Toronto...***

## Scene 7 / In Court

**SCOTT:** Now, Mr. Brown, what, if any, experimentation or study did you make of this blouse?

**BROWN:** Well, sir, I was particularly concerned with the missing piece.

**SCOTT:** And did you conduct certain experiments?

**BROWN:** Yes, I did, sir. Yes.

**SCOTT:** May it please you, My Lords, I would ask that the witness be permitted to give a demonstration on a model with a blouse of this nature.

**TASCHEREAU, CJ:** Yes.

**SCOTT:** Would you indicate please to the honourable members of the Court what you are doing, sir, as you proceed?

**BROWN:** Yes, sir. I would like to place this on the model... Now... if I grasp the blouse thusly, ripping the seam lengthwise... and if I were now to do this [*He ties the blouse around the model's neck.*] I am not putting a great deal of pressure. So.

**SCOTT:** Yes, would Miss Degan turn around, please, so the court can see it as it is now about her throat. Yes, now, what do you do next, sir?

**BROWN:** Well, I then make a cut, just to the side of the knot, like so and ——

**SCOTT** (*quickly*): Well, I'm sorry, sir, something just fell down.

**BROWN:** Yes, the piece that fell is the left half, including the top two buttons, leaving the blouse in a condition similar to the one that I received in 1959.

**GREENSPAN:** ***So a procedure Isabel Le Bourdais had described as impossible had been shown to be quite clearly possible. This was the Crown's demonstration, but Arthur Martin had arranged for some tests of his own, on a far more significant point. At trial in 1959 the Crown had led the following police evidence...***

## Scene 8 / In Court in 1959

**TREMBLAY:** As I was standing on the bridge with Steven a grey car with an Ontario licence passed over the bridge and proceeded towards Number 8 Highway. I fixed my eyes on the licence plates and as the car drew farther away they kept getting smaller and when the car stopped at Number 8 Highway I couldn't see the licence plates at all.

**GREENSPAN:** ***The Crown had also filed a photograph taken from the bridge in which a car stopped at Number 8 Highway looked too small for anyone to have recognized it. Arthur Martin's first steps in the Supreme Court were designed to cast serious doubt on these aspects of the Crown case...***

## Scene 9/In the Supreme Court

**MARTIN:** Mr. Labrash, you are now a private investigator?
**LABRASH:** Yes, sir, I am.
**MARTIN:** Did you perform certain tests at the bridge over the Bayfield River just south of Highway 8 this year?
**LABRASH:** I did, sir.
**TASCHEREAU, CJ:** Was this witness heard at the trial?
**MARTIN:** No, My Lord Chief Justice, this is new evidence.
**TASCHEREAU, CJ:** New evidence. Yes, go on.
**MARTIN:** Very well, Mr. Labrash, what was the purpose of the tests you made?
**LABRASH:** First of all, to see if we could recognize a 1959 Chev as such from approximately the centre of the bridge to the stop sign on Number 8 Highway, and then to determine whether or not we could distinguish colours at this distance.
**MARTLAND, J:** Colours of what?
**LABRASH:** Of licence plates, My Lord.
**MARTIN:** All right, first of all, what is your observation as to whether you could distinguish a 1959 grey Chevrolet from other cars that were similar in design?
**LABRASH:** Well, my observation was that you could distinguish a 1959 Chevrolet at this distance from other cars.
**MARTIN:** What did you do next?
**LABRASH:** I then went to the rear of this car and...

**GREENSPAN:** ***Labrash explained that he placed two associates on the bridge while he laid a sequence of coloured cards over the place where a licence plate would be on the test car. The test was done three times, and each time both of the men on the bridge recorded correctly when***

*a yellow card was used. But Arthur Martin wasn't finished yet with this aspect of his evidence. At the trial Hays had filed the famous Exhibit 21 — the photograph taken from the bridge. Now Martin called an engineering expert in optics...*

**MARTIN:** Professor Henderson, were you able to come to any conclusion as to whether Exhibit 21 actually represents what you could see of a car at the intersection from the bridge?
**HENDERSON:** No, it does not.
**MARTIN:** What defect do you find therein?
**HENDERSON:** The perspective is extremely distorted. The car would appear about one-third of its size in the picture as it would if you were actually looking at it from the bridge.

**GREENSPAN:** *None of this evidence was trivial. The Truscott jury, faced with police evidence and that distorted photograph, would have almost had to conclude that Steven was lying about what he saw from the bridge. Martin's new evidence, while it certainly didn't prove that Truscott had been telling the truth,* **did** *establish that he* **could** *have been...*

*But now the time had come, seven years down the road from 1959, for the most important witness of all, and one who had not testified at the trial...*

**MARTIN:** Mr. Truscott, you were born on the 18th of January, 1945, in Vancouver?
**STEVEN:** Yes, sir.
**MARTIN:** And in 1959 when you were fourteen, what grade were you in at school?
**STEVEN:** I was in Grade seven.
**MARTIN:** Did you know Lynne Harper?
**STEVEN:** I knew her from school, yes.
**MARTIN:** Was she in the same class?
**STEVEN:** Yes, she was.
**MARTIN:** Do you remember very much about her?
**STEVEN:** Other than seeing her in school I knew nothing about her.
**MARTIN:** Very well. Do you recall the occasion of giving Lynne Harper a ride on your bicycle?
**STEVEN:** Yes, I do.
**MARTIN:** You remember that day, do you?
**STEVEN:** Yes, sir.

**MARTIN:** You had your supper at home that night, did you?
**STEVEN:** Yes, sir.
**MARTIN:** And after supper where did you go?
**STEVEN:** I went out on my bicycle.
**MARTIN:** Now what time would this be?
**STEVEN:** Approximately 6:30.
**MARTIN:** Now was there any particular time that you were supposed to be home?
**STEVEN:** I was supposed to be home at 8:30 to babysit my younger sister and brother.
**MARTIN:** Now, after you rode your bicycle for a time, where did you end up?
**STEVEN:** I stopped by the school and I was watching the Brownies who were having a meeting there, and Lynne Harper came over to the bicycle and asked me if I was going down by the river and I replied that I was and she asked me if she could have a lift down to the highway. And several minutes later we proceeded to the County Road and I gave her a ride to Number 8 Highway.
**MARTIN:** And when you got to Number 8 Highway, what did you do?
**STEVEN:** I let her off at the highway.
**MARTIN:** And why did you let her off there?
**STEVEN:** That's where she asked me to give her a lift to.
**MARTIN:** Now, I may be a little out of sequence, but, ah...as you rode north with Miss Harper can you recall seeing anyone?
**STEVEN:** I passed Douglas Oats on the bridge on the County Road.
**MARTIN:** Did you know Douglas Oats?
**STEVEN:** I had seen him at school.
**MARTIN:** Was he your age or older or younger?
**STEVEN:** He was quite a bit younger.
**MARTIN:** Do you remember anyone else you saw?
**STEVEN:** Not on the way down.
**MARTIN:** Did you see anyone on the way back?
**STEVEN:** Yes, I did. I saw Butch George and Gordon Logan at the swimming hole east of the bridge.
**MARTIN:** After you let Lynne Harper off at Highway 8, do you know where she went or what happened to her?
**STEVEN:** I got...I got back to the bridge and I turned around and there was a car pulled in off the highway and she got in the front seat.
**STEVEN:** What was the description of the car?
**STEVEN:** It was a grey '59 Chev.

**MARTIN:** Is there anything else you noticed?
**STEVEN:** It had a lot of chrome on it, and also when it pulled out there appeared to be a yellowish coloured...it appeared to be a licence plate.
**STEVEN:** Now, what familiarity did you have with cars at this time?
**STEVEN:** I knew pretty near every car that was out.

**GREENSPAN:** ***And so, Steven Truscott, now twenty-one years old, told his account of the evening of June 9, 1959, in court for the first time. None of it was new, but Arthur Martin had two other areas of examination, and both of these were new...***

**MARTIN:** I want you to listen to this next question very carefully and apply your mind to it. What did the condition of your penis look like when you first noticed that there was something unusual?
**STEVEN:** It was about six weeks before I was picked up, and it started off as what appeared to be little blisters and it continued to worsen.
**MARTIN:** Now, when you first noticed this, did you tell your father about it?
**STEVEN:** No, I didn't.
**MARTIN:** Was there any reason why you didn't?
**STEVEN:** I was too embarrassed.
**MARTIN:** Have you ever had any condition like that before that time?
**STEVEN:** No, I haven't.
**MARTIN:** Have you ever had a similar condition on any part of your body since?
**STEVEN:** Yes, I have. Ah...on my back and on the side of my neck.
**MARTIN:** When did you have those?
**STEVEN:** While I was in the penitentiary. And finally I went down to the skin specialist to see if I could get it cleared up.

**GREENSPAN:** ***Steven's evidence on this point was later corroborated by a number of doctors who testified that he had been treated while in jail for various skin conditions, including nummular eczema which was characterized by coin-shaped blisters. At trial doctors Brooks and Addison had testified that the lesions on Steven's penis could have resulted from rape. That evidence obviously would have had a profound impact on the jury... Martin's final area of examination involved an attempt to neutralize a potentially dangerous piece of new evidence...***

**MARTIN:** Steven, did you make an application for parole?
**STEVEN:** Yes, I did.
**MARTIN:** And did you write out your own application?
**STEVEN:** Yes, I did.
**MARTIN:** All right, in that application you say, quote, "I have paid five years" ——
**FAUTEUX, J:** Mr. Martin, may I ask you the date of it?
**MARTIN:** August 4, 1964. Quote, "I have paid five years of my life but this has taught me that crime does not pay, so all I ask is please grant me one chance to make a success of my life and prove that one dreadful mistake does not mean I will ever make another one," end quote. Did you sign that application?
**STEVEN:** I did.
**MARTIN:** And did you intend to make any admission of guilt in that application?
**STEVEN:** No, I didn't.
**MARTIN:** What message then were you trying to get across to the parole board?
**STEVEN:** That I knew that crime doesn't pay.
**MARTIN:** As a result of what?
**STEVEN:** Of my observations of all the rest of the people in the penitentiary.
**MARTIN:** What was your understanding of whether the parole board had anything to do with whether you were guilty or innocent?
**STEVEN:** I knew from my observations that they had nothing to do whatsoever with whether I was innocent or guilty.
**MARTIN:** Very well. My Lords, I am requesting that the report of Mr. Haggerty, who was Mr. Truscott's classification officer, be filed along with this application for parole.
**TASCHEREAU, CJ:** Very well, we will admit these two documents.
**MARTIN:** Thank you, My Lord Chief Justice. May I now then refer to this sentence in the last paragraph of the Haggerty report: quote, "Truscott still claims innocence of the present offence but accepts his sentence with the feeling that nothing can be done now," end quote. Mr. Truscott, does that statement describe your attitude at that time?
**STEVEN:** It does describe my attitude at that time.

**GREENSPAN:** ***This issue of the parole application is an interesting and disturbing one. In the light of Haggerty's assessment it appears that***

***Steven had done no more than try to tell the parole board what it wanted to hear. Don Scott's cross-examination of Steven was low-key but purposeful...***

**SCOTT:** In giving your evidence earlier, sir, you indicated that the first time you discussed with anyone those lesions on your penis was apparently with Mr. Martin and Mr. Jolliffe, your lawyers, earlier this year?

**STEVEN:** That's correct.

**SCOTT:** And I think your answer was that — in answer to a question of Mr. Martin's — that you were too embarrassed to tell your father?

**STEVEN:** Yes, sir.

**SCOTT:** Now, you were present at your preliminary hearing in July 1959, is that correct, sir?

**STEVEN:** Yes, sir.

**SCOTT:** When Dr. Brooks and Dr. Addison gave a considerable amount of evidence relating to these penis injuries?

**STEVEN:** Yes, sir.

**SCOTT:** And you didn't tell your father at that time — after the issue had been raised in considerable detail — what had caused them?

**STEVEN:** I do not remember whether I told him anything or not.

**SCOTT:** Well, your previous answer, sir — and I just went over it specifically for that purpose — was that you had talked to no one until Mr. Martin and Mr. Jolliffe this year. Now, what do you say as to it?

**STEVEN:** I do not recall mentioning this subject to anyone other than Mr. Martin and Mr. Jolliffe.

**SCOTT:** And then at your trial, when Dr. Brooks and Dr. Addison gave further evidence relating to the penis injuries, even at this time you didn't tell your father or anyone how they occurred?

**STEVEN:** No, I didn't.

**GREENSPAN:** ***Very effective cross-examination from an expert in the art. Even though all the medical evidence seemed to be that the injuries were not the sort acquired during rape, Don Scott had still managed to find a way to make those injuries damaging to Steven Truscott, because it did indeed seem implausible that he would not have told his lawyer or his father how he got them, given the terribly damaging evidence of the two doctors in 1959. And Scott wasn't finished yet...***

**SCOTT:** Sir, do you recall a Mrs. Geiger giving evidence?
**STEVEN:** No, sir.
**SCOTT:** Well, do you recall a Kenneth Geiger giving evidence?
**STEVEN:** No, sir.
**SCOTT:** Do you recall Paul Desjardine giving evidence?
**STEVEN:** No, sir.
**SCOTT:** Do you recall Arnold George giving evidence?
**STEVEN:** Yes, sir.
**SCOTT:** And I gather you disagree with that evidence.
**STEVEN:** Yes, sir.
**SCOTT:** Do you recall Richard Gellatly giving evidence?
**STEVEN:** No, sir.
**SCOTT:** Now, you will agree with me, I'm sure, that this was a most serious charge you were facing in 1959?
**STEVEN:** Yes, sir.
**SCOTT:** Yes, I am wondering, frankly, Mr. Truscott, bearing in mind the nature of their evidence and bearing in mind the nature of the charge against you, why you cannot even recall these people giving evidence.
**STEVEN:** I don't recall them giving evidence.
**SCOTT:** I know that, sir. My question was, Mr. Truscott, why don't you recall?
**STEVEN:** Because I have forgotten.
**SCOTT:** That concludes my cross-examination, My Lords.
**TASCHEREAU, CJ:** Ah, Mr. Martin?
**MARTIN:** I have no questions in re-examination, My Lord.

**GREENSPAN:** ***After the evidence of Steven Truscott, the reference moved to the single most contentious and critical issue of all: the question of when Lynne Harper had died. Dr. Penistan, the pathologist who had done the autopsy, had placed her time of death at no later than two hours after she had eaten, which meant no later than 7:45 on the evening of June 9 — a finding which, perhaps more than any other fact, had convicted Steven Truscott. Now the two sides began to wheel out a spectacular procession of international pathologists, experts flown in from all over the world, to give their opinions. First was Dr. Charles Petty of Maryland, for the defence…***

**MARTIN:** The question I want to ask you, Doctor, is, can in your opinion the time of death be put within such narrow limits, based on the stomach contents?
**PETTY:** Based on the appearance of the stomach contents I would find myself completely unable to pinpoint any time, a figure such as 7:00 o'clock to 7:45.

**GREENSPAN:** ***Dr. Milton Helpern, the Chief Medical Examiner of the City of New York, a man who had done some 20,000 autopsies, undoubtedly the most famous pathologist in the United States, for the prosecution...***

**HELPERN:** In my opinion, from the amount of food in the stomach I would conclude that death had occurred no more than two hours after the food was ingested.

**GREENSPAN:** ***Dr. Frederick Jaffe of Toronto, the most distinguished and respected pathologist in Canada, for the defence...***

**MARTIN:** Dr. Jaffe, what is your opinion as to whether the facts as to stomach contents would enable you to place the time of death between 7:00 and 7:45?
**JAFFE:** I would certainly not put the time into this period with any degree of certainty.

**GREENSPAN:** ***Dr. Samuel Gerber, the coroner for the City of Cleveland, a man who was both a lawyer and a doctor, for the Crown...***

**SCOTT:** Based on what you have heard, sir, about the volume, nature, and consistency of the stomach contents, have you any opinion as to how long that food had been in the stomach?
**GERBER:** I do, sir.
**SCOTT:** What is that?
**GERBER:** Less than two hours.

**GREENSPAN:** ***A level of disagreement among experts that virtually calls into question the legitimacy of expert opinions in a courtroom. But the pathologists weren't finished yet, and the controversy and the drama of the Supreme Court reference was to peak with the evidence of two formidably distinguished doctors from England. Dr. Francis Camps of the University of London, an associate of Harvard University, the***

***forensic-medicine consultant to the British Army and the Ministry of Defence, was the editor of one of the most widely cited textbooks in legal medicine in the world. He had more than thirty years of experience in the courtroom, and he came to Ottawa to testify for the defence...***

**MARTIN** (*somewhat deferentially*): First of all, Dr. Camps, what is your opinion as to whether the contents of the stomach is a reliable guide to the time of death?

**CAMPS:** It is so variable that this generally has been described as being of no value in assessing the time of death.

**MARTIN:** Assuming the correctness of Dr. Penistan's observations of the stomach contents, what is your opinion as to whether you could, on the basis of those observations, state with any reasonable degree of certainty that the time of death of the deceased was between the hours of 7:00 and 7:45 p.m., having regard to the fact that the victim finished her last known meal at 5:45 p.m.?

**CAMPS** (*confidently*): I would say it's quite impossible and, in fact, I would say it could be dangerously misleading to the investigating officers. Had I been there, having found the stomach contents in that condition — which would indicate death at the end of one hour or up to nine or ten hours — and with other observed post mortem changes, I would put my time of death closer to ten hours than to one.

**MARTIN:** Yes. Your witness.

**SCOTT:** Dr. Camps, it appears that you have had considerable experience in these matters. I suggest to you that you yourself might have given the police a similar time of two hours.

**CAMPS:** I should not have, actually.

**SCOTT:** Well, do you agree that this girl could have died within that period of Dr. Penistan's?

**CAMPS:** She could have died within two hours. Could have been nine, ten, eleven hours. But I do not think you can say she died, fixing a time within half an hour.

**SCOTT** (*cautiously*): Very well... Now, please sir, I am trying to be very cautious here. I do not wish to reflect on your integrity at all, Doctor, please accept that, but I do feel bound to ask you if you really made up your mind about this matter long before you heard any of the evidence or had anything to go on except a book for which you wrote a review in England saying the medical evidence couldn't possibly stand up?

**CAMPS:** Well, it is partly...but almost completely untrue. I wrote to a very...to a gentleman who had asked my advice...and all I said, I wanted to make it clear...subject to my reading the evidence...

**SCOTT** (*firmly*): May I have a moment, My Lords. Thank you.

*Scott searches through his files.*

**SCOTT:** Yes. I have a copy, sir, of the letter you're referring to: I quote: "I have read *The Trial of Steven Truscott* with considerable interest. As you appreciate more than anybody else, books of this type have a certain emotional involvement of the author with the subject and hence require considerable objective detachment. This I have attempted to achieve and on such a basis I do not think the medical evidence for the prosecution can possibly stand up to scrutiny. I should be prepared to support this in writing or in evidence. I have no objection to any communication of my views on the Truscott case," end quote.

**TASCHEREAU, CJ:** This is written to whom?

**CAMPS:** The Lord Chancellor of England as a result of a personal letter from him. I had no idea it was ever to be divulged.

**SPENCE, J:** Well, the suggestion of the letter...that you have no objection to a...

**SCOTT:** Yes, that's the section I have just read, My Lord, quote, "I have no objection to any communication of my views..." end quote.

**CAMPS:** I'm sorry, I must have misunderstood.

**ABBOTT, J:** I can't hear you, Doctor.

**TASCHEREAU, CJ:** When *did* you read the evidence, Doctor?

**CAMPS:** I read the book and it must have been somewhere around that date. I read the evidence as soon as it was sent over to me.

**SCOTT:** I don't wish to pursue this, but frankly it seems that your statement that the medical evidence cannot possibly stand up is made long before you read the evidence. That's my simple question.

**CAMPS:** I'm afraid your simple question is very misleading. Your simple ——

**FAUTEUX, J:** I would like an answer to that. I...as far as I'm concerned ——

**CAMPS:** I don't like to have him suggesting that my integrity is ——

**SCOTT:** No, sir. I am not.

**CAMPS:** My Lord, the answer was that...this was a personal letter but what I had read led me to believe that — and I wasn't saying the evidence was wrong; I simply said it didn't stand up to close scrutiny. In other words it...required more...scrutiny... That was the object of...since...since then I have...I...

**SCOTT** (*soothingly*): All right, sir. All right.

**GREENSPAN:** ***One of the most complete destructions of a professional witness on record. It was reported that when Camps left the stand he literally ran from the room. Scott had just smashed the defence's star, and things got even better for the Crown, because their next witness was the only man in England more distinguished in his field than Francis Camps. Scott called the most famous forensic pathologist in the world, Cedrick Keith Simpson...***

**SCOTT:** In addition to your many academic distinctions, Dr. Simpson, have you done yourself a number of autopsies in the thirty-some-odd years that you have been in this particular branch?

**SIMPSON:** Yes, I have personal records of some 100,000 autopsies which I have performed myself.

**SCOTT:** Thank you, Doctor. Now, ah, very generally, what do you... well, what is your view as to the medical evidence as presented at the original trial of this matter?

**SIMPSON:** I think, My Lords, I would say that with my experience in these matters — extending over thirty years — I would say that Dr. Penistan and the officers responsible appear to have performed a very competent and conscientious investigation pertaining to the timing and cause of death.

**SCOTT:** Yes I see. And what do you say as to the conclusion Dr. Penistan arrived at that the stomach contents he examined had been in the stomach between one and two hours?

**SIMPSON:** I would say that... My Lords, it appears to me in this case most creditable that Dr. Penistan paid particular attention to this matter. In my own experience this is not always so. I would say that he was right to conclude that it was likely that death had taken place up to two hours after eating that last meal.

**GREENSPAN:** ***And so Dr. Simpson had lent the considerable weight of his authority to the support of Dr. Penistan's original findings. He did something more though, in a completely different area, and in the process he showed how an experienced, alert expert witness can be of immeasurable aid to a lawyer...***

**SCOTT:** Finally, Dr. Simpson, I think you have heard the evidence relating to penile injuries to the accused. Have you any comments regarding these, sir?

**SIMPSON:** Yes, sir. When I first read the description of these I found them perplexing, for I would agree with the evidence before this court that they are not the kind of injury one sees in forcible or difficult sexual intercourse. But having heard the evidence of Steven Truscott that he already had some condition of soreness on his penis, this seems to me to give a clue to the rather curious nature of those two patches.

**SCOTT:** In what way, Dr. Simpson?

**SIMPSON:** I would say that something caused these pre-existing patches to become more sore...to weep or crust...and I would regard that as being consistent with a part of a sexual assault.

**GREENSPAN:** ***And this testimony was an outright gift to the Crown from an expert who had been paying close attention to the other evidence and who was quick enough on his feet to incorporate it into his testimony. Arthur Martin rose to cross-examine this immensely formidable, experienced, and assured witness. What he did has become a part of the history of Canadian courtroom confrontations...***

**SCOTT:** Your witness, Mr. Martin.

**MARTIN:** Dr. Simpson, I believe you wrote a review of the book *The Trial of Steven Truscott*?

**SIMPSON:** Yes, sir.

**MARTIN:** And had you read the evidence when you ——

**SIMPSON** (*interrupting*): No, sir. This was a review of a book.

**MARTIN:** Yes. I didn't intend to put this to you, but in view of the fact that my friend put the questions he did to Dr. Camps... Ah...did you not form opinions from the book which you expressed?

**SIMPSON:** I formed an opinion *about* the book, sir.

**MARTIN:** You also expressed an opinion about the medical evidence from the book *without* having read the evidence, didn't you?

**SIMPSON:** Perhaps you'd care to quote the section?

*Martin searches through his files.*

**MARTIN:** Well, yes I...would. I quote, "This critical review of a

Canadian case is so biased by the outraged feeling of the authoress that it is difficult to weigh the facts... Medical and scientific evidence given seemed to us surprisingly sound, coming as it did from quite moderate experts and we do not subscribe to the feelings of outrage that are repeatedly called for in this account of the Truscott case," end quote. Now, sir, did you not form an opinion that the medical evidence was quite surprisingly sound?

**SIMPSON:** It seemed to me from what I had read to be surprisingly sound.

**MARTIN:** You formed that opinion?

**SIMPSON:** I formed the opinion from the book.

**MARTIN:** From the book, yes. Before you read the evidence, that is the opinion you formed from the book?

**SIMPSON:** Yes, sir.

**MARTIN:** Yes... Now, Dr. Simpson, I've read a good many of your books and one of them is entitled *Forensic Medicine* and, as my learned friend Mr. Scott says, it has gone through five editions now?

**SIMPSON:** Yes.

**MARTIN:** Do you, anywhere in this book, suggest that the stomach contents and the state to which digestion has proceeded is a reliable guide to the time of death?

**SIMPSON:** No, sir. I think that it is, as may be evident to you, a short book for the student.

**MARTIN:** It would not have made it much bigger to put in a sentence indicating that stomach contents were a reliable guide.

**SIMPSON:** No, sir. I appreciate that. It is not intended to be a comprehensive work, of course.

**MARTIN:** Well, it should contain those things upon which there is some consensus and ——

**SIMPSON:** I think you may expect the next edition, sir, to contain some reference.

**MARTIN:** Ah...you are going to change the next edition?

**SIMPSON:** Why I think that is how one improves one's textbooks — by experience.

**MARTIN:** And when did you decide to change the next edition?

**SIMPSON:** Each time I am writing I am learning.

**MARTIN:** Oh, then I will throw this away and buy the next edition... You also deal with stomach contents in the twelfth edition of Taylor, which you have edited?

**SIMPSON:** There is a reference to the stomach contents there: it is a more comprehensive book.

**MARTIN:** Very well. On page 210 under the heading "Inferences As To Time of Death" —

**SIMPSON:** I think I know the passage you are referring to.

**MARTIN:** You write, quote: "Examination of the body of a woman strangled at about 11:00 p.m. one February night showed meat, peas, mint leaf and potato still present in the stomach together with some apple pips. Very little had passed into the duodenum. She had had her last major meal of roast lamb, peas, potatoes, mint sauce, apple tart and custard at 2-2:30 p.m., no less than nine hours previously," end quote.

**SIMPSON:** Yes, I remember the case.

**MARTIN:** The description is remarkable. First of all, the cause of death was strangulation?

**SIMPSON:** Yes.

**MARTIN:** The cause of death in this case was strangling. And the description of the stomach contents — is it not very much like Dr. Penistan's?

**SIMPSON:** Yes.

**MARTIN:** Very little had passed into the duodenum, you write. Again, that is very like Dr. Penistan's?

**SIMPSON:** Yes.

**MARTIN:** In fact, the process seems to have gone further in the case of Lynne Harper because he used the phrase, quote, "very little had passed *through* the duodenum," end quote. Is that correct?

**SIMPSON:** Yes.

**MARTIN:** So you have all these analogies in these two cases and yet in yours you wrote that death occurred *nine hours* after the last meal?

**SIMPSON:** Yes.

**MARTIN:** So you get very healthy variations, don't you, in the emptying process of the stomach?

**SIMPSON:** Yes. I must comment...we don't know what the facts were in my case. There must have been some explanation but we did not find out ——

**MARTIN:** You do not know what the facts were with respect to Lynne Harper either do you?

**SIMPSON:** No, sir. I am saying this is ——

**MARTIN:** So, we have *another* parallel.

**SIMPSON:** Sir, not a parallel.

**MARTIN:** Because you have no more evidence as to what duress or fear or things of that nature were working on this girl prior to her death than in your other case?

**SIMPSON** (*subdued*): No...

**MARTIN:** Thank you.

**SIMPSON:** All I am saying is that when Dr. Penistan gave his views they, ah, seemed to be an ordinary, usual, and ah, ah, reasonable view...

**GREENSPAN:** ***As neat an example of handling an expert witness as one is likely to find. Martin didn't break Dr. Simpson, he* stretched *him. Neither of the two distinguished British pathologists can be said to have fared very well when confronted with two superior Canadian cross-examiners... But where did that leave the Supreme Court of Canada? In a moment we shall see the view they took, but before the evidence portion of the reference ended, one more doctor, a psychiatrist this time, provided an extraordinary moment. The Crown called Dr. James Hartford, who was consultant to the Guelph Reformatory at the time when young Steven Truscott was first sent there. Hartford gave evidence that Steven was, in his view, a guarded, unemotional person who could well deceive people by appearing calm in situations where most people would be clearly upset. The doctor went on to suggest that Steven Truscott had paranoid and psychopathic tendencies and on this point, Arthur Martin zeroed in...***

**MARTIN:** You found the boy had paranoid tendencies?

**HARTFORD:** Yes, sir.

**MARTIN:** And on what did you base this?

**HARTFORD:** Well, this was a very suspicious boy.

**MARTIN:** Would you not *expect* someone who had been through what he had just been through to be suspicious of people?

**HARTFORD:** Well, he didn't talk with rancour about the Court or his conviction.

**MARTIN:** What? He complained about the police, did he not?

**HARTFORD:** Yes.

**MARTIN:** He complained about a doctor giving testimony that he felt was deceitful?

**HARTFORD:** Ah, yes, sir. I found that very peculiar.

**MARTIN** (*with some sarcasm*): You did. I see. You also say in your report that he had some psychopathic tendencies, didn't you?

**HARTFORD:** Yes, sir.

**MARTIN:** Yes. And let me read to the Court what you have here, I quote: "In addition there are some things that suggest a mild suspiciousness, some petulance, and some psychopathic flavouring. This latter is indicated by his apparent philosophy that guilt is something that has to be proved and the onus is not on him to establish his innocence," end quote.

*Laughter breaks out among the judges.*

**MARTIN:** *That* was what suggested to you that he was a psychopath?
**HARTFORD:** Well, I...this note is not...I did not expand on this particular idea very much...

**GREENSPAN:** ***If that makes a psychopath, then the good doctor would have had to add everyone in this country who believes that someone is innocent until proven guilty — and at the head of that list would have been the highly amused judges of the Supreme Court of Canada. But the amusement was short-lived, as the Court and lawyers passed from evidence to argument. For two and a half days Arthur Martin presented the case for Steven Truscott. When Martin concluded Bill Bowman took another day and a half to make his points. When Bowman finished, Chief Justice Taschereau said the only thing he could say...***

**TASCHEREAU, CJ:** Gentlemen, we will reserve our decision.

**GREENSPAN:** ***It was not until three months later, on May 4, 1967, that the Supreme Court of Canada announced what that decision was. It would be pleasant to call their conclusions a shining hour for justice in this country. The bald facts, though, are that by a margin of eight to one they upheld the conviction of Steven Truscott. The heart, the kernel of the majority decision, lay in one simple, short sentence...***

**TASCHEREAU, CJ:** There were many incredibilities inherent in the evidence given by Truscott before us and we do not believe his testimony.

**GREENSPAN:** ***And so, for eight judges, the jury conviction was correct. What would they have done if Steven Truscott had not testified? I don't know. I do know that the dissenting judge, Mr. Justice Emmett Hall, would have done and said exactly what he did say, in one of the most passionate, blistering dissents ever registered in the Supreme Court...***

**HALL, J:** Having considered the case fully I believe the conviction should be quashed and a new trial directed. I take the view that the trial was not conducted according to law. Even the guiltiest criminal must be tried according to law. Applying the foregoing to the trial under review I find that there were grave errors brought about principally by the Crown counsel's method in trying to establish guilt. There was no evidence to support what the Crown counsel said in his address to the jury, referring to Truscott's having called for Jocelyne Goddette, quote: "and I suggest to you, Gentlemen, that if they were late having their supper it was God's blessing to that girl," end quote, and when he followed this with a reference to Lynne Harper and said that, quote, "she went with him to the bush and to her doom," end quote, the damage was done. Crown counsel was pursuing a planned course of action that included the subtle perversion of the jury to the idea that Truscott was sex hungry that evening and determined to have a girl in Lawson's Bush to satisfy his desires. It was inevitable that this horrible crime would arouse the passions of the whole community. When the Court is dealing with a crime that cries out for vengeance then comes the time of testing. It's especially at such a time that judicial machinery must function objectively, devoid of inflammatory appeals, with the scales of justice held in the balance. In addition, real and irreparable harm was caused to the accused by the learned trial judge's charge to the jury. His introduction of the theory that Truscott may have taken Lynne to the highway and brought her back to the bush had not the slightest foundation in the evidence. It came wholly out of thin air. These directions must on any objective reading of what was said compel acceptance of the argument that the most vital issue in Truscott's case was actually withdrawn from the jury at this late time in the trial. For all of these reasons, as stated at the beginning, I would quash the conviction and direct a new trial.

**GREENSPAN:** ***But this was only a dissent, one judge against eight, and the majority prevailed. Was justice done? Well, without necessarily sharing Isabel Le Bourdais' passionate belief that Steven Truscott was innocent, I* can *say that I* do *share Mr. Justice Hall's equally passionate belief that he was unfairly tried. Did he kill Lynne Harper? I don't know. Did he deserve a new trial? I think he did. There was, however, no new trial. On October 21, 1969, after serving the minimum ten years of his***

*sentence, Steven Truscott was given a new name and paroled. Truscott has since married; he has two children and lives anonymously in the province of Ontario. His children do not know his true identity. And it is apt, perhaps, that we end on this note because, in the final analysis, the Truscott case is a children's tragedy. It is a story of twelve-year-old Lynne Harper who died much too soon, and of fourteen-year-old Steven Truscott who either lived an uneventful, perfectly normal life with the exception of one twisted half hour in his adolescence, or — and this would be worse — who was inexorably caught up in a malfunctioning justice machine. We cannot know for certain, and it is likely we never will, for it is more than twenty-five years now since those two children took that bicycle ride together in the summer of 1959...*

# Producer's Notes

Before the Truscott story we have only found it necessary in one other instance to present a case in two parts. This was the famous case of Peter Demeter, the Toronto developer convicted for the murder of his wife, Christine, in 1974. That script (included in Volume 1 of *The Scales of Justice*) was prepared for radio by Guy Gavriel Kay and Ian Malcolm. We decided to turn to Kay again for the preparation of the Truscott script.

Currently the associate producer of "The Scales of Justice," Winnipeg-born Kay is a lawyer as well as a writer, in addition to being a radio producer and director. He articled in Toronto with Edward L. Greenspan. At Oxford he collaborated with J.R.R. Tolkien's son in the preparation of the great fantasy writer's posthumous bestseller *The Silmarillion*. His own fantasy-trilogy, *The Fionavar Tapestry*, is being simultaneously published in Canada, England, and the United States.

Scripting the Truscott case required the gifts of an overachiever like Kay. No other crime in Canada has divided public opinion as much as the 1959 murder of twelve-year-old Lynne Harper for which Steven Truscott, then fourteen, was ultimately convicted. Eminent politicians, lawyers, doctors, and writers, not only in Canada but around the world, had formed firm opinions on Truscott's guilt or innocence.

Our program has always tried to look at the evidence and the workings of Canada's legal system in an impartial way, regardless of the emotional climate surrounding a particular case. In the two episodes re-creating the tragic story of Lynne Harper and Steven Truscott we sought to achieve this not only through Kay's meticulously researched script and host Edward L. Greenspan's thoughtful commentary but also by assembling the finest cast of Canadian performers.

One of the keys to a dispassionate examination of a hotly contested issue is good acting: performances that are all the more powerful for being realistic and understated. This described, I believe, Eric Peterson's brilliant portrayal of Steven Truscott. Long established as outstanding among Canada's younger actors, in this program Peterson confirmed his reputation.

Similar excellence characterized the performances of Frank Perry and Harvey Atkin, in the roles of Truscott's first defence lawyer J. Frank Donnelly and prosecutor Glenn Hays. Notable also were Pierre Berton (playing himself) and Michael J. Reynolds as OPP Inspector Graham. The late Sean Sullivan, a fine and versatile actor, portrayed Truscott's father with power and sensitivity.

Part 1, entitled "The Children's Hour," was also a showcase for young Canadian talent, including Reena Schellenberg as Lynne Harper and the exceptionally gifted child-actor Torquil Campbell as defence witness Douglas Oats. Terri Hawkes, though no longer a child, conveyed the texture of a fourteen-year-old girl's voice perfectly in the role of Crown witness Jocelyne Goddette.

In Part 2, "The Darkest Hour," dealing with Truscott's appearance before the Supreme Court of Canada, the courtroom duel was between Henry Ramer and Michael Tait, two fine actors who work with the mind as well as the heart. They played, respectively, Truscott's lawyer (now the eminent jurist) Arthur Martin and Crown Attorney Don Scott. Their devastating cross-examinations of two world-famous English pathologists, Dr. F.E. Camps and Professor Keith Simpson — played by veteran actors Sean Mulcahy and Gillie Fenwick — re-created a truly memorable moment in Canadian courtroom history.

As once before on "The Scales of Justice," the radio artist Max Ferguson treated the production to a *tour de force* by playing all the voices of the jurists on the Supreme Court, with the exception of the dissenting judgement of Mr. Justice Emmett Hall. This judgement was delivered with reasoned passion by Mavor Moore. The role of Isabel Le Bourdais, the author whose book resulted in the unique hearing, was performed by Nonnie Griffin. True to what has by now become almost a Canadian show-business tradition, Gordon Pinsent played the role of a member in the House of Commons.

The success of the Truscott show, which was among the ACTRA award nominees for the best radio program of 1984, was in no small measure due to its crisp stereo sound, the work of the talented young sound engineer John McCarthy.

G.J.

# By Reason of Doubt

*Ellen Godfrey*

## The Cast

Commentary by Edward L. Greenspan, Q.C.

| | |
|---|---|
| **CYRIL BELSHAW** | Gerard Parkes |
| **BETTY BELSHAW** | Maureen Fitzgerald |
| **DIANA BELSHAW** | Susan Hogan |
| **M. HEIM** for the prosecution | David Calderisi |
| **M. PASCHOUD** for the defence | Esse Ljungh |

With the support of (in alphabetical order): Jean Marc Amyot, Harvey Atkin, Jean Cavall, John Douglas, Alan Fawcett, John Gilbert, François Klanfer, Robert LaChance, Diana Leblanc, Bill Lynn, Richard Monette, Nicole Morin, Denis O'Connor, Frank Perry, Michael J. Reynolds, and Paul Soles

## Scene 1 / In the Paris Métro

**CYRIL:** All right then, Betty. I've decided upon our plans for the day. We'll meet at the Galeries Lafayette for an aperitif before lunch.

**BETTY:** Well... I guess, yes...

**CYRIL:** That will be most convenient as I'll be shopping there all morning.

**BETTY:** Well, that ought to be all right.

**CYRIL:** Of course it will be all right. You should easily have your reader's card by noon.

**BETTY:** Yes... It ought to go smoothly, I suppose.

**CYRIL:** And then, in the afternoon, you'll be all ready to begin research on your book.

**BETTY:** It's just that I've waited so long to begin work on this book... and now, if something were to go wrong...

**CYRIL:** Nothing will go wrong.

**BETTY:** I don't know why I let myself get nervous about things like this.

**CYRIL:** Really, I know you'll find it quite straightforward.

**BETTY:** Yes... yes, of course. Now let me see...

**CYRIL:** Yeah?

**BETTY:** Here's my passport — they'll need that for identification — and letters from UBC. Yes, that should be everything.

**CYRIL:** All right now, Betty, don't worry about a thing... I'll see you in a while. Bye.

**CONDUCTOR:** Bourse...

**BETTY:** See you at one o'clock.

**GREENSPAN:** ***And that, according to world-renowned University of British Columbia anthropology professor Cyril Belshaw, was the last he ever saw of his wife, Betty Belshaw, alive.***

*Cyril and Betty Belshaw were on a sabbatical in Europe. On that cold January morning in 1979 Betty, an English instructor, was on her way to the National Library to do some research for a book on Katherine Mansfield. Dr. Belshaw, the New-Zealand-born anthropologist, had also been working during his sabbatical. But, he was planning to do some shopping at the famous Parisian department store, Galeries Lafayette, that day.*

*Now, the distance is no more than two hundred metres between the subway station and the National Library. Yet Betty seems to have never reached the library. She vanished...disappeared from the busy Paris streets, in broad daylight. What did happen to Betty Belshaw? My name is Edward Greenspan, and the story you are about to hear is reconstructed from the book* **By Reason of Doubt** *by Ellen Godfrey, and from her interviews with Canadian, French, and Swiss authorities, as well as from additional interviews with some of the main participants in the case.*

## Scene 2 / In Cyril Belshaw's Hotel Room

**CYRIL** (*answering the telephone*): Cyril Belshaw here.
**DIANA:** Dad? Dad, is that you?
**CYRIL:** Yes.
**DIANA:** I got your message. Is there...is something wrong, Dad?
**CYRIL:** It's the most bizarre...
**DIANA:** Dad? What is it? What's the matter?
**CYRIL:** I can hardly bring myself to tell you...You won't believe it...It's your mommy. She's...I don't know where she's gone!
**DIANA:** What do you mean? I...I don't understand.
**CYRIL:** Yesterday she was supposed to meet me for lunch...and she didn't show up. I'm worried. Now, that's not like your mommy, not like her at all...
**DIANA:** It certainly isn't.

*Both laugh uneasily.*

**CYRIL:** And she didn't come back to the hotel, and I checked...and she never arrived at the library. And then, I waited all night, and today...still no sign of her! I'm dreadfully worried.
**DIANA:** What a night for you, Dad. What a terrible night.

**CYRIL:** I've talked to the police, but you know they haven't got back to me yet. They say thousands of women disappear in Paris each year. They shrug their shoulders; they hardly seem to care. They... They think she's taken off with a man!

**DIANA:** They don't know Mommy. Do they?

*Both laugh.*

**CYRIL:** I went to the Canadian Embassy... and I gave them every det... every little detail. I stayed up all night remembering, worrying, writing out every detail in her description, thinking [*His voice breaks, as if he is trying not to cry*]...

**DIANA:** Dad, I'm flying over to Paris.

**CYRIL:** No. It... it's not necessary. I... Oh, there's nothing you can do. You have your job. The play you're in in Calgary, is... is it still running?

**DIANA:** Yes.

**CYRIL:** I find myself thinking that something dreadful must have happened like...

**DIANA:** Oh...

**CYRIL:** I... I don't want to think of that... but... logically the idea can't be avoided.

**DIANA:** Dad... Dad, just hang in there. Okay? I love you. And I'll do anything I can to help.

**CYRIL:** What could have happened? If it had been an accident, a mugging...

**DIANA:** Try not to worry. You're certain to hear something later today.

**CYRIL:** Yes, you're absolutely right. I'll call again, as soon as I have any news.

**DIANA:** And I'll come there, Dad, whenever you need me. But, you'll see, she'll turn up. She might have taken too much of one of her medicines, you know...

**GREENSPAN:** ***But Betty Belshaw did not turn up. And so, three days after her disappearance, Cyril Belshaw made the long drive back to Switzerland to the little mountain town where he and Betty were spending his sabbatical... to wait, and to worry.***

***And then, on March 28, two and a half months after Betty's disappearance, on a deserted mountain road more than sixty kilometres from the Belshaws' apartment in Montana-Vermala, road workers, who had been clearing rocks and debris from the roadside, called the police...***

## Scene 3 / A Mountainside in Switzerland

**POLICEMAN 1:** Hey, over here...Jean! Look!

**POLICEMAN 2:** Oh...Looks like one of the farmers has been dumping livestock again...

**POLICEMAN 1:** Let's have a look...Jesus!

**POLICEMAN 2** (*very softly*): Better leave it...it's human...we'd better get the *Sûreté* down here. *Sacré*.

**POLICEMAN 1:** She's been here a while, I'd say.

**POLICEMAN 2** (*calling*): Hey! You, *cantonnier*! Drive out and get the *Sûreté* and step on it.

**POLICEMAN 1:** Never have found her, never, not in a million years...

**GREENSPAN:** ***The grisly discovery under the bridge near the small Swiss village of Le Sépey caused a sensation. The newspapers of Lausanne and other towns near where the body was discovered published the details as the magistrate was prepared to make them public: "Middle-aged woman, light-coloured hair, well-cared-for teeth, four gold crowns. Age between 35 and 45...wrapped in garbage bags tied with twine..." And at the headquarters of the Police de Sûreté, in Lausanne, the young officer on the case, Sergeant Wyss, was getting nowhere.***

## Scene 4 / At a Swiss Police Station

**WYSS:** Hey, Guignard!

**GUIGNARD:** Yes, Sergeant Wyss!

**WYSS:** Anything on that Le Sépey corpse yet?

**GUIGNARD** (*flipping through papers*): Nothing today, sir. Let's see...uh...We've been through more than two hundred missing-person reports and no luck. Nothing.

**WYSS:** I got a call from the guys over in the Valais today, you know?

**GUIGNARD:** Yeah?

**WYSS:** Seems they got a telex from Berne. Some woman missing in Paris in January. Her husband is living in the Valais, in the ski resort, Montana-Vermala. Know the place?

**GUIGNARD:** Yeah, well I know where it is...Never been there, I don't think, but,...ah, what's that got to do with this Le Sépey thing?

**WYSS:** I know, doesn't seem likely there'll be a connection but Reichen from the Valais *Sûreté* wants to go check it out. Go along with him and look into it, will you? Here's the file...

## Scene 5 / In Belshaw's Apartment

**CYRIL** (*answering the door*): Yes, gentlemen, can I do something for you?

**REICHEN:** Are you Professor Belshaw?

**CYRIL:** Yes, I am.

**REICHEN:** I'm Sergeant Reichen from Sierre, and this is Sergeant Guignard from Lausanne.

**GUIGNARD:** How do you do, sir?

**REICHEN:** We want to ask you a few questions about the disappearance of your wife...in Paris.

**CYRIL:** Yes? Is that right? Well, come in, officers...Come in here and sit down. I must admit I'm surprised to see you. It's the first time anyone in Switzerland has shown the slightest interest in the matter.

**GREENSPAN:** ***Exactly who said what at this important interview was later disputed at Belshaw's trial. But all agreed it was a polite interview. Belshaw was co-operative, exact with details...***

**CYRIL:** And that's the story, then. Not a word from her since that day in Paris, January 15, 1979, to be precise. Now here is a picture of her. Quite a clear one, as a matter of fact. Good colour.

**REICHEN:** Would you have dental records, sir?

**CYRIL:** No, I would not have dental records. It's not the sort of thing one keeps around the house. But I could obtain them from her dentist.

**REICHEN:** Could you give us his name and address?

**CYRIL:** Of course, of course...but, if you don't mind, why don't I write for them? The dentist is a friend of mine; it will be much faster. Yes, that's...that's what I'll do, write to the dentist. How will that be?

**REICHEN:** That will be just fine, sir, thank you...

## Scene 6 / In the Lausanne Police Station

**GUIGNARD:** Oh, Sergeant Wyss, we've got those dental records from that Canadian professor in Montana-Vermala. Reichen sent them over from Sierre. Here, let's have a look...

**WYSS** (*slowly, unwillingly, as if puzzled*): No...there is no way. Just isn't the same person.

**GREENSPAN:** ***But Sergeant Wyss wasn't satisfied. He came back to those dental records and finally, acting on a hunch, he sent via INTERPOL another request to Vancouver for Mrs. Belshaw's dental records.***

***In the meantime, Cyril Belshaw had returned to Vancouver. On August 24, eight months after Belshaw had reported Betty's disappearance, Constable Smith of the RCMP detachment at the University of British Columbia called him.***

## Scene 7 / Telephone Conversation

**CYRIL** (*answering the telephone*): Professor Cyril Belshaw here.

**SMITH:** This is Constable Smith from the U.B.C. RCMP detachment.

**CYRIL:** Oh yes, Officer. What can I do for you?

**SMITH:** We've received a telex from Switzerland, Professor Belshaw. They, ah, need some information there in regards to the disappearance of your wife last winter?

**CYRIL:** Yes?

**SMITH:** Ah, can you give me the name of your dentist, Professor Belshaw?

**GREENSPAN:** ***The next day, Cyril Belshaw telephoned the detachment. Later he came over with a written statement:***

**CYRIL:** "I wish to make the following statement in order to correct information which I supplied to the Swiss police authorities. The Swiss police authorities requested me to obtain my wife's dental charts, in connection with the search resulting from her disappearance in January. These did not reach me until later than anticipated, and in fact a few days before I had to leave in May for London and Paris, and ultimately Vancouver. When they arrived I felt I could not face the psychological trauma of possibly identifying my wife without the presence of family and friends or the delays in returning to my home and family after many months of hope that my wife might be found alive. On impulse I altered the charts during the copying process, before distributing them. While this has probably not had material consequences for the investigation, it is clear that it might have done so, and it is important for me to express my regrets for a foolish action and to clarify the matter for the authorities. I understand that the correct dental chart is now being forwarded by the RCMP."

**GREENSPAN:** ***The consequences of Dr. Belshaw's impulsive act may or may not have been material to the investigation. But there is no doubt that they came to be so regarded by the Swiss authorities. On the basis of the new dental chart forwarded by the RCMP, the Swiss police concluded that the remains found by the mountain road at Le Sépey were indeed those of Betty Belshaw. Whether or not this conclusion was correct, and whether or not in arriving at it they had been influenced by Professor Belshaw's acknowledgement that he had falsified the set of dental records, the Swiss police became very anxious to interview the Canadian professor...***

## Scene 8 / In a Lausanne Police Station

**CHATELAIN** (*from behind door*): Yes? Yes? Who is it?
**WYSS:** It's Sergeant Wyss, Magistrate. You said you want to see me.
**CHATELAIN:** Ah, sit down. I want to discuss this Belshaw case with you.
**WYSS:** Yes, sir.
**CHATELAIN:** Since we identified the body as Mrs. Belshaw's, the authorities here in Vaud have tried to get co-operation from the Canadians. I'm sorry to say, Sergeant, that we have not been successful.
**WYSS** (*surprised*): But why is that, sir? The professor has confessed to falsifying those dental records.
**CHATELAIN:** I know, it's hard to understand. But it seems their law is very different. But, of course, we can't let it drop. As is my right as a magistrate, I have declared a *Commission Rogatoire*. You and Sergeant Fischlin are to go to Canada and investigate.

**WYSS:** But of course. When do we start?

**CHATELAIN:** Right away. I want you in Vancouver by the 23rd of September.

## Scene 9/In the RCMP Office at U.B.C.

**GREENSPAN:** ***And so it was that Professor Belshaw found himself summoned to an interview — suddenly, with no warning — at the RCMP detachment on the campus of the University of British Columbia. Present were Fischlin and Wyss from Switzerland, Constable Smith from the RCMP, another RCMP officer, and a translator. The interview you are about to hear is a dramatization reconstructed from testimony at Belshaw's trial.***

**CYRIL:** Yes, yes, I am Professor Belshaw. You say you have news of my wife?

**WYSS:** I am Sergeant Wyss, from Lausanne *Sûreté*, and this is my colleague Sergeant Fischlin...and yes, Professor Belshaw, we have news of your wife...as if it is news to you!

**CYRIL:** What do you mean?

**WYSS:** I mean she's dead, Professor Belshaw. It was her body, all along at Le Sépey as you ——

**CYRIL:** Oh my God!

**WYSS:** —— knew very well when you falsified her dental records.

**CYRIL:** I...dead! Betty dead! There's no question, then? She's been...identified? Incontrovertibly...iden...identified?

**WYSS** (*suddenly, almost shouting*): Don't play that game with us, Professor! Why did you kill her?

**CYRIL:** I didn't...I ——

**FISCHLIN:** Don't bother us with that! We know you did it!

**CYRIL:** But...you can't be serious...I...

**FISCHLIN** (*without pausing for Belshaw*): Come on...Come on...don't play games with us, Professor, what did you do — strangle her first?

**CYRIL:** Betty, dead?

**WYSS** (*annoyed with Fischlin, as there is no proof of cause of death*): We know you did it, Professor, you might as well tell us all about it.

**CYRIL** (*emotionally*): How could you suspect me of such a thing? After a long hard day, to call me down here like this, without any warning and tell me... Betty dead... and to suspect *me*... it's unbelievable...

**FISCHLIN** (*opening his briefcase*): Here, let me show you what I brought over from Switzerland... How do you like these pictures, Professor?

**CYRIL** (*making a slight gagging noise, trying to speak*): I...I...

**WYSS** (*hectoring*): Pretty disgusting, aren't they? Aren't they, Professor?

**CYRIL** (*recovering himself*): Yes, dreadful. Dreadful. There's no need to shove them under my nose. I get the point.

**WYSS:** Well, Professor Belshaw? What have you got to tell us about this?

**CYRIL** (*angry, surprised, frightened at this attack*): But she disappeared in Paris... I tell you I had nothing to do with this!

**FISCHLIN:** Don't treat us like fools! We know the truth, Belshaw! You killed your wife...

**CYRIL:** No! No...

**WYSS:** And you killed her in Switzerland...

**FISCHLIN:** And wrapped her in garbage bags... a brand which is to be found only in Switzerland... only in the neighbourhood of Montana. It's no use trying to pretend anymore, Professor...

**CYRIL:** But... it's not possible... (*more calmly*) She disappeared in Paris.

**WYSS:** Are you a religious man, a Christian, Professor Belshaw?

**CYRIL:** What? A Christian? No, as a matter of fact, I'm an atheist.

**WYSS:** Maybe that explains it then.

**CYRIL:** Explains, Sergeant? What do you mean, explains?

**WYSS:** Explains you, Professor Belshaw. Explains how you can be so cool, so calm, so lacking in normal Christian feeling. I find it... unbelievable... that, having committed such a horrible act... you feel no remorse... no guilt...

**CYRIL:** Nonsense! Nonsense!

**SMITH:** Professor Belshaw, may I ask you a few questions?

**CYRIL** (*relieved*): Yes, of course, Constable Smith.

**SMITH:** Tell me Professor, is there another woman in your life?

**CYRIL** (*composed*): Of course not. That's an absurd idea.

**SMITH** (*kindly*): Wouldn't it be better, in the long run, for you to tell us the truth?

**CYRIL:** But I am... Why do you persist with this?

**SMITH:** Believe me, Professor Belshaw, the truth would be better for all of us. If you continue to deny it, we are going to have to investigate you... thoroughly...

**WYSS** (*interrupting*): Now, why don't you just tell us the truth, Professor. You're wasting everyone's time. We already know you killed your wife. These denials won't do you any good.

**CYRIL** (*calmly*): The truth is, Sergeant Wyss, that I had nothing at all to do with the death of my wife, and it doesn't matter how many times you ask me, I'm going to tell you the same thing!

**FISCHLIN** (*exasperated*): If you were in Switzerland you wouldn't get away with this, I can tell you that, Professor. We'd have the truth.

**GREENSPAN:** ***This unbelievable and, under Canadian law, totally improper interview proceeded for two hours and ten minutes. Then, the officers drove out with Belshaw to his home and, with his permission, searched through Betty's things. In the days that followed, they conducted a thorough investigation, talking to all of Belshaw's friends and colleagues. But when they wanted to interview Belshaw again, his lawyer told him that his advice to Belshaw was not to agree to another interview. This of course was sound advice, as well as being a fundamental right of anyone under our law from which no adverse inference could possibly be drawn. To the Swiss it was a sign of guilt — the first and perhaps the main indication in their eyes that Belshaw was not an innocent man. When Fischlin and Wyss returned to Switzerland, they reported to the examining magistrate, Monsieur Chatelain.***

## Scene 10/In Magistrate Chatelain's Office

**CHATELAIN:** So, Sergeant Wyss, you say the Canadian police, they agreed? They agreed Belshaw didn't have to answer?

**WYSS:** Yes, Magistrate. But they say that's how it goes there.

**CHATELAIN:** And when you asked him why he falsified the dental records?

**WYSS** (*sarcastically*): Oh, he was upset, didn't want to believe she was dead... He didn't know what he was doing... He's so sorry...

**CHATELAIN:** Well then, we must get to the bottom of it... We must investigate. We must follow up the leads you found in

Vancouver...talk to everyone who knew the Belshaws there... check in Montana...check on their route to Paris, on the route to Le Sépey...in London...

**GREENSPAN:** ***In Lausanne, and in Montana-Vermala, the police launched an exhaustive investigation. Every move of Belshaw's while in Switzerland, every expenditure was examined and all the details of a person's life, including those details that in Canadian law would be totally irrelevant and inadmissible but in the eyes of the Swiss could amount to evidence started to fill the dossiers of the examining magistrate in Vaud.***

***Meanwhile, in Vancouver, Professor Belshaw was facing a difficult decision. He had an important conference to attend in Paris, in November. His suspicion of the Swiss system of justice made him apprehensive, yet professionally he felt he*** **had** ***to go to Paris. As his defence lawyer was later to say: Why should a man, found guilty of nothing, and, we might add, not even charged with any crime, be a prisoner in his own country? And so, Belshaw made up his mind...***

## Scene 11/Jetway in the Paris Airport

**PARIS POLICE OFFICER:** *Bonjour, Monsieur*, are you *Le Professeur* Belshaw?

**CYRIL:** Yes, er *oui, Monsieur.*

**PARIS POLICE OFFICER:** I am of the airport police, *Monsieur*, and I hereby arrest you under an international *mandat* of the Swiss government...

**GREENSPAN:** ***Belshaw was put into prison to await his extradition hearing. There, defended by one of the most famous lawyers in France, Robert Badinter, now the Minister of Justice, he fought his extradition. The Swiss found this another suspicious circumstance. Why, they wondered, if he was innocent, did he not wish to come to Switzerland to tell his story?***

***Finally Belshaw's extradition hearing took place. The French court found that there was reason to believe that Betty Belshaw had been murdered, and reason to believe that this murder took place in Switzerland.***

*This apparently satisfied the French that Belshaw should be extradited. For the next seven months, the Canadian anthropologist was imprisoned in a Lausanne jail while the Swiss police continued their investigation.*

*On December 3, 1980, under a blaze of publicity in Switzerland, England, and Canada, the trial opened in the Canton of Vaud.*

## Scene 12 / In Court

**PRESIDENT:** Do you promise to give the most serious attention to the proceedings which are here beginning, not to falter in the exercise of your duty neither through interest, nor through weakness, nor through fear, nor through favour, nor out of hatred; to make your decision entirely upon these proceedings, according to your own conviction...

**GREENSPAN:** *The Swiss system, which had held Belshaw in prison for many months before charging him with any offence, is a system very different from our own. The Canadian system, like the American, is rooted in the Common Law. It is shaped by a British tradition of justice. It makes at least an attempt to put the individual citizen on an equal footing with the state and appoints an impartial body, a judge and jury of his peers, to resolve the question of his innocence or guilt. Our system does not regard the state as infallible and does not assume that its servants, the prosecutor and the police, are necessarily free of error or malice. On the contrary, it presumes that whoever is accused of a crime is innocent unless, on relevant evidence, the prosecution can prove his guilt beyond a reasonable doubt. The Swiss system, however, has roots both in German law and in French law, a law which was shaped by the Napoleonic Code. This inquisitorial system, or Civil Law as it is also called, is accordingly imperious and affords fewer safeguards for personal and civil liberties. It is a system that assumes that the state, the prosecutor, and the police are both wise and benevolent. Under the Civil Law, once the accused is sent to trial, there is an enormous presumption of guilt.*

*After swearing in the jurors, the President read out the charge...*

**PRESIDENT:** Between the 6th and 13th of January, 1979, perhaps following a dispute due to the discovery, by Betty Joy Belshaw, of the liaison of her husband with another woman, Cyril Belshaw, by a means which has not been determined, in the couple's apartment in Montana-Vermala — or en route between Montana and Paris — intentionally killed his wife.

**STOUDMANN:** *Monsieur le Président*, I must ask to be allowed to raise an objection at this time...a *most* serious matter...

**PRESIDENT** (*surprised*): Ah...Yes? Go ahead, *Maître* Stoudmann.

**GREENSPAN:** ***The man who took the unusual step of raising a procedural point before the President could call the first witness, unusual that is in a Swiss court, was the Swiss criminal lawyer Eric Stoudmann, the younger of Dr. Belshaw's two defence counsels.***

**STOUDMANN:** *Monsieur le Président*, contrary to our law, contrary to our justice, the Lausanne police and the RCMP taped the first interview with Belshaw. Then, Your Honour, worse and worse, important parts — threats by the police, Your Honour! — were removed from the files!

**GREENSPAN:** ***This was a serious charge; under Swiss law* everything *which happens between the accused and the police must be in the files...***

**PRESIDENT** (*in an avuncular manner*): Is this true, Professor Belshaw? Did you feel yourself threatened? Were the accounts of the interview in the dossier incorrect?

**CYRIL:** Yes, Your Honour. At that first interview they threatened me. They said, "You wouldn't be able to get away with things like this in Switzerland."

**PRESIDENT:** You saw that as a threat, did you?

**CYRIL:** Yes, Your Honour.

**PASCHOUD:** *Monsieur le Président?*

**PRESIDENT:** Yes, *Maître* Paschoud.

**GREENSPAN:** ***Jean Philippe Paschoud was Dr. Belshaw's senior defence counsel, head of an old, established Swiss family firm whose clients included Chaplin, Chanel, and other celebrities. Paschoud very seldom practised criminal law.***

**PASCHOUD** (*emotionally*): *Monsieur le Président*, the defence feels this is extremely important, a crucial matter. Our police have behaved most incorrectly.

**STOUDMANN:** Your Honour, we have read the transcription of that interview... It is contrary to law, and contrary to justice. It was a savage interview. And, Your Honour, it was illegal according to our procedures.

**HEIM:** *Monsieur le Président?*

**PRESIDENT:** Yes, *Maître* Heim?

**GREENSPAN:** ***Willy Heim was the prosecutor. A high-ranking and very experienced official in the Swiss justice system.***

**HEIM:** Speaking for the prosecution, we feel it would be against logic and common sense to remove the edited transcript of the tape from the files after the prosecution and the President of this tribunal have both seen it.

**GREENSPAN:** ***However, somewhat to the surprise of the Swiss, who seldom exclude evidence from the files, no matter how improperly obtained, the President upheld the defence objection and the transcripts were thrown out. The President then continued reading the articles of accusation, including a deposition from the Vancouver Mounted Police...***

**PRESIDENT:** On July 19, 1979, Constable Fleet of the RCMP was driving around a secluded part of the university at 11:00 p.m. There was a car parked where it would not easily be seen. Constable Fleet approached the car, which appeared to be empty. As he approached he saw a man climb off a woman. Her clothes were in disarray. The couple showed their identification. They were Professor Belshaw and a woman named Margery Wilson.

**GREENSPAN:** ***Later, Dr. Belshaw was to dispute this account bitterly. When the President finished, the examining of the witnesses began. The forensic dentist was the first to testify...***

**IMOSTERBERG:** We examined the teeth of the corpse, and the dental records. We found the records were falsified with Liquid Paper and then photocopied. The records first deposed were altered charts. But in the correct charts we found that the body had four gold crowns. The evidence was conclusive. The body was that of Madame Belshaw.

**PRESIDENT:** And you are certain of this identification — you're absolutely certain? There is no doubt whatsoever in your mind?

**IMOSTERBERG:** I confirm it absolutely.

**GREENSPAN:** ***The Swiss forensic dentist may not have had any doubt in his own mind. But since the defence never challenged this vital evidence — the only evidence of identification — to this day we have only the Swiss doctor's word for the Le Sépey corpse's being, in fact, Betty Belshaw. At this point the medical evidence was interrupted while the President began questioning the accused — common practice in the inquisitorial procedure.***

**PRESIDENT:** Let us admit, Professor Belshaw, that anyone in a moment of passion could kill his wife. But to let her remains lie, unclaimed — this, I can't understand. I have for you all the sympathy a magistrate can have for an accused, but this! It's...it's beyond understanding!

**CYRIL** (*slowly*): I couldn't support the psychological trauma of such an identification without my family. I was alone in the apartment. I wanted to think of my wife living. And then, I was irrational during that time, up and down, and... with the dental records before me, so technical, so cold and technical... Something...involuntary...came over me. That dental chart. It had nothing to do with a living being!

**PRESIDENT:** So you mean... did you intend to remain forever uncertain about the fate of your wife?

**CYRIL:** I didn't want to think of something like that.

**PRESIDENT:** If you had killed your wife ——

**CYRIL** (*interrupting*): I didn't kill my wife! I thought only of the dental record! And the possibility that my wife might be dead, and at that minute I couldn't bear... I was cowardly, I know.

**HEIM:** *Monsieur le Président?*

**PRESIDENT:** Yes, go ahead, *Maître* Heim.

**HEIM:** Professor Belshaw, it was fifteen days between the time you wrote for those records and the day you falsified them. Fifteen days! How can you say you did it involuntarily, in an emotional state?

**PRESIDENT:** You say you wanted to have an identification, couldn't go on, but it's *you* yourself who prevented that. That is what is so horrible.

**CYRIL:** It was wrong. It was serious, what I did. My conscience weighs upon me.

**PRESIDENT** (*angrily*): Let us admit, Professor Belshaw — how many people when told about the finding of a body say they can't face it and falsify the record? Wives, husbands, sons, daughters, how many of *them* falsify the record? How many do you think? How many? How many?

**CYRIL:** Very few, very few.

**PRESIDENT:** Less than zero per cent! In fact it has never happened.

**CYRIL:** How many people have had their wives disappear as mine had done...and then lived through the events after, having their hopes raised...and then dashed?

**GREENSPAN:** ***The prosecutor and the President continued hectoring Belshaw, trying to break him, to catch him out. They did not succeed. The medical evidence continued as Dr. Genillard took the stand...***

**GENILLARD:** The body was found stretched out, on its side, naked, wrapped in a plastic sack.

**GREENSPAN:** ***Progressor Marc Henri-Thélin, forensic doctor, gave his testimony...***

**HENRI-THÉLIN:** We could not determine the cause of death.

**PASCHOUD:** Then how can you be sure she met with foul play?

**HENRI-THÉLIN:** But she was naked...wrapped in garbage bags.

**PASCHOUD:** *Oui, Oui,* but what medical proof do you have? Isn't it possible she died a natural death and then somebody else came along and denuded the body and disposed of it?

**HENRI-THÉLIN** (*reluctantly*): Yes, yes, I suppose so.

**GREENSPAN:** ***Unfortunately the evidence of Alex-Rudolphe Guger, the toxicologist, was inconclusive...***

**PRESIDENT:** And did you examine the body for poisons, *Monsieur* Guger?

**GUGER:** Yes, *Monsieur le Président.* But the body was in such an advanced state of putrefaction we could determine nothing with certainty.

**GREENSPAN:** ***All experts called in from Switzerland and abroad failed to agree with any certainty on the cause of death. Then...***

**PRESIDENT:** Call Madame Wuest.

**MADAME WUEST:** Yes, I knew Madame Belshaw. Both of them. I looked after the renting of the apartment where the Belshaws lived in Montana-Vermala. They seemed agreeable tenants.

**PRESIDENT:** Did you ever see Professor Belshaw with a woman other than his wife?

**MADAME WUEST:** Oh yes. I remember very clearly. The summer before Professor and Madame Belshaw came to stay he came to look over the apartment. He had a "lady" with him, a *petite amie* as we say...*you know*...and right in front of his lady friend he said that the apartment looked fine to him, but that he would have to telephone his wife.

**PRESIDENT:** And why do you remember that so clearly?

**MADAME WUEST:** It was not a thing one forgets, to say *that* in front of a lady friend like that...I remembered.

**GREENSPAN:** ***At this point the President gave Dr. Belshaw a chance to explain about his relationship with Mrs. Wilson, and the incident of the car on the U.B.C. campus. Her deposition was read to the court. She claimed that their love affair provided relief for her from a difficult marriage, but that neither she nor Belshaw intended to leave their spouses...***

**PASCHOUD:** Do you confirm Mrs. Wilson's statement, Professor Belshaw?

**CYRIL:** Yes, it is exactly correct. But, I must say one thing, what Constable Fleet said is disgusting to me. His story about us in the car is not true. We were in the car next to the physics lab; it was well lit. The car lights were on. We were discussing an exam. I have admitted that we were having an affair. But...something like that? Sex in a car? That's absolutely disgusting!

**GREENSPAN:** ***Then the President tried to prove that Belshaw never contacted the Swiss police...***

**PRESIDENT:** And so, you testify you contacted the French police when your wife disappeared; you contacted the Canadian Consul in Paris; you called friends in London and in Canada. (*slowly, accusingly*) But you never contacted the Swiss police!

**CYRIL:** I thought the Canadian embassy would contact the Swiss police.

**PRESIDENT:** You claim that you were anxious to know what happened to your wife, yet you refused to co-operate with the Swiss police. Why?

**CYRIL:** Never! Never!

**PRESIDENT** (*suddenly compassionate, helpful*): You know, under our law there are three possible verdicts: you can be convicted, acquitted totally, or acquitted because there is a reasonable doubt. If, after all that has happened, there is a choice of condemnation or acquittal, could you accept acquittal by the benefit of doubt?

**CYRIL** (*with conviction*): It's not what I want. I had nothing to do with the death of my wife. Only an acquittal would be just. [*Cyril strikes the table for emphasis.*] (*Frantically*) It's unbearable that people could suspect me of such a thing!

**HEIM:** I would like to ask you a few questions, Professor Belshaw, on behalf of the prosecution.

**CYRIL:** Yes, *Maître* Heim?

**HEIM:** I know we have heard depositions from Vancouver that say you were happy with your wife, but you showed off your affair. You displayed your mistress. You spent twelve days with her at Montana when you knew your wife was coming there later.

**CYRIL:** No, it was not like that. It was low season, there was almost no one there.

**HEIM:** Oh come, you slept with your mistress there. Someone who saw you together that summer might later say to your wife, "Madame, how you have changed since last summer." Let's admit it, you were indifferent to whether your wife found out.

**CYRIL:** No, *Maître* Heim. I considered that danger. I decided the risk was slight.

**HEIM:** And...what would have happened if your wife had found out?

**CYRIL:** If she found out? She would have criticized me; she would have complained bitterly; there would have been a scene, an argument...

**HEIM** (*interjects quickly*): There was such a scene?

**CYRIL:** No.

**HEIM:** Have you ever struck your wife?

**CYRIL:** Never. Never in our life.

*Heim searches through the papers in front of him.*

**HEIM:** Yes, well, I read from your own words, quote: "I may have struck her, she may have struck me," end quote — you said that about a fight in the early 1960s...Now this infidelity...how *could* she have borne it?

**CYRIL:** You must keep in mind that my wife was not intolerant towards things like that. She did not attach much importance to the physical act.

**HEIM:** Tell me, Professor Belshaw. Tell me this. Why, when your wife did not return to the hotel in Paris on January 15, why did you not phone the concierge at your apartment in Montana to see if she had not returned home? It seems the very first thing you would do.

**CYRIL:** I was completely at sea...The idea never entered my head. I just never imagined that my wife would run away.

**HEIM** (*with scorn*): A pretty answer!

**GREENSPAN:** ***Strange and wholly improper as the Swiss method of presenting the prosecution's case may seem to us — the prosecutor and the President arguing with the defendant, demanding that he offer alternate hypotheses to prove his innocence, and making sarcastic remarks if his answers failed to satisfy them — this was what Professor Belshaw had to endure until the defence's turn came to call its witnesses. The most important defence witness was Belshaw's daughter — the Canadian actress Diana Belshaw...***

**DIANA:** Our family is very private: we keep ourselves to ourselves. We find it difficult to show our emotions...But just because we are reserved doesn't mean we don't feel. There was so much warmth, so much affection in our family!

**PRESIDENT** (*solicitous, considerate*): Now tell us, Mademoiselle Belshaw, how would your mother have felt if she had heard of your father's liaison?

**DIANA** (*her voice trembling with emotion*): She would have been hurt, disappointed... She would have been wounded to the heart. And she would have been angry!

**PRESIDENT:** Could she have accepted it?

**DIANA** (*after a long silence, very softly*): I don't know.

*Sighs and murmurs from the spectators.*

**PRESIDENT:** Would she have stayed with him if she had known he had a mistress whom he saw once a month?

**DIANA:** My mother loved my father very much and he loved her. I can't answer that.

**PRESIDENT:** *Maître* Paschoud, you may question your witness.

**PASCHOUD:** Tell the tribunal, Mademoiselle Belshaw, who was it who unpacked your mother's things...the things she had taken with her on the trip to Paris?

**DIANA** (*close to tears, her voice breaking*): It was I who did that... It was I who had to unpack her things... I had to sort them...

**PASCHOUD:** Was there soiled lingerie in those suitcases?

**DIANA:** Yes, I had to wash it...

*Excited murmurs from the spectators.*

**GREENSPAN:** ***This answer electrified the court. It was the first evidence that Mrs. Belshaw had actually made that trip to Paris.***

**PASCHOUD:** How was your father when he first telephoned to inform you of your mother's death? Was he, as the prosecution has contended, cool, flip, indifferent?

**DIANA:** Oh no, he was lost, devastated, upset, tormented. He didn't know what to do, where to turn. He needed someone. People say...people say he is cold...indifferent... Well, that is because they don't know him. And also, we hoped, each minute, each day, if she came back...well, everyone wouldn't have to know...

**PASCHOUD:** Could your father have killed your mother?

**DIANA** (*firmly, with absolute conviction*): It is not possible.

**PASCHOUD:** That is all, *Monsieur le Président*.

**GREENSPAN:** ***The prosecution wisely enough decided to leave Diana Belshaw alone. Willy Heim did not cross-examine her. Instead he rose for his closing address to the tribunal...***

**HEIM:** *Monsieur le Président*, judges, gentlemen of the jury...on the 15th day of January, 1979, Professor and Madame Belshaw eat breakfast and then they leave the Novotel Hotel... At ten o'clock they part, and she gets off the train at the Bourse, two hundred metres from the National Library...where she never arrives. Abruptly Betty Belshaw decides to return to Montana. Without going back to her hotel for her suitcase she takes the next train home. Let us imagine what she does...

**GREENSPAN:** ***The prosecutor then proceeded to describe an imaginary scene...***

## Scene 13 / In a Small Train Station

**BETTY** (*worried*): Oh, how am I to get home from the station... I should have... No car... Perhaps I should take the funicular, but then of course, I...

**MALE VOICE** (*seductive, charming*): Perhaps Madame would like a lift...

**BETTY** (*nervous*): Oh, no, no. I couldn't...

**MALE VOICE:** But surely you remember me, Madame Belshaw. I have seen you on the streets in Montana; you live there do you not?

**BETTY:** Yes, but — I couldn't possibly...

**MALE VOICE:** But first, we will have something to eat, no? The food on the train...impossible. I know a charming restaurant...an *intime* little bistro where they...

**HEIM:** And so the stranger takes Betty in his car, makes advances...

## Scene 14 / Inside a Car

**MALE VOICE:** Come over and sit closer to me...

**BETTY** (*frightened*): Why are we going this way? This is not the way to Montana. Why are you stopping?

*The car pulls onto the gravel shoulder and stops.*

**MALE VOICE** (*angry*): I said, come over here!
**BETTY:** No!

*Betty screams and struggles with her attacker.*

## Scene 15 / In Court

**HEIM:** And this unknown person kills her, drives to Le Sépey, removes all her clothes, including her rings — with great difficulty, they were very tight — wraps her up in three garbage bags he happens to have with him...

If only there had been an investigation then! Perhaps some traces of these events might have been found. But on his return to Montana, Professor Belshaw strenuously avoided telling the Swiss police of his wife's disappearance, although he persistently pursued every avenue of search in Paris and London. And why?

Because Professor Belshaw never believed in his wife's disappearance from Paris!

Now, consider this, *Monsieur le Président*, judges, gentlemen of the jury. If Madame Belshaw disappeared in Paris the discovery of her body — not in Paris but in Switzerland — precludes all explanations except the one I have just given. Remember, she was wrapped in *Swiss* garbage bags. (*Sarcastically*) Is it likely she was killed by someone in Paris who would risk taking her body to Switzerland for disposal? Why? The idea is totally implausible.

So you see, we come, almost irresistibly, to the extraordinary conclusion: *Madame Belshaw never was in Paris!* The defence has tried to find a trace of Madame Belshaw on this journey. But no one saw her.

As for the charming Diana's saying that she found the used lingerie of her mother — the fact that the story comes out for the first time yesterday renders it suspect. Why, I ask you, gentlemen of the jury, was this not brought out before? (*Pause*) No, no. Professor Belshaw, is it not more likely that in your Swiss apartment, you — perhaps in a sudden fit of temper, perhaps without meaning to... I don't see you as a calculating...

**GREENSPAN:** ***Here Heim presented the prosecution's theory in a purely speculative manner, based on no evidence whatever...***

# Scene 16 / In the Apartment

**CYRIL** (*bored*): Yes, dear?

**BETTY** (*getting angry*): Put down that paper! I said I want to talk to you!

**CYRIL:** All right, all right, I'm listening.

**BETTY:** Mrs. Wuest came by today...

**CYRIL:** Hardly an earthshaking event...

**BETTY:** I'm serious, Cyril. She told me something...about you... about last summer, when you were looking for a place for us to stay.

**CYRIL:** The woman is an arrogant, ignorant fool.

**BETTY:** You promised me, Cyril. And I believed you, that it would never happen again, like it did...in the sixties... *That* almost killed me, Cyril!

**CYRIL:** Betty...

**BETTY** (*shouting*): You promised! You promised! And you did it again! You were having an affair with someone else. Here. While I was at home, working...

**CYRIL:** Please, Betty ——

**BETTY:** Please, Betty, please Betty! Is that all you can say? How dare you do that? How dare you? You've humiliated me in front of everyone and I won't put up with it. I'll tell everyone... I'll...

**CYRIL:** You don't mean that, Betty. You know I love you...

**BETTY** (*crying*): Oh... What are you saying? How dare you, you... you're horrible. Get away from me! Don't touch me!

**CYRIL** (*trying to comfort her*): I'm sorry, really I am. It won't happen again...but if you think it would be better...a divorce...

**BETTY** (*screaming*): A divorce! Never! I'll kill myself first! Left for another woman. I'll kill myself...and, and, and... I'll tell everyone at the university...tell them what a monster, what an animal you are...

**CYRIL:** Betty, don't distress yourself.

*She strikes him on the shoulder with her fists.*

**BETTY** (*screaming*): Keep away! Keep away from me!

**CYRIL** (*suddenly losing his temper*): Stop it! Stop hitting me. You're mad. You're hysterical.

*Betty screams hysterically and Cyril hits her.*

**CYRIL** (*very softly*): Betty? Oh my God.

## Scene 17/In Court

**HEIM:** Without meaning to, perhaps exasperated beyond measure... he loses control and kills her. It is after that that he sets out to dissimulate. So he undertakes the required task of hiding his crime. And this good wife and mother is abandoned, thousands of miles from her family, her friends, and her country, to the mercies of the wild beasts. Gentlemen: you must have the courage of your experience of life, the courage of your convictions. Don't be misled by vague doubts. I ask you, gentlemen of the tribunal, to convict Cyril Belshaw for murder, and to sentence him to twelve years in prison!

**GREENSPAN:** ***When Willy Heim finished, the more senior of the two defence lawyers, Jean Philippe Paschoud, rose to speak...***

**PASCHOUD:** I am not a great trial lawyer like my colleague, *Maître* Heim... I am just an ordinary lawyer, but it is with my heart that I will try to convince you. For the Belshaw case is a difficult, a tragic matter. It concerns the death of a woman, and now the life of a man, her husband. It has deeply upset me, and totally preoccupied me...since I found myself for the first time, before Cyril Belshaw, in the terrible prison of Fleury Mérogis in Paris...

## Scene 18/In Belshaw's Prison Cell

*The guard unlocks the cell door.*

**GUARD:** A Swiss lawyer to see you, Professor Belshaw.
**CYRIL** (*politely*): Thank you for coming, *Maître* Paschoud.
**PASCHOUD:** I was in Paris when your message came through.
**CYRIL:** I am very glad you can help.

**PASCHOUD:** No, no, just a minute... We must talk first. There are some questions I must ask you. You must tell me, Professor Belshaw, frankly, man to man, if you are guilty. It would be better for you to tell me now. You can then find another lawyer. But as for me, if I ever come to believe you are guilty I will renounce my responsibility and your position will be... extremely dangerous.

## Scene 19 / In Court

**PASCHOUD:** Cyril Belshaw swore to me with tears in his eyes that he had not killed his wife. And since then, until this very moment, step by step, day after day, my conviction of his innocence has been reinforced. Nothing has happened to shake it. Let me read to you, gentlemen, notes from Betty Belshaw's journal written but two weeks before her disappearance...

## Scene 20 / In a Car on a Highway

**BETTY** (*calmly*): As I sit in the car which is moving at great speed southward I think of this fragile thread by which we are held to life, and I think of what I would like to leave behind for those I love. Not only material things, which will come to them in any case, but the knowledge of what is beautiful in life: The love of children, of husband, and the joy that they have given me.

I hope that they will remember me in the good years of laughter and adventure, not in the years when I was half-ill with fatigue, and the ill humour that goes with it... The special places we were happy... Long Beach, the Okanagan, School... The sun shines... It's hard to write. Another day I will write all these memories for you...

**GREENSPAN:** ***After reading the journal entry Paschoud sat down. And then it was the turn of the second defence lawyer, Eric Stoudmann. As a criminal lawyer, it was his task to rebut the essentials of the prosecution's case...***

# Scene 21 / In Court

**PRESIDENT:** You may begin, *Maître* Stoudmann.

**STOUDMANN:** The Belshaw case is an enigma. And our epoch does not like enigmas. So the temptation is great to gloss over such mysteries — to give a rational explanation where none exists. But truth is not always logical, reasonable.

Let us return to earth. The accusation is that he killed her. But we don't know *if* she was killed, or *how* she was killed, or *when* she was killed, or *where* she was killed. To accept the prosecution's case we must accept so many unproven hypotheses: *one*, that Mrs. Belshaw knew of the affair; *two*, that she reacted in a violent way; *three*, that he would have responded violently himself. And as for the contention that Mrs. Belshaw was never in Paris: remember, the *defence* retraced the entire journey of the couple with a picture of Betty and one of Cyril. *Neither* were remembered, so what does it prove that Betty was not remembered?

Gentlemen, who killed Betty Belshaw? Let us remember *that* is not the question. Did Cyril Belshaw kill Betty? To answer this we must discover if there is enough proof or if there is not.

*Monsieur le Président*, judges, jurors, in the end, when the prosecutor demands that you have the courage to convict, he demands something monstrous; he demands that you have the courage to err, to convict an innocent man!

**GREENSPAN:** ***And then, after brief rebuttals by the prosecutor and defence, Belshaw had the final word...***

**CYRIL:** I loved my wife and I still love my wife. I have not committed murder. I have not hurt my wife. I could not do such a thing. Gentlemen, I am in your hands.

**GREENSPAN:** ***The trial ended on Friday, December 5, three days after it began. And as scheduled, on Monday, December 8, at 5:00 p.m., the court reconvened for the reading of the judgement. The President recounted all the events which had occurred since the disappearance of Madame Belshaw in Paris. The judgement discounted Belshaw's explanation of his behaviour and lent its support to the prosecution's view of Belshaw's behaviour after his wife disappeared.***

# Scene 22 / In Court

**PRESIDENT:** The contradictory attitude of the accused, logically inexplicable and morally shocking, incurred upon him an enormous presumption of guilt which justified the opening of the enquiry and its being remitted to the tribunal... But in this case, an analysis of the facts and their interpretation is confronted with the obstacle of the foreign nature — to our mentality — of the character of the accused and his conceptions of justice founded on the Anglo-Saxon law. So, an absolute conviction of guilt, with the severe consequences which would flow from it, in the presence of the constant and firm denials — however suspect these may be *à propos* of major and immediate facts — is confronted by a very slight doubt.

In consequence the tribunal refuses to find the accused guilty of murder, although it is convinced of disloyal and morally shocking manoeuvres...

**FEMALE VOICE:** What does it mean? Ah, what does it mean?

**DIANA:** He's free. Oh daddy! It's over...

**GREENSPAN:** ***Commenting after the trial, the public prosecutor and the defence lawyer Paschoud said:***

**HEIM:** Professor Belshaw's behaviour would have been cause for suspicion in a Swiss, but it was proper for an Anglo-Saxon. If he had been Swiss, he would have been condemned.

**PASCHOUD:** It is not what I would have liked... this verdict. But, remember this: He is a man like you or me now... he is a free man.

**GREENSPAN:** ***For us, the benefit of a reasonable doubt is not a gift conferred by a benevolent court. In our system it is everyone's birthright. In our country, on this evidence, Professor Belshaw would probably not even have been charged, let alone committed to stand trial. The Swiss court acquitted him, which is to its credit, though it did assess costs against him in the amount of about $15,000 to help defray the expense of his prosecution, a prosecution to which he should scarcely have been subjected in the first place. To our sense of justice, Dr. Belshaw was as much a victim as Betty Belshaw, whatever may have happened to her, and the woman whose remains were found at Le Sépey, whoever she may have been.***

# Producer's Notes

Unlike the United States or Great Britain where criminal trials often attract outstanding authors and journalists — examples range from Truman Capote to Auberon Waugh — in Canada it is rare for real-life crime to capture the interest of accomplished writers. As a result the judicial process is seldom portrayed with any degree of insight in this country.

Fortunately for our program, in 1980 the scholarly West-coast writer Ellen Godfrey became interested in the case of a Canadian professor, Dr. Cyril Belshaw, who was being tried for the murder of his wife in Switzerland. Though the trial attracted much media attention, only Godfrey researched it exhaustively. She took meticulous, verbatim notes of the French-language proceedings. The book, *By Reason of Doubt*, which she wrote about the case became the basis of the script we later commissioned her to write for "The Scales of Justice".

Dr. Belshaw's trial was also of special interest to host Edward L. Greenspan. He regarded it as a particularly vivid example of the difference between the inquisitorial system of the European and the adversary system of the Anglo-Saxon traditions. Though the aim of both systems is to achieve justice, the route they take is divergent, and it reflects the different view each system has of the relationship between the individual and the state.

The Swiss authorities accused Dr. Belshaw on evidence so scant as to preclude his extradition from Canada, and they could only bring him to trial by having him arrested during a visit to France. Not surprisingly, he was acquitted in the end. But the procedure employed to weigh his guilt or innocence, though in strict conformity to Swiss law, might have seemed to many Canadians little more than a mockery of justice.

Outrage, however, is a poor substitute for understanding, and we have attempted to present the trial of Dr. Belshaw, as well as the events leading up to it, with the utmost fairness to the positions of both the prosecution and the defence. Gerard Parkes in the role of Cyril Belshaw and Maureen Fitzgerald as his wife, Betty, enhanced the production with their sympathetic, low-key performances, as did David Calderisi playing the Swiss prosecutor *Maître* Willy Heim.

Diana Belshaw, Cyril Belshaw's daughter, is an accomplished Canadian actress who has performed in several other episodes of "The Scales of Justice". We would have preferred her to play her own role in the trial as a defence witness, and regretted (though fully understood) when she turned us down. In the program Diana Belshaw's role was portrayed in a very sensitive performance by Susan Hogan.

Jean Philippe Paschoud, Belshaw's senior lawyer in Switzerland, was played by an unusually eminent figure in Canadian broadcasting — the actor, director, and one-time head of CBC drama, Esse W. Ljungh. Along with such legendary producers as the late Frank Willis and Andrew Allan, it was Esse Ljungh who put public broadcasting on the map in Canada during the Golden Age of Radio. His old drama studio "G" has been altered beyond recognition since his retirement. It was a pleasure to see that, sitting in front of far more modern microphones at the age of eighty, he could still teach us a great deal about acting with class, power, and restraint.

G.J.

# I'm Not Living Like This Anymore

*John G. Douglas*

**The Cast**

Commentary by Edward L. Greenspan, Q.C.

| | |
|---|---|
| **JANE STAFFORD** | Nicky Guadagni |
| **BILLY STAFFORD** | Frank Moore |
| **ALLAN WHYNOT** | Angelo Rizacos |
| **MR. FERRIER** for the defence | Neil Munro |
| **MR. ALLABY** for the Crown | Paul Soles |

With the support of (in alphabetical order): John Bethune, Lally Cadeau, Gordon Clapp, John Douglas, Alan Fawcett, Kay Hawtrey, James Morris, Frank Perry, Wayne Robson, Cedric Smith, and Murray Westgate

## Scene 1 / Inside a Truck Outside the Stafford House, Bang's Falls, Queens County, Nova Scotia, March 11, 1982

**JANE** (*opening truck door*): We can't sit in the truck all night, Billy. You can get out my side.

**BILLY** (*drunk and vicious*): Old woman, you stay right where you are! You gonna get outta this truck without I tell you?

**JANE** (*quietly*): No, Billy.

**BILLY** (*peering drunkenly*): Goddamn rain. Can't see. Her light still on?

**JANE:** Whose?

**BILLY** (*raging*): You know damn well whose! Marg Joudrey's. You hear that old bag tell me this afternoon that land of mine from here to the road is hers? *My land!* I'm gonna take that can o' gas in the back of the truck, light 'er up, and throw it in her trailer window down there! She'll never even have a chance to get out!

**JANE:** Please, Hon... Please...!

**BILLY:** And when I'm done with her, I'm gonna deal with your goddamn son Allan — him, too. Might as well clean up everything in one night!

**JANE:** You can't do that! Now, leave Allan alone! You can't do that to Margaret; she's been just like a mother to me!

**BILLY** (*savagely*): You're telling *me* what I can do? You...*you* bitch.

*Billy strikes her.*

**JANE** (*cowering*): Billy, no, please — !

**BILLY** (*grunting, as he rains blows on her*): No-good... goddamn... gonna teach you...who's boss...you...

**JANE** (*crying and moaning*): No... Billy, no!

*Truck horn blares as he pushes her against it.*

**BILLY** (*still striking her*): I'll smash your head...through...the goddamn...wheel!
**JANE:** Please...God, God...please!

*A shotgun blasts.*

**JANE** (*gasping, after a moment of silence*): White...someone in white... wet...Billy...why...is everything...wet? (*screams with horror*) *Billy*! Oh God, the blood! (*calling*) Come, somebody, for God's sakes, come!

*The truck horn blares, long and steadily.*

**JANE:** Somebody's shot Billy... Please, help!

*Someone approaches.*

**JANE:** Who's there? Allan, is that you?
**ALLAN:** It's me, Ma.
**JANE:** Is that...our shotgun?
**ALLAN:** Yes, Ma.
**JANE:** Al, I don't know what we're going to do. But I'm going to take the rap for this.
**ALLAN:** No!
**JANE:** Yes!

**GREENSPAN:** ***The body of Billy Stafford, his head almost blown away by a 12-gauge-shotgun blast, was found about 7:30 on the morning of March 12, 1982, sprawled across the seat of his pick-up truck on the River Road about ten miles from his house in the little settlement of Bang's Falls, near Liverpool, in Nova Scotia. The scene you have just heard was described by the woman who had been Stafford's common-law wife, thirty-three-year-old Jane Marie Whynot Stafford, and it pointed to the guilt of the victim's stepson, Allan Whynot, Jane's own sixteen-year-old son by her first marriage, who lived with his mother and Billy. The case was to be far more complex than that though, in every possible way. My name is Edward Greenspan, and what follows has been reconstructed from the transcripts of the trial in the Nova Scotia Supreme Court and the judgment of the Nova Scotia Court of Appeal.***

***That Billy Stafford died violently, by the hand of someone who knew him well, would have surprised no one in the area around Bang's Falls, a hamlet of fewer than twenty people, about fifteen miles from the Atlantic seaport of Liverpool. Over six feet tall, weighing more than 250 pounds, and correspondingly strong, Stafford was feared and hated by almost everyone in the neighbourhood for his bullying and savage temper. Before Jane Stafford described the murder scene, there was already a strong sense, as yet unspoken, that Billy's killer had saved the community a lot of future trouble. Most of the neighbours could only guess how much Jane had had to endure from him. There was widespread sympathy for her, shared even by the first police investigators on the scene, as Corporal Howard Pyke indicated to his superior, Staff Sergeant Peter Williamson, at the RCMP Detachment, Liverpool...***

## Scene 2 / At the RCMP Offices, Liverpool, March 12

**PYKE:** I met Mrs. Stafford outside the Joudrey residence, you know, the neighbour that lives at the foot of their lane ——

**WILLIAMSON:** Unh-huh.

**PYKE:** ...and, ah, we were walking up the driveway towards her house. I told her we'd traced the truck licence, and she recognized the description of the clothing. There was no question that the dead man was her husband. She...more or less fainted. I had to catch her body from falling and carry her up to the house...

**WILLIAMSON:** Mmmm. And there's nothing to suggest the fainting wasn't genuine?

**PYKE** (*mildly surprised*): No. It was only natural she'd be shocked... Hadn't seen him since he drove off sometime last night — she said.

**WILLIAMSON:** Okay. Who was up at the house when you got there?

**PYKE:** Her son, Allan Whynot, and the boarder, Ronnie Wamboldt, couple of in-laws, and her little boy, Darren Stafford, the son she had by Billy — about four, I'd guess — never moved a muscle all the time we were there...tense little kid...

**WILLIAMSON** (*grimly*): Yeah, wouldn't you be if you were *that* guy's son?

**PYKE:** Yeah, I suppose I would. Bad customer, Billy Stafford. Surprised we didn't have more trouble with him than we did.

**WILLIAMSON** (*impatiently*): If you'd been around here as long as I have, you'd know we *would* have — *if* anybody'd been willing to testify. We'd have got him half a dozen times on deer-jacking if he hadn't bullied somebody else into taking the rap. Drunk, disorderly, threatening — nobody'd say a thing!

**PYKE:** Makes you wonder what his wife went through, doesn't it?

*Williamson grunts.*

**PYKE:** She supported him, didn't she? Only one in the house who worked?

**WILLIAMSON:** She had to. Found out he was blacklisted from the scallop fleet he used to work on. Mutiny. Charges dropped, of course. (*Bitterly*) Nobody would testify.

**PYKE:** Scared almost everybody. Some..., ah, some even wilder rumours I've been picking up about Billy... Have you heard any?

**WILLIAMSON:** Like... ah, murder?

**PYKE:** Yeah. Heard any details? Well, do you think it's true?

**WILLIAMSON:** Eh... We'll never know. We looked into it a long time ago. When they wouldn't have Billy any more in Liverpool, he worked the fishing boats out of Lunenburg. One night, about two years ago, a sailor called Jimmy LeBlanc went overboard — officially, suicide... When Billy was drunk or drugged, he used to boast he'd done it.

**PYKE:** Charming guy.

**WILLIAMSON:** Yeah. Hated just about everybody in the world, Billy Stafford did... You know, if he'd lived... we'd have had to have a showdown with that one... sooner or later...

**PYKE:** You mean a shoot-out?

**WILLIAMSON:** Something like that maybe, yeah... That's why I'm sorry... but there's a job to be done.

**PYKE:** Sorry?

**WILLIAMSON:** I want you to go out to the Stafford house in Bang's Falls again tonight... We've got about a dozen officers on the case now, and they're finding things that, ah, indicate... Jane Stafford...

**PYKE:** What have they turned up on her?

**WILLIAMSON:** In May of last year she took out an insurance policy on the whole family with Canada Life. Billy, herself, the kid. If she or the kid died, Billy got the money. But if Billy went first ——

**PYKE:** *She* gets it. How much is the policy worth?

**WILLIAMSON:** Twenty thousand dollars. And apparently there's only *her* signature on it. Jane signed for Billy. No evidence he even knew it existed.

**PYKE:** I guess I'd better pay her another visit.

**WILLIAMSON:** I think so. Any...ah, tension there this morning? Anyone nervous, over-excited?

**PYKE:** Not a bit. It was almost eerie how quiet and calm everybody was. Mrs. Stafford seemed half in another world. We were very gentle with her.

**WILLIAMSON:** Good. Stay that way.

**GREENSPAN:** ***Corporal Pyke and other officers confirmed the details of the life insurance policy that night, and then returned to Liverpool, leaving Jane with her family. But over the next two days, more and more leads began to deepen their suspicion that Jane Stafford was heavily involved in the murder of her husband, particularly indications by the friends of a fishing-boat crewman called Beverly Taylor. Taylor himself was at sea the night Billy was killed, but two days later, when he landed, the RCMP made contact with him...***

## Scene 3 / At the RCMP Offices, March 14

**TAYLOR:** Ah, I met Billy and Jane Stafford around Christmas 1981, one time only. So I was surprised when she called me in January, couple of months ago, said I should pay her a visit, not at home but where she worked — Greenfield old folks' home in Bang's Falls. Said it'd mean a lot of money for me. Well, she kept calling, and calling, and never saying what it was, so finally I went up to Greenfield, sometime late January, 9:30, 10:00 in the morning...

**GREENSPAN:** ***According to Taylor's evidence, this was his conversation with Jane Stafford...***

# Scene 4 / In a Room in Greenfield, January 1982

**JANE:** Come in. They won't disturb us here.

**TAYLOR:** Okay. Sure.

**JANE** (*very tense and edgy*): Sit down. Please.

**TAYLOR:** Ah, thanks... Ah... Mrs. Stafford...

**JANE:** Jane. Please.

**TAYLOR:** Jane. Right... Well, ah, if you wanted to see me — here I am. What can I... ah, you know?

**JANE:** Okay. [*There is an agonized pause while she gets the strength to take the plunge.*] I want you to kill Billy for me.

**TAYLOR:** What... What's that?

**JANE:** I want you to hit Billy. Kill him.

**TAYLOR:** And, ah, just why do you want me to do that?

**JANE:** Because... because...

**TAYLOR:** Does... does he beat you?

**JANE:** Most every day, but that don't matter so much. My little boy, Darren, Billy's driving him crazy. He's going to be crazy and he's only four! And he threatened... Billy said if I left him, he said he'd kill my mother and father. He's got to be done away with.

**TAYLOR:** Look, Mrs.... Jane, I'm afraid I'm not interested in anything to do with killing Billy. If it's that bad, why in hell don't you phone a lawyer?

**JANE:** What's the point of that? He'd get revenge on me — hurt Mum and Dad.

**TAYLOR:** I'm sorry, but, ah...

**JANE:** There's twenty thousand dollars for you if you kill him!

**TAYLOR:** What —— ?

**JANE:** Billy's insurance. I'll give it all to you ——

**TAYLOR:** I'm sorry, Jane, but the answer's still no.

**JANE:** But, Billy jacks a lot of deer. You could shoot him when he's out in the woods. Nobody'd ever know who done it... He's got so many enemies ——

**TAYLOR:** Look, why are you asking *me* to do this?

**JANE** (*helplessly*): You look like a guy who would help a person... out of a bad situation.

**TAYLOR:** Look, Jane,... ah, what about the police?

**JANE:** They can't help me. I'd never run far enough to get away from him.

**TAYLOR:** Well, Billy trucks dope back and forth on the gypsum boats, doesn't he? Everybody knows that.

**JANE:** Yeah.

**TAYLOR:** Well, you know...have him put away for a couple of years.

**JANE:** Maybe...No. No. You met Ronnie Wamboldt, the guy who lives with us, when you visited before Christmas?

**TAYLOR:** Un-huh.

**JANE:** He'll do anything Billy tells him. If Billy got busted for dope then Ronnie would take the charge...and Billy would still be there...Do you see?

**TAYLOR:** Yeah, I'm afraid I do. (*Grunting, as he gets up*) I...ah, I guess that's all I can say, Jane. Believe me, I'd like to help if I could ——

**JANE:** Can I phone you? Talk to you again about it?

**TAYLOR:** Look Jane, if you won't use the law or the police, there's nothing to be done — nothing at all.

**GREENSPAN:** ***Between the 12th and the 13th of March, the police collected more details tending to close the net around Jane Stafford. Late on the evening of Saturday, March 13, six RCMP officers came to Bang's Falls, questioned Jane again, and asked her to come with them. Shortly after midnight, the car carrying Jane and the police drove away from the house...Although Jane was not yet charged with murder, the formal police caution was read to her in the car...***

## Scene 5 / Inside the Police Car

**POND** (*reading*): "You need not say anything. You have nothing to hope for any promise or favour, and nothing to fear from any threat, whether or not you say anything. Anything you do say may be used as evidence." You do understand what I've just read, Mrs. Stafford?

**JANE:** Yes. May I smoke?

**POND:** Of course.

**GREENSPAN:** ***For nine hours through the night of March 14, from approximately 1:00 a.m. until 10:00 the next morning, a number of policemen questioned Jane at RCMP headquarters. Shortly after 6:00 a.m., Jane asked a question that puzzled the officer who was with her...***

# Scene 6/In a Small Room in the RCMP Offices

**JANE:** If...if I'm going to say anything...Can I have Lamont here?
**POND:** Can you have who?
**JANE:** Lamont Stafford...Billy's father.
**POND** (*incredulously*): But...Mrs. Stafford...Your *own* father's here...Maurice Hirschman...Surely you want ——
**JANE** (*stubbornly*): I want Lamont Stafford. I can trust him. I want him to hear what I have to say.
**POND:** But, Mrs. Stafford, it's 6:15 in the morning. There's no way I'm going to drag somebody out of bed at this hour. Of course you know you're entitled to a lawyer if you wish.
**JANE:** I just want Lamont.
**POND:** I'll have someone call him...in an hour or two.

**GREENSPAN:** ***Much as it may have surprised the police, Jane Stafford was closer to her father-in-law than to her father, Maurice Hirschman. Jane was always attracted to strong, assertive men, but Lamont Stafford may have been one of the few such men in her life who was also consistently kind to her. Whatever the cause, she asked to see him three times in those early morning hours. He was finally brought into the RCMP offices about 9:15 that morning and was left briefly alone with her...***

**LAMONT:** Janey.
**JANE:** Oh, thank you for coming.
**LAMONT:** Guess I had to.
**JANE:** You...don't hate me?
**LAMONT:** Why would I?
**JANE:** You think now...I killed Billy. (*Frantically*) It wasn't me! It was someone else!
**LAMONT** (*gently*): I figured...since you're here in the police station, there was something more come out of it than what you told me in the first place.
**JANE:** You...understand, then?
**LAMONT:** Ah, you know I do...Now, Janey, the sergeant out there is going to ask you to make a statement. Now, you just tell him the truth, whatever it is, and everything's going to be all right.
**JANE:** I wish I could...

**LAMONT:** You know you can trust me. I'll be right there beside you. And so will your dad.

*Corporal Pond enters the room.*

**POND:** Mrs. Stafford, Mr. Stafford, Sergeant Williamson would like to see you now in the coffee room, if you're ready.

**LAMONT:** C'mon now, Janey, I'll help you. Just you tell them exactly what happened. You know everything's going to be okay...

**GREENSPAN:** ***While they moved towards the coffee room, a number of witnesses overheard Sergeant Williamson address someone from another area:***

**WILLIAMSON:** Jane Stafford should be given a medal for what she did. She probably saved two or three of your lives!

**GREENSPAN:** ***No one was ever able to be sure whether Jane overheard this remark or not. If she had, a court might have considered it an "inducement" for her to confess, and could have ruled any statement she made inadmissible. But, apparently unaware of anything around her, she entered the coffee room and sat down with her father and father-in-law on either side of her...***

## Scene 7 / In the Coffee Room

**WILLIAMSON:** Well now, Mrs. Stafford, gentlemen... Mrs. Stafford, what can you tell us about this matter?

**LAMONT:** You're not going to get anything out of her that way!

**WILLIAMSON:** I beg your pardon?

**LAMONT:** Janey here just bogs down if there's too much pressure put to her. If you don't ease up, you're not going to get any statement anyway! (*Turns to Jane*) Now Janey, did you kill Bill?

**JANE:** Yes.

**WILLIAMSON** (*quietly*): Would you repeat that, Mrs. Stafford?

**JANE:** Yes. I killed Bill... (*Rapidly, with a sense of urgency*) You've no idea what he was like... He was right crazy. He beat all of us all the time. He beat me sometimes so bad I couldn't get out of bed for days. Darren, my four-year-old... Darren, he was just going crazy; he got a beating put on him so often...

GREENSPAN: *The admission you've just heard was never placed before the jury at the trial. The fact was that Staff Sergeant Williamson took down, for Jane's signed statement, only what she said about the murder itself, leaving her reasons in her own defence unrecorded. The incompleteness of the record caused the trial judge to rule the whole statement inadmissible. But the judicial removal of this confession was months in the future: Jane had, after all, admitted that she'd killed Billy. Two days after she did so, on March 16, Jane Marie Whynot Stafford was formally charged with first-degree murder. But nine days later, on Thursday, March 25, accompanied by her lawyer, Alan Ferrier, she came again to the RCMP detachment in Liverpool, and this time her signed statement differed from her earlier one in several crucial respects:*

JANE: "We left Leona Anthony's house (where we'd been having a few drinks), at approximately 9:00 p.m. on March 11, 1982. I was driving the Jeep truck. Bill Stafford, my common-law husband, was seated next to me and Ronnie Wamboldt (who lived with us) occupied the passenger's seat..."

GREENSPAN: *This second statement is the one you heard dramatized at the beginning of this episode: a story in which Billy is drunk but fully conscious when the truck arrives home; in which he beats Jane savagely and then is shot by a third party Jane cannot see, except for a flutter of white shirt; a story in which her son, Allan Whynot, approaches with a "smoking gun" and his white shirt visible in the darkness — a story in fact that exonerates Jane and points the finger of guilt straight at the sixteen-year-old Allan.*

*Jane was not believed. The police had too much information coming in from neighbours worried about being cast as accomplices, and in the yard by the Stafford house they found recent ashes containing zippers and clasps indicating the remains of a woman's recently burned clothing. Jane was taken into custody that night, and next day driven to Halifax for a polygraph, or lie-detector test, with her own and her lawyer's consent. Results of a polygraph test are not admissible as evidence in court, but in this case they would not have been needed anyway. When Jane was told that the test indicated that several points in her story of Allan killing Billy were not true, she broke down at last...*

## Scene 8 / In the Interrogation Room, RCMP Headquarters, Halifax, Saturday, March 27, 1982

**PYKE** (*gently*): Corporal Innis has told you about the results of the polygraph test, Mrs. Stafford?

**JANE** (*weeping quietly*): Yes.

**PYKE:** He says that you want to make a full statement now?

**JANE:** Yes, I do.

**PYKE:** Now I'll be writing as you talk, so if you don't mind, just go along slow.

**JANE:** All right.

**PYKE:** Now, what can you tell me about Billy Stafford's death on the night of March 11, 1982...

**GREENSPAN:** ***And here, reconstructed from Jane's third statement and her testimony at trial, is the* real *story of what happened on that night...***

## Scene 9 / Jane's Narration of Events of March 11, 1982

**JANE:** We were down to a friend's place that night. Billy'd brought a case of beer, and I had one, I guess, and there was a joint passed around. We left to go home at around nine o'clock, me driving the truck, Billy beside me, and Ronnie Wamboldt by the passenger door, loaded as usual. Billy'd been drinking rum all day, and his mouth was still running on about the same thing he'd said all the way down. He started right in again on the way back...

**BILLY** (*muttering*): Burn her out...

**JANE:** What, Hon?

**BILLY:** Joudrey bitch... Your friend... Stole my land... burn...

**WAMBOLDT** (*chanting happily*): Burn... Burn... Burn...

**BILLY:** Shut up.

**WAMBOLDT:** Ah, beautiful deer... I... shot...

**BILLY** (*threateningly*): When I say shut your fuckin' mouth, Ronnie, you *shut it*!

**WAMBOLDT:** S... sorry... Billy...

**JANE:** Please, Hon, we're almost home...

**BILLY:** And yer son... goddamn Allan... Mounties come out to talk to 'im. *Why*?

**JANE:** I'm sure it's okay, Billy, Allan's a good boy.

**BILLY:** Yeah, he'd better be. Take care o' Joudrey first... Take that can o' gas in the back of the truck, light 'er up, 'n throw it in her trailer window down there! She'll never have a chance to get out!

**JANE:** Ah, no, no, Billy... Please... Billy...

**BILLY:** And when I'm done with her, I'm gonna deal with Allan — him, too... Might as well... clean up everything... in one night... in... one... night...

**WAMBOLDT** (*giggling*): Billy's out... He's out... out...

**JANE:** Here's the bridge, Ronnie. We're almost home.

**WAMBOLDT:** Ah... home!

**JANE:** Allan's to home and asleep, Ronnie. And Darren. Don't wake them when you go in.

**WAMBOLDT:** When I get to bed... I'm... dead... dead...

**JANE:** Go on now, Ronnie. You know when Billy passes out I have to stay with him till he wakes up. Go to bed.

**WAMBOLDT:** Okay.

*Wamboldt lurches out of the truck and heads for the house.*

**WAMBOLDT:** Good night.

**JANE:** Good night.

**WAMBOLDT:** Good night... Good night, ever'body... good night...

**JANE:** I waited a little while, I don't know how long, maybe twenty minutes, half an hour. I just sat there in the cab, with him slumped against me, and the words, everything he'd been saying, just started sinking in... Margaret Joudrey and Allan, what he was going to do. I just said to hell with everything. I'm just not living like this anymore. I blew the horn on the truck, and in a couple of minutes my son, Allan, came...

**ALLAN** (*calling softly*): Ma? What is it? Is something wrong?

**JANE:** Al, get me the gun — the shotgun — and load it.
**ALLAN:** Okay, ma.

**JANE:** When Allan left, I got out of the truck. He came back with the gun, I took it from him, and he went back inside. I held the gun in the driver's window... and pulled the trigger... It was just... a big mess. I was covered with blood and... stuff... I went to the door and laid the gun on the ground...

**JANE** (*calling softly through the front door*): Al... Al!
**ALLAN:** I'm here, Ma.
**JANE:** Come on out.
**ALLAN:** What do you... What...
**JANE:** Go get me some clean clothes... in a plastic garbage bag.
**ALLAN:** Okay.
**JANE:** Then you go down there to Margaret Joudrey's and call... You call my mother and tell her to meet me in her car out by the Satellite Station.
**ALLAN:** Unh-huh.
**JANE:** There's blood on the gravel here, maybe on the house wall... You clean it up and get rid of the gun.
**ALLAN:** Yeah.
**JANE:** And tell Margaret that everything's going to be all right... And tell her that he won't hurt her no more. Now get the clothes.
**ALLAN:** All right. Just a minute...

**JANE:** When he brought me the clean clothes, I got in the truck and I drove away — just drove... I don't... I don't remember that drive — the blood, or Billy, or anything. I know the road was in bad shape. I didn't see anything. Everything was just like it was nothing. I just looked straight ahead and kept on driving... till I got to the Satellite Station Road... I got out, with the clothes bag in my hand. I thought Mom and Dad would be there, but I didn't see nobody. I walked across the one road, and I then walked across the other, and I saw the car coming down from the Satellite Road... and I knew it was Mom.

**JANE** (*climbing into her mother's car*): Take me over to your house.
**GLADYS HIRSCHMAN:** Janey, what's the matter... What's wrong with ——
**JANE:** Don't ask me anything. Don't talk to me. Just take me to your place, quick!

**JANE:** Well, they didn't ask any more. They drove me over to their trailer in Danesville and I went in and it was dark, and I went into the bathroom and I took off my stained clothes and had a bath, and I put the old clothes back in the same bag, including my towel and facecloth. Then they drove me home as far as the Bang's Falls Road. I told them to let me out there, and I cut up through the woods on foot and over to my place. When I got in I put the bag with all the stuff in it into the stove, and I went to see if my little boy was all right.

**JANE** (*softly*): Darren? [*The child whimpers in his sleep.*] Okay, sweetheart. Just checking.

*Jane checks on Wamboldt.*

**JANE** (*softly*): Ronnie? [*Wamboldt is snoring loudly.*] Thank God.

**JANE:** There was a note on the table from Allan and he said he was down at Margaret's, so I flicked the lights on and off 'cause Margaret can see it from her trailer. A couple of minutes later they all come up...there's Allan and Margaret and her boarder, Roger Manthorne...

**MARGARET:** Janey, Janey for godsake love, what happened?

**JANE:** I don't want to talk about it.

**MARGARET:** I figure you want me right now, dear. I know you want me up here.

**JANE:** I do.

**MARGARET:** Janey, everything's going to be all right! (*Hugging her*) There...there darling...

**JANE:** It's all over. I blew his fuckin' head off.

**MARGARET:** Now, come on, now Janey. Now go over to the table and sit down. Just sit down. Eh? Okay.

**JANE:** Okay.

**ROGER:** Al and I broke the gun down and threw it in the river, Janey.

**ALLAN:** Three pieces. Right off the bridge. River's in full spate. They'll never find it.

**ROGER:** And we cleaned up the yard and the side of the house.

**MARGARET:** Yeah, where's Ronnie, too? Where's Ronnie Wamboldt?

**JANE:** With the liquor he got into him, he won't wake up till mornin'.

**MARGARET:** Okay, good.

**ROGER:** Janey?

**JANE:** Yeah, Rodge?
**ROGER:** Can I have some tea?

**JANE:** Roger and Margaret left soon. I just went in the bedroom. Al crawled in bed in the same room. I just sat there on the foot of the bed... I sat there all night. Al and I never talked. It's just silent. He dozed off and on, but I didn't. I didn't believe in my own mind that Bill was dead. I waited for that truck just to come up the driveway. I waited... all night.

**GREENSPAN:** ***The trial of Jane Marie Stafford on a charge of first-degree murder began in the old courthouse in Liverpool, Nova Scotia. It attracted nationwide publicity, not only because of widespread sympathy for the accused, but because her case seemed to many a perfect battleground in the struggle for women's rights and against male oppression. The opposite view was maintained just as hotly: That however impossible Billy Stafford may have been, his wife had no right to act as his judge and executioner, and the law must take its course. The task of the Crown attorney, Blaine Allaby, was to convince the jury beyond a reasonable doubt that Jane Stafford was guilty of murder in the first degree. This meant that they must agree Billy's killing was "planned and deliberate". To support this theory, Allaby emphasized the importance of Jane's meeting with Beverly Taylor, three months before Billy had died...***

## Scene 10/In Court

**ALLABY:** Mr. Taylor, what happened in that little room where you met with Jane?
**TAYLOR:** Hm... I asked her why she wanted to see me and... ah, she said she wanted to hire somebody to hit Billy.
**ALLABY:** And by "hit" ——
**TAYLOR:** Hit as in kill.

**GREENSPAN:** ***The thrust of the defence case, on the other hand, was to suggest that Jane's killing of her husband was the result of "provocation" —— that is, of a "wrongful act or insult sufficient to deprive an ordinary person of the power of self control". If the jury believed that Jane had acted out of long-accumulated desperation,***

***brought to flashpoint by Billy's threats to harm her friend and neighbour Margaret, and her son Allan, or had a reasonable doubt about that, then the appropriate verdict would be manslaughter —— and a much lighter sentence. Defence counsel Alan Ferrier pressed Taylor on the details of Jane's distraught state of mind when she had asked him to kill Billy...***

**FERRIER:** Now, you had this conversation with Mrs. Stafford at the senior citizens' home...hm...how would you describe her emotionally at that point?
**TAYLOR:** Quite upset, excited.
**FERRIER:** Desperate?
**TAYLOR:** Yes.
**FERRIER:** Trapped?
**TAYLOR:** Yes.
**FERRIER:** Is that the feeling you got from her?
**TAYLOR:** Yes, it was.

**GREENSPAN:** ***When Allan Whynot was called to the stand, his testimony differed from his mother's in one key respect. Jane had said that when she asked Allan to bring the gun out to the truck on the night of the murder, he brought it out*** **at once.** ***Prosecutor Allaby drew out a slightly different story...***

**ALLABY:** What did your mother tell you?
**ALLAN:** She just told me to get the gun.
**ALLABY:** And what did you think at that point?
**ALLAN:** I don't know.
**ALLABY:** So, what did you do?
**ALLAN:** I went back in and got the gun and put a shell in it...and put it under my bed.
**ALLABY:** Why did you do that?
**ALLAN:** Well, I went out to make sure she still wanted it or not, you know... So, I just put it under and went out to see if she still wanted it, that's why. She did.
**ALLABY:** So, you took the gun out and you gave it to your mother?
**ALLAN:** Yes. Then I went back to the house. I went in and stood by the sink a minute until I heard a shot. After maybe twenty-five seconds, I went outside and looked.
**ALLABY:** And what did you see?
**ALLAN:** My mother standing there with the gun.

**ALLABY:** Could you see the truck or see into the cab of the truck?
**ALLAN:** I didn't... You couldn't have paid me enough to look in that truck!

**GREENSPAN:** *This was potentially damaging testimony because by making his mother ask* **twice** *for the weapon, Allan had given her more time to think. Along with her own testimony that she had waited twenty minutes to half an hour before calling for the gun, it would be, if the jury believed Allan, powerful evidence for the "deliberation" which is an essential element of first-degree murder. In his cross-examination, Defence Counsel Ferrier took Allan back again and again to Billy's brutality with Jane and all her family. He was building a case for insupportable pressure on Jane, the kind of pressure that might make the most controlled person explode...*

**FERRIER:** Mr. Whynot, can you tell the court what you found on a night in January 1981?
**ALLAN:** I found my mother laying on the kitchen floor, about two in the morning. She wouldn't wake up.
**FERRIER:** Was she clothed?
**ALLAN:** Yes.
**FERRIER:** Was she bleeding?
**ALLAN:** I don't remember.
**FERRIER:** Did you try to wake her up?
**ALLAN:** Yes, I threw a cup of water in her face.
**FERRIER:** Do you know how she got there?
**ALLAN:** Bill put her there.
**FERRIER:** Did she look like she'd been beaten?
**ALLAN:** Well, it was dark in the house. I didn't put no lights on. I just threw the water in her face and shook her a few times and she wouldn't wake up, she just laid there.
**FERRIER:** Did you have any doubts about her, or whether she was alive?
**ALLAN:** Yeah, I did.

**GREENSPAN:** *But Billy's savagery was not confined to Jane. Ferrier went on to ask Allan about his step-father's treatment of the whole family...*

**FERRIER:** Did he ever abuse you or others at the dinner table?
**ALLAN:** Yes.

**FERRIER:** Can you tell this Court and the jury why?

**ALLAN:** Well, my little brother Darren, he's four, he couldn't eat very fast. So one day, Bill, he was in one of his mean moods, and Darren never finished when we did, so Billy started feeding it to Darren himself. Spoonful after spoonful, and Darren threw up, and Billy just scraped it all back in the plate and made him eat it again, vomit and all. And then Mom said, "You know he can't eat very fast, Hon," and Bill just got up and smashed all the plates and cracked me on the head and went over and started beating Ma again with his fists. He went over and he gave little Darren a good beating. He said, "When I'm talking to these f—in' kids", he said, "I don't want your mouth to open."

**GREENSPAN:** ***Although the Crown quite properly insisted that Billy Stafford was not on trial — his widow was — his behaviour was so important to establishing Jane's state of mind at the time, that her defence counsel pressed her to the most painful testimony on the stand...***

**JANE:** He would sometimes tie my hands, sometimes just my feet, sometimes both, and he would want to do it like dogs do it, back ass to — I don't know...

**FERRIER:** Can you speak up a bit?

**JANE:** ...anal sex, and he did. It was just like somebody tearing you apart, and he said, "I'll fix it so you get used to this," and he went and brought in a piece of pipe...plumbing pipe...

*A murmur ripples through the courtroom.*

**BURCHELL:** I'm sorry? I didn't hear her?

**FERRIER:** I think she said "plumbing pipe", My Lord.

**BURCHELL:** Yes...Continue.

**FERRIER:** Was there anything he did to you that you thought more disgusting than that?

**JANE:** One time he came in, he tied my hands behind my back, and I was down on my knees on the floor, and he had the dog leash around my neck, and he just led me around the room. He brought... We had a St. Bernard dog... He went and brought the dog in... He brought...

**FERRIER:** Can you speak up, Mrs. Stafford? I know it's difficult but can you please speak up?

**JANE:** He... made the dog do it to me...

*A gasp echoes around the courtroom.*

**GREENSPAN:** ***In his summation to the jury, Defence Counsel Ferrier stressed Jane's slowly accumulating desperation. Billy's last threat to "burn out" Margaret Joudrey and his threat to "deal with" Jane's son Allan were only the straws that broke the back of her self-control. Ferrier was clearly aiming for a reduced verdict of manslaughter by reason of provocation. If the jury did not accept provocation, Ferrier told them, then they had only one option...***

**FERRIER:** Now, if for any reason you conclude that you are satisfied without a doubt that there was *no provocation*, then in fact there has been murder. If you come to the conclusion that murder has occurred...

**GREENSPAN:** ***After telling the jury that their only choices were murder or manslaughter, Ferrier then made a passing reference to a completely different section of the Criminal Code, that dealing, not with provocation, but with self-defence. This was inconsistent with his earlier statement because self-defence leads to a complete acquittal...***

**FERRIER:** Section 37, subsection 1, reads, quote: "Every one is justified in using force to defend himself or any one under his protection from assault, if he uses no more force than is necessary to prevent the assault or the repetition of it," end quote. That may be a relevant consideration for you to deal with in this matter. We have a situation where Billy Stafford had indicated to his wife an intention to harm her neighbour and her son Allan.

**GREENSPAN:** ***This almost casual reference to a completely different ground of defence would have momentous consequences for the case. After this brief mention of self-defence, Jane's lawyer returned immediately to his main argument of provocation.***

***To succeed in this defence he had to raise a doubt in the jury not only that Billy's behaviour had caused Jane to lose her self-control, but that any reasonable person would also have lost self-control...***

**FERRIER:** I would suggest to you all, as ordinary people, knowing Billy Stafford, not from your position as his wife, but as an ordinary member of this community in Queens County, that you would take his threats seriously. You would react if your own mother's life was in jeopardy, and there is evidence to suggest that Mrs. Joudrey was in fact like a mother to Mrs. Stafford. I suggest to you that it would very firmly establish the loss of control, that it would cause loss of control in any ordinary person who knew Billy Stafford as he was.

The case generally requires you to consider the syndrome of a battered wife — that feeling of putting up with incredible abuse, but staying for reasons that made absolutely no sense to a person who was outside of that relationship. Jane has given evidence that, in fact, Billy threatened her if she ever left — as his first two wives in fact had left him — that he wasn't going to be a "third-time loser". And, of course, she was aware that he had brutally attacked her father on a previous occasion, as well as both her sons. So, when he said to her, "I'll get your parents, and I'll get your family," she believed him, and if you were in her shoes, wouldn't you have believed him?

I would suggest to you very, very strongly that the issue of provocation is substantial enough in this case to raise a doubt, and I want you to know that the law is the Crown must *disprove* provocation. It is not for the defence to prove it. The Crown must establish that this murder happened and without any doubt, without provocation. If you have any doubt whatsoever about provocation, you must exercise that in favour of Mrs. Stafford, and as a result it is acquittal on the charge of murder and a guilty finding on manslaughter. I urge that on you in the strongest way, after hearing all the evidence you've heard.

**GREENSPAN:** ***So, a manslaughter verdict by reason of provocation was what the defence was asking for. The defence summary may have been a bit overstated: a jury must have "reasonable doubt" in order to give the accused its benefit, not just "any doubt whatsoever". But Crown Counsel Allaby was equally forceful in his insistence that the killing of Billy Stafford was a considered and deliberate act...***

**ALLABY:** The Crown is suggesting to you that Jane Stafford was waiting her chance to kill her husband, and that she took it on this particular night, and that what she did was planned and what she did was deliberate. Look at the facts: She sat in the truck for twenty minutes or more before calling for the gun. The instant she completed the act, she had a plan all ready, orders for her son — clean up the yard, get rid of the gun, go call my father and mother to pick me up. And think of the insurance policy, which according to the evidence, Billy never even knew existed. My learned friend would suggest to us that his client was so upset, so intent on protecting her friend Margaret Joudrey and her son Allan, that she lost control of herself. This woman, who was so concerned with her neighbour and her son, two weeks later was prepared to sacrifice that son. She was prepared and maintained for two days that it was her son *Allan* who had shot Billy Stafford and not herself.

I would submit that in this case we have to say to Jane Stafford that we sympathize with your situation, nobody's questioning the fact that you had one hell of a life with that man, but the law is the law. What you did was planned and deliberate, was not provoked, and was first-degree murder!

**GREENSPAN:** ***Following the summary for the prosecution, the jurors retired. Mr. Justice Burchell conferred with both counsels about their arguments and his own forthcoming charge to the jury. And it was then that events began to take an unusual twist...***

**BURCHELL:** I looked at the defence of self-defence last night, Mr. Ferrier — the section raised briefly — and I must say I had great difficulty. It's — of course — and I won't say this to the jury, but...but, of course, it is a secondary matter as far as you're concerned, Mr. Ferrier?

**FERRIER:** Well, hm... Quitc frankly, My Lord, the section might have *some* bearing...ah, not so much in terms of whether or not it meets all tests in this particular case, but...ah, whether or not the accused *believed* that that was the case in terms of provocation, or in terms of intent to kill. In...in other words ——

**BURCHELL:** Well, presented in that way it creates the problems. Either there's foundation for it or there is not. It...it's vexatious from the standpoint of confusing the jury to present them with an additional defence argument if there's no foundation...

**FERRIER:** Well, what I'm wondering...ah, My Lord ——

**BURCHELL:** I take it that you're wondering whether you really *want* to advance that as a defence or not, Mr. Ferrier?

**FERRIER:** Well, actually — upon reflection, My Lord — maybe it's something that should be dealt with. I guess my problem is that I initially was not...quite honestly, I...I didn't consider that it was a relevant issue, and it's something that only really came to me last night.

**BURCHELL:** Very well. I'd like to think overnight about how to present it to the jury.

**GREENSPAN:** ***In the final days of Jane's trial, a number of people seem to have had a good many second thoughts overnight. In his charge to the jury the next morning, the judge's discussion of aspects of self-defence covered nine pages of the court transcript:***

**BURCHELL:** Section 37 of the Criminal Code provides... (*fumbling*) Bear with me, I thought I had it marked... Yes, quote, "Every one is justified in using force to defend himself or *any one under his protection* from assault, if he uses no more force than is necessary to prevent the assault or the repetition of it," end quote. Now, if that applies, I must tell you it would afford a complete defence to the charge against the accused. If you conclude that she did kill Mr. Stafford in self-defence, or if there is any reasonable doubt in your mind as to that, then in either case you must find her not guilty.

**GREENSPAN:** ***But was self-defence really available? After all, on Jane's own testimony, Billy Stafford was unconscious and, at that moment at least, no threat to anyone. In the ensuing five hours while Justice Burchell exhaustively reviewed the testimony, it seems that he never related this fact to the self-defence theory. The jury retired to consider their verdict on November 20, 1982. The next morning, having deliberated a total of three and a half hours, they returned...***

**COURT CLERK:** The Jury is all present, My Lord.
**BURCHELL:** Thank you.
**CLERK:** Mr. Foreman, have you reached a verdict?
**FOREMAN:** Yes, we have.
**CLERK:** Mr. Foreman, what was your verdict?
**FOREMAN:** Not guilty.
**CLERK:** As one say, so say you all — not guilty?
**JURY** (*in unison*): Not guilty!

*There are cheers in the courtroom.*

**GREENSPAN:** ***But the Jane Stafford case was not yet over. In the light of those last-minute developments in the defence argument, as presented by Justice Burchell to the jury, the Crown appealed against her acquittal. On November 30, 1983, just over a year after the jury had freed Jane, Mr. Justice H.A. Hart of the Nova Scotia Court of Appeal, delivered that court's unanimous judgement:***

**HART, CJ:** A person who seeks justification for preventing an assault against himself or someone under his protection must be faced with an *actual* assault, something that he must defend against, before the self-defence provisions of section 37 of the Criminal Code can be invoked. That assault must be *life-threatening* before he can be justified in killing in defence of his person, or that of someone under his protection. I do not believe that the trial judge was justified in placing section 37 of the Code before the jury. In my opinion no person has the right, in anticipation of an assault that may or may not happen, to apply force to prevent the imaginary assault. The jury should not have been permitted to consider a possible assault as a justification of Jane Stafford's deed.

Since the jury was improperly instructed on the law relating to the offence alleged against the defendant, and since that improper instruction may well have permitted them to reach a conclusion that would not otherwise be open to them, I would allow the appeal, set aside the verdict of the jury, and order a new trial upon the original indictment of first-degree murder.

**GREENSPAN:** ***But the new trial never took place. Instead, with the Crown's consent, Jane Stafford pleaded guilty to the lesser charge of manslaughter — the result her lawyer had sought all along...***

**FERRIER:** At that last point in time, Mrs. Stafford, when he was at his worst, can you tell the Court whether or not you wanted Mr. Stafford dead?

**JANE:** Yes, I wanted him dead. I hated him. He was a maniac.

**FERRIER:** Why didn't you leave him?

**JANE:** ..There was no leaving him to my mind. His first two wives had left him... Pauline, and the other one... Sometimes, when he was right crazy and beating me, he'd call me "Pauline"...

I told him once before that I was going to leave him, and he said he was never going to be a third-timer loser. He said, "Wherever you go, old woman, you'll be back." And he said, "You'll bring that bastard of a kid back with you," he said, "because I'll just start with your mother and your father and your sisters, and on and on," he said... "until you come back." So there was no way... no way...

**GREENSPAN:** ***On February 15, 1984, Jane Stafford was sentenced to six months in jail and two years probation by a judge who declared that Billy Stafford had been a man on the outer fringe of a definition of humanity. The range in manslaughter cases is from a suspended sentence to life imprisonment. While the sentence in this case is clearly on the low end of the scale, it is not unprecedented. On April 26 of the same year, Jane Stafford was released on full parole after serving the minimum two months of her sentence.***

# Producer's Notes

The case of Jane Stafford became widely discussed in the media. The impression created was that Mrs. Stafford, charged with first-degree murder in connection with the death of her abusive husband in the spring of 1982, was unjustly or at least insensitively treated by the legal system. The legal process is at times capable of being unfair, and for us it is irrelevant whether this is a rare or frequent occurrence. One case of unfair treatment is one too many. We wanted to find out if Jane Stafford's treatment may have been an example of it.

After reading the trial transcripts, we asked John Douglas to write the script. Douglas, one of the most experienced broadcast dramatists in Canada, turned in a meticulously crafted drama-documentary on the tragic events leading to Billy Stafford's death and Jane Stafford's ultimate conviction for manslaughter. In the end, we could find no fault with the legal system's treatment of the case. Though Billy Stafford was, in the words of the trial judge, "a man on the outer fringes of humanity", it was clear that he was asleep when Mrs. Stafford shot him. Further evidence indicated that she had, on an earlier occasion, tried to hire another person to kill her husband. The evidence also showed that she had taken out life insurance on him, and that at first she tried to blame the killing on her son. In light of this evidence, the prosecution probably had no choice but to proceed with a charge of first-degree murder.

On the other hand, a spirited defence amply demonstrated what Jane Stafford had to endure from Billy, a drunken and violent domestic tyrant, before she killed him. Manslaughter rather than murder — which the defence had asked for all along, and to which Jane Stafford pleaded guilty after the Nova Scotia Court of Appeal overturned the jury's acquittal — was undoubtedly the proper result.

The six-month sentence also reflected the system's understanding and sensitivity in this sad and difficult case.

Nicky Guadagni is one of the finest actresses of the younger generation. Her portrayal of Jane Stafford was a model of compassion and control. Other outstanding performances included those by Angelo Rizacos in the role of Jane's son, Allan; Frank Moore as her husband, Billy; and Cedric Smith as the Crown witness Beverly Taylor. Neil Munro as defence lawyer Alan Ferrier and Paul Soles as Crown Attorney Blaine Allaby demonstrated how suspense and realism can go hand in hand in a courtroom drama. Not content with merely writing a first-rate script, John Douglas also gave us a first-rate performance as Judge Burchell.

"I'm Not Living Like This Anymore" received several nominations, and in 1985 it won the Gabriel Award for the best radio entertainment program in North America. In no small measure this was due to the work of sound- and musical-effects technician Stephanie McKenna and to the flawless and unintrusive stereo operation of veteran sound engineer Derek Stubbs, whose work has enhanced many episodes of "The Scales of Justice".

It would be difficult to overestimate the influence of production assistant Nina Callaghan on any of our productions. In this episode her evident sympathy for Jane Stafford's plight may even have influenced the compassionate commentary of host Edward L. Greenspan.

G.J.

# The Scopelliti Case

*George Jonas*

## The Cast

Commentary by Edward L. Greenspan, Q.C.

| | |
|---|---|
| **ANTONIO SCOPELLITI** | Harvey Atkin |
| **MR. JUSTICE SAUNDERS** | Eric House |
| **CROWN** | Jim Morris |
| **SERGEANT HOUGH** | Ken James |
| **EDWARD L. GREENSPAN** (in scenes) | Al Waxman |

With the support of (in alphabetical order): Zoe Carter, Celestino De Juliius, Roger Dunn, Jayne Eastwood, David Ferry, Barry Flatman, Thomas Hauff, Jim Henshaw, Ken James, Geza Kovacs, Peggy Mahon, James Rankin, Tony Rubes, Dixie Seatle, and Michael Tait

## Scene 1 / In the Sutton Home

**DAVE:** Hey, Mom. I'm off now.
**MOM:** Are you taking the truck, Dave?
**DAVE:** Yeah.
**MOM:** Have you got some job interviews lined up?
**DAVE:** Yeah, and I'm dropping in at Manpower.
**MOM:** All right. I'll see you later.
**DAUGHTER:** Are you driving back to the shop, Dad, or are you going to wait for me?

## Scene 2 / At the Skating Rink

**SCOPELLITI:** Ah, what time your lesson finish?
**DAUGHTER:** Same time.
**SCOPELLITI:** Road bad today. I wait. I watch you skate.

## Scene 3 / In the McRae Home

**MRS. MC RAE** (*answering the telephone*): Hello?
**DAVE:** Is Mike there?
**MRS. MC RAE:** Ah, just a minute... (*calling*) Mike, telephone.
**MIKE** (*taking the receiver*): Yeah, is that you, Dave?
**DAVE:** Yeah. What are you doing?
**MIKE:** Having supper. Just got off work. You?
**DAVE:** I'm pickin' up a case of beer, takin' it over to Shawn's. Are you comin'?
**MIKE:** Yeah, sure. Soon as I'm finished.
**DAVE:** See ya.

**GREENSPAN:** ***Monday, January 22, 1979, was a winter day like any other in the small Ontario town of Orillia — an Italian shopkeeper was taking his little daughter to her figure-skating lesson; a teenage boy was coming home from work and having supper at his parents' home; another teenage boy was picking up a case of beer... Yet before ten o'clock that evening, two of these people would be dead, and a third would face the charge of having murdered them.***

***My name is Edward Greenspan, and the story you are about to hear is based on one of my own cases. The material has been reconstructed from the trial notes, as well as the transcripts and judgments in the Supreme Court of Ontario and the Ontario Court of Appeal. In the dramatized sequences, my role will be re-enacted by Al Waxman.***

***It was at 9:57 that evening that Bell Canada operator Joanna Groves received the first of three telephone calls...***

## Scene 4 / The Bell Exchange/Phone

**GROVES:** Operator. May I help you?
**SCOPELLITI:** Send the police to Gold Star Trailer Park...

**GREENSPAN:** ***The caller hung up immediately, but Joanna Groves, an experienced operator, kept the line open, expecting him to pick up the telephone again...***

**SCOPELLITI** (*breathing heavily*): Send ambulance...
**GROVES:** Send what?

**GREENSPAN:** ***The caller seemed so excited that the operator could not even tell for certain if it was a man's voice or a woman's. However, she stayed on the line, and in another second the caller returned...***

**SCOPELLITI:** Hello, you send ambulance...
**GROVES:** Stay on the line, please, stay on the line, okay? Now, you tell the police what you want. I'm connecting you to the police.
**EDGETT:** Constable Edgett speaking.
**SCOPELLITI:** Okay, police officer, come over here, Gold Star Trailer Park. I got two guys in the store. I think they take ambulance...
**EDGETT:** Gold Star Trailer Park?
**SCOPELLITI:** Yes.
**EDGETT:** All right.

**GROVES:** What number are you trying now, please? I'll connect you.
**SCOPELLITI** (*still excited*): I try Orillia Curling Club...
**GROVES:** Hold the line, just a minute...
**JOE ZITO:** Hello?
**SCOPELLITI:** Giuseppe, Giuseppe...
**ZITO:** Yeah, it's me, Tony. What'sa matter?
**SCOPELLITI:** It's better you come over here. I just shoot two guys.

**GREENSPAN:** ***As it happened, the police dispatcher, Constable Edgett, immediately recognized the excited, Italian-accented voice on the telephone as the voice of his neighbour, the small, mild-mannered owner of the Gold Star Food Market and Variety Store, Antonio Scopelliti. However, constables Lawrence and James, the two Orillia policemen who arrived at the variety store two minutes after Scopelliti's call, did not know the Italian shopkeeper. What they saw at the scene would later be elicited in court by Crown Attorney J.H. Madden...***

## Scene 5 / In Court

**CROWN:** ...When you went into the store, Constable Lawrence, what did you see?
**LAWRENCE:** After opening the door, the front door of the store, I observed two male persons lying on the floor near the door. One was lying closest to the door with his head against an ice cream freezer. I could see blood coming from a hole in the right side of his face... The other person was lying to my right as I stood at the doorway.
**CROWN:** Did you find any signs of life?
**LAWRENCE:** Shortly after my entry into the store the bleeding from the first person stopped and I could not feel any pulse from him or the other person.
**CROWN:** And was there a third person in the store?
**LAWRENCE:** A third person was standing on the other side of a counter at the rear of the store.
**CROWN:** And what did you do next?

# Scene 6 / In the Store

**LAWRENCE:** You better go to the cruiser and get an ambulance...
**JAMES:** Okay...
**LAWRENCE** (*calling*): And radio the sergeant. (*To Scopelliti*) Is there a telephone here? A telephone?

# Scene 7 / In Court

**LAWRENCE:** I asked the person that was standing beside the counter if there was a telephone, and he pointed to a doorway at the rear of the store.
**CROWN:** Now, the person you're talking about is the accused?
**LAWRENCE:** Yes.
**CROWN:** And what happened when you went back to the area to phone the police station?

# Scene 8 / In the Store

**LAWRENCE** (*softly*): See that gun on the shelf under the counter? I noticed it while I was on the phone.
**JAMES** (*also softly*): Yeah, I see it.
**LAWRENCE:** I don't want to touch it, but that guy's still standing right next to it... See if you can walk him to the window.
**JAMES:** Okay. (*Normal voice*) Ah, could you step over this way, sir? Ah, come with me, please.
**LAWRENCE:** Okay, what happened here?
**SCOPELLITI** (*calm, in a flat voice*): I shoot them. They gave me hard time... I go out now turn off my car? I lock car door.
**JAMES:** I'll turn it off for you, sir. Just give me the key.

**GREENSPAN:** ***In a sense, the reason I became involved in the Scopelliti case was this conversation, at least as Constable Lawrence recollected it. Because if Antonio Scopelliti shot and killed two young men only because they gave him a hard time, a jury of his peers might find him guilty of murder, the charge on which he was committed to stand trial. But was Constable Lawrence's recollection correct?***

# Scene 9/In Court

**JUSTICE SAUNDERS:** Mr. Greenspan?

**GREENSPAN:** Thank you, My Lord...Constable Lawrence, I would like you to look at this piece of paper. This is the piece of paper on which you wrote down what was being said, isn't it?

**LAWRENCE:** That's right.

**GREENSPAN:** And it says, "10:05 p.m.," right?

**LAWRENCE:** Yes.

**GREENSPAN:** Quote, "After entering the store and observing what was there I said to the suspect, 'What happened here?', answer was, 'I shot them'. At this time P.C. James was with me," unquote. That's all in the same ink pen, right?

**LAWRENCE:** That's right.

**GREENSPAN:** Now in a different ink pen and tucked in in this sentence is, quote, "They gave me a hard time," end quote — right?

**LAWRENCE:** That's right.

**GREENSPAN:** It's not part of what you wrote when you first wrote down what was said, correct?

**LAWRENCE:** That's right.

**GREENSPAN:** But you obviously used another pen and wrote this in much smaller print at a later time, right?

**LAWRENCE:** Right.

**GREENSPAN:** And that is your recollection of what was said in the presence of Officer James, right?

**LAWRENCE:** That's what I heard the accused saying, yes.

**GREENSPAN:** My Lord, I wonder if I might file this sheet of paper as an exhibit for the jury?

**JUSTICE SAUNDERS:** It will be Exhibit 44, I believe.

**GREENSPAN:** ***Exhibit 44 symbolized, in a sense, the Crown's entire case against Antonio Scopelliti. There was no question that the little Italian storekeeper shot the two young men in his store; he admitted it to the police right away; he told his brother-in-law Joe Zito on the telephone immediately after the shooting. But did he shoot them because they gave him a hard time? Did Scopelliti say what the police thought he said; and if he did, did he know enough English to understand their questions and his own answers? Because Constable James, standing next to Constable Lawrence, remembered the exchange differently...***

**GREENSPAN:** Constable James, you wrote down that Constable Lawrence asked Mr. Scopelliti, quote, "What happened here?" unquote, and that he said, quote, "I shoot them," unquote; because he spoke in an Italian accent, right?

**JAMES:** Yes.

**GREENSPAN:** And that's what you heard?

**JAMES:** Yes.

**GREENSPAN:** Okay. And if you had heard anything else — you would have written it down, right?

**JAMES:** Yes.

**GREENSPAN:** ***So Constable James did not recall Scopelliti saying, "They gave me a hard time"; if he had, he said, he would have written it down. But the question was far more complex than that. Why would a storekeeper gun down two men in his shop; and whether Scopelliti said what Constable Lawrence heard him say or not, why would the police come to believe that he might have done so just because they gave him a "hard time"? To answer those questions, it became important to know who Antonio Scopelliti was...***

**SCOPELLITI:** Me, Antonio Scopelliti — say like that. I was born the 24th April, nineteen hundred forty-two, inna village of Fiumara, Italy. My mother, my father has six children. I was the third one and they was farmer and they raised a — how you gonna say this? — sheeps. I was go to school for grade three, and then I was start to work at the farm... My father was no so healthy, so the childrens help him... When I was twenty, I go to Switzerland. I work in the factory and learning the trade, welding, in the night school... For six years I work very hard and live by myself, and send the money to my mother and my father. In 1968, I got married to a girl what I was grow up with in Fiumara, is the name Rose Zito. She emigrate to Canada and I was away so I come there and then we were marry and again I working for the welder... My son, Dominic, was born nineteen hundred sixty-nine, and my daughter, Paola, nineteen hundred seventy. I was make $110 a week and stop my job welding because my brother-in-law and me, we buy our own business, is called the Gold Star Trailer Camp, and I move my family in the back of the store from the time until when the police arrest me, and I work seven days every week in the store and I don't take time off, from 8:30 in the morning until it close up 11:00 in the night except the last three months I close the store at 10 o'clock... I was never charge with criminal problems before in my life and I am a Roman Catholic.

## Scene 10 / In the Law Office

**BUHR:** And that's the statement he gave me for his bail application.
**GREENSPAN:** Accurate as far as we know?
**BUHR:** Yep.
**GREENSPAN:** No record, wife and two kids, saves his money, works seven days a week? Did all his life?
**BUHR:** Oh yes.
**GREENSPAN:** No clouds, no complications?
**BUHR:** There are always clouds.

**GREENSPAN:** ***Chris Buhr, a law student working in my office at the time, was right: there are few criminal cases with no clouds on the defence's horizon, and Antonio Scopelliti's case was no exception. One cloud was that the victims, two local boys named David Sutton and Michael McRae, were only seventeen years old. The evidence indicated that Scopelliti fired seven shots at them, three of which, including the fatal shot, may have hit David Sutton in the back. The two young men were much bigger and more powerful than the shopkeeper, but — except for a small knife one of them carried on his belt — they were unarmed. They had no guns. And perhaps the darkest cloud was the conversation the police said occurred after Mr. Scopelliti was taken from the scene of the shooting to the police station...***

## Scene 11 / In the Police Station

**HOUGH:** Come in, Tony, you can sit over there... I'm Sergeant Hough. I know you from the store; I go in sometimes...
**SCOPELLITI** (*very flatly*): I know you, yeah...
**HOUGH:** And this is Staff Sergeant Smith, and you know Constable Lawrence... Okay, before we start, I want to caution you, if you have spoken to any police officer, anyone in authority, I don't want it to influence you in making a statement. Do you understand that?

**SCOPELLITI:** I don't know too much...
**HOUGH:** Okay, it just means, if you talked to another policeman, I don't want it to influence you in talking to me about this incident. Do you understand?
**SCOPELLITI:** I understand...
**HOUGH:** Do you know why you're here?
**SCOPELLITI:** I know...
**HOUGH:** Do you realize you're in custody for shooting those two youths in your store?
**SCOPELLITI:** Yes, yeah. I shoot them; I call cops.
**HOUGH:** Well, you told Constable Lawrence what happened, so you can tell me.
**SCOPELLITI:** Just before I close I was...
**HOUGH:** What time was that?
**SCOPELLITI:** Five to ten, about, I go out to start the car to warm him up. I close at ten... Two guys come inside the store and tried to hit me, slap me, but I duck, he miss.
**HOUGH:** Which one?
**SCOPELLITI:** The tall one, one in blue...
**HOUGH:** And where was the other one?
**SCOPELLITI:** His foot, he had on chocolate bar display. I say move, three time; he go get magazine. The tall skinny one, he try to open the till, I said to him to get away and other one say, "You don't have to pay him"...
**HOUGH:** Well, what did they buy?
**SCOPELLITI:** Some twenty-five-cent chips and bubble gum.
**HOUGH:** And what happened next?
**SCOPELLITI:** I reach under the counter where was the gun.
**HOUGH:** Was the gun loaded?
**SCOPELLITI:** Yeah, loaded... Yeah...
**HOUGH:** Then what happened?
**SCOPELLITI:** I shoot one in blue first...
**HOUGH:** And what did the other one say or do then?
**SCOPELLITI:** He call me son of a bitch, bastard. I shoot him too.
**HOUGH:** Did he try to get at you at all?
**SCOPELLITI:** No...
**HOUGH:** Well, did they indicate to you as if they were going to rob you?
**SCOPELLITI:** Don't say, but I don't know if they rob me or they're just horsing around...

**GREENSPAN:** ***If Antonio Scopelliti did, in fact, say what the police claimed he did, and if his emotional state and his knowledge of English enabled him to really understand Sergeant Hough's questions — and if the policemen could understand his answers — the Crown might indeed have a case against him. And there was more...***

## Scene 12 / In the Law Office

**BUHR:** Well — there seems to be some evidence that he knew these guys.

**GREENSPAN:** Scopelliti knew them?

**BUHR:** Apparently he had trouble with them before in the store... Small incidents, over the last year or two... The boys lived in the neighbourhood, and on one occasion they may have thrown snowballs and broke a light over the door; another time one of them may have stolen some gas from the pump outside; and once they bought some bottles of Coke and spit it all over the floor... Scopelliti had called the police on them.

**GREENSPAN:** I see. You think the prosecution may contend that he shot them in revenge?

**BUHR:** Possibly. After all, he is charged with first-degree murder, which involved planning and deliberation...

**GREENSPAN:** You'd have to be a prosecutor to believe that...

**GREENSPAN:** ***Over-charging defendants is, of course, a fact of life. The Crown often lays charges over an incident that are far more grave or more numerous than the evidence would warrant by any stretch of the imagination — not out of malice, as a rule, but simply as a tool in plea-bargaining. Rather than face the risk of a conviction for first-degree murder, which carries an automatic life sentence with no eligibility for parole for twenty-five years, a defendant might plead guilty to a lesser charge of second-degree murder or manslaughter. However, I had reason to believe that, on this evidence, the judge at Scopelliti's preliminary hearing would not commit him to trial for first-degree murder.***

# Scene 13 / In Court

**JUDGE MONTGOMERY:** I have given this serious consideration, but I still cannot find the planning that I feel is required and within the jurisdiction of the provincial court judge to decide at this stage of the matter and, accordingly, I commit the accused for trial before a court of competent jurisdiction in respect to charges of second-degree murder.

**GREENSPAN:** ***But second-degree murder is still a very serious charge and it, too, carries a mandatory sentence of life imprisonment. The only difference in punishment is that parole may be available after ten years of incarceration, instead of twenty-five. And, on the facts, I believed that Mr. Scopelliti had an excellent defence on the charge of second-degree murder as well. Ironically, his case might have appeared in a worse light to the prosecution through the efforts of the very people who were trying to help him... It was in February 1979, shortly after I had been retained, that Scopelliti's brothers-in-law, Rocco and Joe Zito, came to see me...***

# Scene 14 / In the Law Office

**BUHR:** Mr. Zito, please tell Mr. Greenspan what you told me.

**ROCCO ZITO:** You know, Mr. Greenspan, our sister Rosie is married to Tony, and...ah, we're partners inna Gold Star Trailer Park, too... Tony's a good man... When Sergeant Hough, he comes to me in barber shop — Joe and me, we got a barber shop inna town — and he tells me about this shooting, I say I'm a very shocked because I tell him I never knew Tony had any handguns; I never saw any handguns in the house...

**GREENSPAN:** And, I take it, this was not true?

**ROCCO:** Not true. Tony has a gun, since ten year or more, from Switzerland. He bought the gun there. I seen it, oh, two, three times.

**JOE ZITO:** At home, in Fiumara, everybody's got a gun, most people... So Tony has gun. But when police ask me, I say same as my brother, Rocco. I never see the gun... I say so to not hurt Tony.

**GREENSPAN:** I see... Mr. Zito, I understand why you and your brother lied to the police. Don't worry about it now, only remember this: When you come to court, you must tell the truth. You must tell the judge that you had lied, and you must tell him why. Do you understand that?
**ROCCO & JOE:** Yes sir... We understand. Bye. Good-bye.
**BUHR:** Thanks very much, gentlemen. I'll be in touch.

*The Zitos leave.*

**BUHR:** Well, what do you think? Possessing an unregistered firearm, importing it from abroad... No wonder they didn't want to tell the police.
**GREENSPAN:** Yes, well, I wish they had... Scopelliti either committed a crime or he didn't. If what he did was murder, it is no less a murder to shoot people with a properly registered firearm. I don't think the judge will let that go to the jury: it is irrelevant to what he is charged with and highly prejudicial. But if his brothers-in-law had told the police the truth, that Scopelliti had owned the gun for ten, fifteen years, the Crown could never argue that he just bought it before the shooting...for the purpose of killing those boys.

**GREENSPAN:** ***To obtain a conviction for murder, something like this had to be the prosecution's argument. However, the facts as we saw them did not support this theory. I did not believe for a moment that a hard-working shopkeeper with a wife and two children, would risk his entire existence in order to avenge a broken lightbulb or a spilled bottle of Coke. Shopkeepers — unless they are crazy, for which in this case there wasn't the slightest evidence — don't lie in wait with guns to kill their customers. My view of the facts was infinitely more supportive of Antonio Scopelliti's own version of the events...***

## Scene 15/In the Store/Phone

*Two men enter.*

**SCOPELITTI:** Yes? (*No reply*)... Please...take your foot from the candy. (*No reply*) Your foot, from the chocolate candy, please, take it off there. (*No reply*)... I said, please, to take your foot away from the chocolate. Okay?

*Second man approaches the counter.*

**SCOPELLITI** (*nervous*): What do you want?
**DAVE:** Gum. Here's a dime.

*He throws the dime on the counter and unwraps the gum.*

**DAVE** (*with gum in mouth, menacingly*): This gum is no good.

*Dave spits the gum out and Mike laughs disdainfully.*

**SCOPELLITI:** This is no good, then take your dime and leave, please. I want to close 'm up the store.
**DAVE:** You son of a bitch...

*He throws a punch at Scopelliti but misses and he thuds into the counter.*

**SCOPELLITI** (*frightened*): Go away. I'm going to call the police...
**DAVE:** I'll kill you before that... Gimme the money!
**SCOPELLITI:** You, you want the money. So there. Take it if you want it...

*Scopelliti fires five shots in rapid succession, then two more. The two men slump to the floor.*

*Scopelliti reaches for the telephone.*

**OPERATOR:** Operator. May I help you?
**SCOPELLITI** (*hysterical*): Send the police to Gold Star Trailer Camp...

**GREENSPAN:** ***This was Scopelliti's story, and it gave rise to some questions. The first and most obvious one was why did he not tell it this way at his first interview with Sergeant Hough after the shooting? There could have been several reasons for that, and some of them emerged from the cross-examination of Sergeant Hough…***

## Scene 16 / In Court

**GREENSPAN:** When you said you knew Mr. Scopelliti three or four years, sometimes you'd go into the store and Tony would be there?

**HOUGH:** Yes.

**GREENSPAN:** You marked down "alias"; you don't mean alias, it's just —?

**HOUGH:** An abbreviated short form of…

**GREENSPAN:** His name is Antonio and he calls himself Tony, right?

**HOUGH:** Yes, yes.

**GREENSPAN:** Did you call him Tony when you knew him?

**HOUGH:** Yes…

**GREENSPAN:** All right… Now, it's your evidence that during the time that you were with him at the police station, that he was very calm, right?

**HOUGH:** Yes.

**GREENSPAN:** Okay. He was very flat, no animation at all, right?

**HOUGH:** He made some expressions.

**GREENSPAN:** You, yesterday under oath, said, did you not, that he was very flat and had no animation?

**HOUGH:** That might have been your terminology.

**GREENSPAN:** No, you said that? You agreed with what I said?

**HOUGH:** Probably, yes.

**GREENSPAN:** So that what I am saying to you is that he was sitting emotionless, he was very flat and had no animation, that you've said this on an earlier occasion under oath, isn't that correct?

**HOUGH:** To a point, yes.

**GREENSPAN:** You didn't say it to a point, you said it under oath?

**HOUGH:** I also said something else as well, sir.

**GREENSPAN:** Well, did you say *that* at least?

**HOUGH:** Probably, yes.

**GREENSPAN:** Okay. Now…

**GREENSPAN:** ***It was important to establish that right after the shooting, understandably enough, Scopelliti was in a state of shock. I was calling medical experts to testify later that in a traumatic shock people can appear outwardly calm, yet their minds are totally scattered and can't focus on questions and answers. I also wished to show that the officers could not reliably understand Scopelliti's fractured English, and that he could not understand them at all...***

**GREENSPAN:** Now, Sergeant Hough, in what room did you and Tony meet the justice of the peace? After your interview?
**HOUGH:** With Tony, in the first interview room adjacent to my open-plan office.
**GREENSPAN:** And what was the justice of the peace's name?
**HOUGH:** Mr. Harris.
**GREENSPAN:** Mr. Harris. Tony thought he was a priest?
**HOUGH:** He asked me later if he was a priest, yes.
**GREENSPAN:** So the justice of the peace comes in to read him the charge to remand him and then Tony asks you whether or not this man is a priest?
**HOUGH:** Yes, that's correct.
**GREENSPAN:** Thank you, no further questions.

**GREENSPAN:** ***There was other evidence that Scopelliti was either too shocked to know what he was talking about at the police station, or the policeman did not understand his English. Sergeant Hough had testified that Scopelliti had talked about David Sutton purchasing "twenty-five-cent chips and bubble gum" before the shooting. But there was no bag of chips anywhere, and Sutton had only twelve cents on him. In all likelihood, the officers had misunderstood Scopelliti in this respect as well. So, unimportant as the bag of chips may have been, it supported Tony's story. But was there anything to support his contention that the two young men had tried to rob and threatened to kill him? To introduce evidence for that, a very contentious legal hurdle had to be surmounted...***

## Scene 17 / In the Law Office

**BUHR:** There is quite a bit of evidence, you know, that these boys were pretty violent characters... Too bad you can't use it.
**GREENSPAN:** Why can't I use it?

**BUHR:** Well, obviously...it would be irrelevant and prejudicial, wouldn't it? The boys were the victims; they're not on trial.

**GREENSPAN:** True, but if Scopelliti knew about their reputation for violence, it would make him all the more terrified. It would affect his state of mind.

**BUHR:** Yes, but he didn't. There is no evidence that he did, anyway...

**GREENSPAN:** Wait a minute. Just think about it. True, the victims are not on trial, but then nobody is trying them... This evidence doesn't go in to show that they deserved to be shot because they were behaving like bullies. And I agree, if Tony didn't know that they had acted violently in the past, it could not have affected his state of mind... But the evidence can still corroborate Tony's explanation. It can help the jury to decide whether or not he is telling the truth.

**BUHR:** Is that the law?

**GREENSPAN:** I don't know. But get out the books; we're going to find out.

**GREENSPAN:** ***As my student-at-law suspected, before the Scopelliti case the law in Canada was far from being settled in this regard. In fact, there was a climate of opinion, especially with respect to rape cases, that considered it unfair to test the disposition or reputation of the victims in any way. I have always disagreed with that. It seems common sense to me that knowing the truth about a victim, as long as it pertains to a relevant issue, can only help the jury in finding out the truth about an accused... I made my arguments; the Crown naturally opposed them; and the decision was up to Mr. Justice Saunders...***

## Scene 18 / In Court

**JUSTICE SAUNDERS:** Before the jury comes in I will give my ruling with respect to the evidentiary matter we discussed yesterday afternoon... The evidence was fully summarized by Mr. Greenspan... If accepted, it tends to show that both victims were predisposed to unprovoked violence... The difficulty is in admitting specific prior acts as evidence of disposition where the accused was unaware of those acts. I was referred to no reported Canadian or English decisions where they would have been admitted.

If evidence of this nature had been offered by the Crown as to the disposition of the accused it would almost certainly have been ruled inadmissible... But in my view, there is a distinction between evidence that may be offered with respect to the disposition of the accused and with respect to the disposition of his victims... In view of the extraordinary nature of the evidence I have decided that it should be admitted as corroborative of the explanation of the accused of the events of January 22.

The jury will have to be charged as to the limited use they may make of the proposed evidence; it is evidence only in support of the accused's explanation of the events, but is not evidence that should be taken into account when they consider the accused's state of mind, nor should they feel that the victims deserved some sort of punishment as a result of their behaviour.

**GREENSPAN:** ***Mr. Justice Saunders' ruling had great legal significance. If upheld by the higher courts, it would have an effect on the law in Canada reaching far beyond the fate of Antonio Scopelliti. But my immediate concern was my client. The fact was that because of the judge's ruling, it became possible for me to call certain witnesses for the defence.***

**GREENSPAN:** Sir, you are twenty-six years of age, married with two children, and are a production operator by occupation?
**HENDERSON:** Yes.
**GREENSPAN:** Okay. I would like to take you back to November 7, 1978. Before that day did you know David Sutton or Michael McRae?
**HENDERSON:** No sir.
**GREENSPAN:** At around 3:30 p.m. that day where were you?
**HENDERSON:** I was on my way to work, drivin' in my car and, going through Floral Park, I come upon a truck doin' about thirty miles per hour... I attempted to pass him and...ah, he sped up to keep me from passin' and I slowed down and...they'd slow down so as I could not get into the proper lane... Then I stepped on the brakes to stop my car and they stopped in the middle of the road, and one of the lads got out, come back to my car, and he said...
**GREENSPAN:** Who was that person who came back to your car?
**HENDERSON:** Well, that was Sutton.

## Scene 19/In the Open Air

**DAVE:** You son of a bitch, you tried to cut me off...
**HENDERSON:** No, I didn't. I...

*Sutton punches Henderson.*

**MIKE:** You wanna try me, I'm pretty good...

## Scene 20/In Court

**GREENSPAN:** You wear glasses. Were you wearing glasses at the time?
**HENDERSON:** Yes.
**GREENSPAN:** What happened to them?
**HENDERSON:** They landed in the back seat.

**GREENSPAN:** ***The next people to encounter Sutton and McRae were not formidable adversaries either...***

**CAROL:** My fiancé and I were coming down Highway 11 and we turned right off by the bypass on West Street and...well, I noticed a car coming up behind us quite fast and we turned — we stopped at the stop sign and they were honking the horn and yelling and we pulled out and they pulled around our right and stopped...

## Scene 21/Outdoors and in a Car

**CAROL** (*frightened*): They're coming back... What do they want?
**BRADEN:** To hell with that, I'm going to the police...

*Braden accelerates.*

**CAROL:** They're chasing us... We've got to get to the station...

## Scene 22 / In Court

**CAROL:** ...and as we got to the police station — we had our doors locked all the time — I said to my fiancé, "We don't have time to get out," and at this point the guys, four guys got out of their car, two on my side and two on his, and they tried to get in the doors...

**GREENSPAN:** May I ask you this: Were those two boys, Sutton and McRae, two of the four boys?

**CAROL:** I only recognized Sutton.

**GREENSPAN:** How terrified were you?

**CAROL:** I was terrified to the point of tears and hysterics...

**GREENSPAN:** ***If this attack made little sense, the incident described by the next witness seemed even more senseless...***

**BRIAN:** I was just going...walking up the street with my girlfriend and Dave Sutton and Mike McRae jumped out of their car and they pinned me up against the wall.

## Scene 23 / Outdoors

**DAVE:** I don't like the looks of you.

**BRIAN:** Why not?

*Sutton punches Brian.*

## Scene 24 / In Court

**GREENSPAN:** Where did he hit you?

**BRIAN:** In the face and the arm.

**GREENSPAN:** And at that point were you afraid?

**BRIAN:** Very, very much afraid.

**GREENSPAN:** ***There it was, four witnesses, none of whom knew Tony Scopelliti, and who hardly knew, or did not know at all, Sutton and McRae before they were attacked by them... There was little doubt that the two boys were very tough, whatever else they may have been, though this in itself would excuse no one for shooting them. But the onus was on the Crown to prove that Scopelliti was not acting in self-defence, and such testimony, coupled with Tony's evidence, might be enough to raise a reasonable doubt about the issue in the jury's mind. But first, the defence had to overcome another hurdle, Rocco and Joe Zito, who had only been trying to help Tony. Now, on the witness stand, they were rigorously cross-examined by the Crown attorney...***

**CROWN:** Mr. Zito, you indicated to Sergeant Hough that, quote, "I was very shocked about the shooting because I never knew Tony had any handguns," end quote. Isn't that what you said to Sergeant Hough?

**ROCCO:** Yes, I did, sir.

**CROWN:** And you tell us today that that, in fact, was a lie, is that correct?

**ROCCO:** Yes, sir, and I'm very sorry. I apologize.

**CROWN:** And you say you did that so that you could assist your brother-in-law, help him?

**ROCCO:** Well, I didn't know what to say; if I say "yes" I hurt the guy, and if I say "no" I hurt the guy, so I rather say nothing, so I say I know nothing about it.

**CROWN:** You didn't say nothing about it! You told the police officer that you'd never seen or heard anything about a handgun.

**ROCCO:** I'm very sorry that I lied to the officer.

**CROWN:** Are you telling us then that you were trying to mislead the police officer so that you could help Tony?

**ROCCO:** Yes, sir.

**CROWN:** Now, when did it come to your attention that, in fact, that statement to the police *wasn't* going to help Tony? When did you find that out?

**ROCCO:** When did I find that out?

**CROWN:** Yes.

**ROCCO:** When our attorney asked us to tell the truth and nothing else but the truth when we come in court...

**GREENSPAN:** ***Not having received much comfort from Rocco Zito, the Crown attorney tried to go a little farther with his brother, Giuseppe Zito...***

**CROWN:** Rocco actually told you that in fact he had lied?
**JOE:** No, he no told me; he was just talking.
**CROWN:** Well, perhaps Rocco didn't know anything about the gun...
**JOE:** No, I don't say he didn't, he just was talking about...you know, come up about the gun...and I say no, when police ask, the same thing, but Rocco, he never say to me to say anything, no.
**CROWN:** You said that you spoke to Mr. Greenspan about it?
**JOE:** Yes, I asked him.
**CROWN:** How long ago was that?
**JOE:** Oh, when the...how long it's ago? It's four, five months ago, maybe more.
**CROWN:** Now, Mr. Zito, perhaps we could cover...
**GREENSPAN:** My Lord, this is... You see, it's going to make me a witness, and, and I think that is an unfair thing to do. There's a privilege. If I differ with this witness, does this mean that I now have to go into the box and say exactly what and when this man told me? I don't think that was fair at all.
**CROWN:** I'm sure, My Lord, that in fact the jury is interested in knowing when indeed such items were accounted...
**GREENSPAN:** As soon as I was retained. You want me to go into the box and talk about that? My friend should know better than that.
**JUSTICE SAUNDERS:** Perhaps we should discuss this in the absence of the jury.

*The jury files out of the courtroom.*

**GREENSPAN:** ***The prosecutor had a reason for raising the matter in this fashion: it was an attempt to bring in through the back door, as it were, the fact that Scopelliti's gun was unregistered and improperly imported into Canada — evidence that His Lordship had previously ruled inadmissible, as it was totally irrelevant to the question before the jury. Now Mr. Justice Saunders ruled on that issue for the last time...***

**JUSTICE SAUNDERS:** The witness cannot be asked any questions that tend to show that the gun was improperly imported or was not registerable...

**GREENSPAN:** ***This ended the matter, and now, finally, it was up to Antonio Scopelliti. Although the law of self-defence is very complex, in the end it boils down to one simple question: Was Scopelliti afraid for his life, and did he shoot the two young men because he believed that he could not save himself from death or grievous bodily harm in any other way?***

**GREENSPAN:** Mr. Scopelliti, before this incident, had you ever been charged or convicted of any criminal offence?

**SCOPELLITI:** I no have a criminal record.

**GREENSPAN:** And you testified that you lived, with your family, in the back of the store until about a year ago, when you bought a house, but your wife would continue to cook dinner for you and your children in the kitchen behind the shop?

**SCOPELLITI:** Yes, sir. Because I work late in the store.

**GREENSPAN:** And on the night of January 22, after you brought your daughter back from her skating lesson, did you all have dinner?

**SCOPELLITI:** Yes, sir.

**GREENSPAN:** And after dinner did your wife wash the dishes?

**SCOPELLITI:** Yes, sir.

**GREENSPAN:** And then she and the children left for home?

**SCOPELLITI:** Yes, sir.

**GREENSPAN:** Now you told us that...ah, five minutes before closing time you started up your car, went back into the shop, and it was then that Sutton and McRae came in... When you told McRae to take his foot off the chocolate bars, did he say anything to you?

**SCOPELLITI:** No, but he look at me...ah, like he no like what I say to him.

**GREENSPAN:** And how did you feel at that point?

**SCOPELLITI:** I start to get nervous and fright.

**GREENSPAN:** And you mentioned Sutton picking up how many packages of gum?

**SCOPELLITI:** Two.

**GREENSPAN:** Now, there has been evidence that when you were in the police station later that night that you said something about a bag of chips?

**SCOPELLITI:** I no remember saying nothing about chips, sir, or seeing chips that night.

**GREENSPAN:** Okay. Now, when Sutton picked up these two packages of gumballs, what did he do?

**SCOPELLITI:** He throw the ten cents, sir, and they...they go on the floor.

**GREENSPAN:** What did you do with the dime?

**SCOPELLITI:** I take it from the floor and put it top the bench.

**GREENSPAN:** Did you open the cash register and put it in?

**SCOPELLITI:** No.

**GREENSPAN:** Why not?

**SCOPELLITI:** I was afraid.

**GREENSPAN:** All right. Now did Sutton do anything with the gum?

**SCOPELLITI:** In that second I pick up the dime, is put the gum inside the mouth and chew and he's take with the fingers and threw in my face... He said what's wrong with the gum.

**GREENSPAN:** Now, did you say anything or do anything after Sutton did that?

**SCOPELLITI:** I pushed towards him the dime, I say to him, "Take dime and leave, please, because I want to close 'm up."

**GREENSPAN:** What did he do?

**SCOPELLITI:** He hit me with a closed fist on my face, and I moved backwards and he no hit me.

**GREENSPAN:** And how did you feel at that time?

**SCOPELLITI:** Sir, I trembled because I was so scared.

**GREENSPAN:** How tall are you, Mr. Scopelliti?

**SCOPELLITI:** Five feet and a half, about.

**GREENSPAN:** How much do you weigh?

**SCOPELLITI:** A hundred sixty pounds, more or less, more or less. I don't know.

**GREENSPAN:** Now, when Sutton missed, did you say or do anything?

**SCOPELLITI:** "Go away, I go to call the police."

**GREENSPAN:** How did you feel after you'd said that?

**SCOPELLITI:** I was more fright because Mr. Sutton, he was more nervous because he miss me, and he put his hand in the pocket and at the same time ask me for the money.

**GREENSPAN:** Did he say anything else to you at that time?

**SCOPELLITI:** Say he's going to kill me before I call the police.

**GREENSPAN:** What happened next?

**SCOPELLITI:** I look at him to see what movement he was do, and at the same time I say, "The money is over there, take it if you want it."

**GREENSPAN:** At that moment did you believe you were going to live or die?

**SCOPELLITI:** I think so they're going to kill me.

**GREENSPAN:** What did you do?
**SCOPELLITI:** Split second, sir, like this with hand, put underneath the counter take the pistol, I shoot. That's all I know.
**GREENSPAN:** Mr. Scopelliti, did you mean to kill David Sutton?
**SCOPELLITI:** No, sir.
**GREENSPAN:** Did you mean to kill Michael McRae?
**SCOPELLITI:** No, sir.
**GREENSPAN:** Are you sorry they are dead?
**SCOPELLITI:** Yes.
**GREENSPAN:** Why did you shoot them?
**SCOPELLITI:** God has created humanity, the people to love each other and not to kill. Death is a horrible thing. Every one of us forgot, you go away from God's commandment, you defend from death.
**JUSTICE SAUNDERS:** I...ah, I'm sorry. I didn't get that last phrase.
**GREENSPAN:** "You defend from death," My Lord.

**GREENSPAN:** ***In his cross-examination Crown Attorney Madden did not pursue too strenuously the suggestion of a revenge-killing, probably realizing that, on the facts, it would have been a very farfetched theory. Instead, the prosecutor tried to elicit support for the view that Scopelliti was a cantankerous person who shot the two young men out of anger and frustration rather than genuine fear...***

**CROWN:** Isn't it a fact, Mr. Scopelliti, when you produced that gun Mr. Sutton tried to turn around to get out of your place?
**SCOPELLITI:** I don't believe that's what he did, sir.
**CROWN:** What did he do then?
**SCOPELLITI:** I don't know for sure, sir, because I do not know what was his intention to do. When I shoot, he start to turn; if he want to hide or if he want to run, I do not know, sir.
**CROWN:** Can you tell me how you shot him three times in the back?
**SCOPELLITI:** I said before, sir, it's a matter of second. I start to shoot; I don't know nothing, where I strike him, how. I don't know...
**CROWN:** All right... You indicated to Sergeant Hough, when he asked whether or not they indicated they were going to rob you, that you said, quote: "They didn't but I didn't know whether they were or not or if they were just horsing around," end quote?
**SCOPELLITI:** Sir, I was frightened, nervous after what did happen, I no explain to Sergeant Rough [*sic*] exactly what they did to me.
**CROWN:** Well, when did you finally realize that you hadn't told Sergeant Hough everything?

**SCOPELLITI:** After about two weeks, sir, when start to clear up my mind.

**CROWN:** When your mind started to clear and think better, did you get back in touch with Sergeant Hough?

**GREENSPAN:** My Lord, I have an objection. I'd like to take it up in the absence of the jury, My Lord.

**JUSTICE SAUNDERS:** Yes.

**GREENSPAN:** ***The trial judge knew, of course, why I was raising an objection. Under our system of law every accused person has the fundamental right to remain silent, and the prosecutor can never make this a subject of comment to the jury. It is up to the authorities to prove a defendant guilty, not up to the defendant to explain or prove his innocence to the authorities...***

**JUSTICE SAUNDERS:** It is akin to making a comment to the jury on his failure to testify; I can't see the distinction. So you must not continue that line of questioning.

**GREENSPAN:** ***After His Lordship's ruling, the Crown did not have many questions left. I asked only one thing in re-examination...***

**GREENSPAN:** Mr. Scopelliti, do you know an English expression "horsing around"?

**SCOPELLITI:** No.

**GREENSPAN:** No further questions.

**GREENSPAN:** ***The defence had presented its case, and the Crown called no evidence in reply. The time had come for me to address the jury. These would be the last words at the trial spoken in Antonio Scopelliti's behalf...***

**GREENSPAN:** May it please Your Lordship, and you, ladies and gentlemen of the jury, at 10:05 p.m. Constable Lawrence asked Mr. Scopelliti in his store, "What happened here?" According to Constable Lawrence, Mr. Scopelliti said, "I shot them. They gave me a hard time." And you will recall Constable Lawrence remembered that last sentence — "They gave me a hard time" — some time after the conversation actually happened. Constable James swears Lawrence is mistaken. All Mr. Scopelliti said was, "I shoot them." Now, I could say to you that Constable

Lawrence simply wrote down that first time what really happened, but that in the strain of the situation and after it was all over Lawrence attributed someone else's idle conjecture to Mr. Scopelliti. I could say that to you — but that would be wrong. That would be speculation and, as His Lordship will tell you, you are not allowed to speculate. You must deal with facts and the only facts we have are that Lawrence, sometime afterwards, wrote in the words "they gave me a hard time" and that Constable James, who was standing right beside Mr. Scopelliti, swears that it didn't happen. But stop for a moment. Suppose Lawrence is right. What does that prove? A man in shock — who less than ten minutes before has just fired a gun seven times, has been completely hysterical calling for an ambulance, an Italian immigrant who has great difficulty speaking and understanding English at the best of times — what does it prove if he said that? Can anything he says under these circumstances mean anything? What will the prosecutor say to that? Hm? For the prosecutor had his opportunity to say that Sutton and McRae weren't really trying to kill Mr. Scopelliti. He could have asked Mr. Scopelliti that in cross-examination. But he didn't. He didn't ask a single question about what happened in that store before the shooting. Not a single question of Mr. Scopelliti. And if he tries to pull that suggestion out of his hat now, don't let him.

But let's continue. At 12:39 Mr. Scopelliti is questioned by Sergeant Hough. Sergeant Hough asked Mr. Scopelliti if he knew why he was there. And the reason, I suggest to you, that question was asked, was because even Sergeant Hough had doubts that Mr. Scopelliti knew what was going on. Whatever Mr. Scopelliti said, he didn't know what he was talking about — or it was just one more example of the police failing to understand his fractured language, like the phrase "horsing around". Remember that? When I asked him if he knew what it meant, he said he had no idea. "Horsing around," indeed!

Now what will the prosecutor say about this interview? He'll say, I expect, that when Sergeant Hough asked Mr. Scopelliti if Sutton and McRae "indicated" they were going to rob him and Mr. Scopelliti said they didn't, but that he didn't know if they were or if they were horsing around, that in some way that's significant. But had the police bothered to ask him if they "indicated" that they were going to kill him, and if he wasn't so disoriented, he would have told them yes, Sutton had threatened to kill him and yes, Mr. Scopelliti had believed they would. Because, after all, he knew them — at least by their faces — and if they did rob him as they were trying very hard to convince him of — they would have to kill him in order not to be identified. That's what Antonio Scopelliti believed. And that is why he grabbed the gun and fired.

But let's go a step further. The prosecutor wants you to believe Antonio Scopelliti went out and cold-bloodedly bought a gun and lay in wait for them to come into his store and then he killed them. That's the prosecutor's theory. On that theory, what's the gumball doing on the floor? Why is David Sutton in that store with twelve cents in his pocket — buying some gum that cost a dime and then spitting it out? But far more importantly, why did Scopelliti, within seconds of the shooting, telephone frantically three times for an ambulance and the police? Why would he do that if he had just satisfied some murderous lust for revenge?

Why did those young men go into the store late that night? No one can ever be sure that they went in there to rob Mr. Scopelliti, but consider this. David Sutton had twelve cents in his pocket — he didn't go in there to buy anything. And Michael McRae carried a knife on his belt. It wasn't a big knife, but how big a knife would it take to completely intimidate a small, quiet shopkeeper?

The fact that David Sutton was shot three times in the back doesn't change that. Antonio Scopelliti swore that both Sutton and McRae turned to the side as he fired. He didn't aim at all. He just fired, his hand shaking as he held the gun. He didn't see anything after he started firing.

I submit to you that, on all the evidence, Antonio Scopelliti has shown you that he acted in self-defence when he fired the gun that killed David Sutton and Michael McRae. I suggest to you that there is nothing more he could do to convince you of his innocence.

You cannot remove his suffering; you cannot bring those boys back. But we would suffer, all of us, if a man in his own place could not be allowed to defend his own life. It is a good law and good sense that a man, when attacked, may defend himself. Antonio Scopelliti acted in self-defence to protect his life. I ask you to acquit him.

**GREENSPAN:** ***After I sat down, the prosecutor addressed the jury. Later the Crown's position was summarized by His Lordship this way...***

**JUSTICE SAUNDERS:** The Crown asks you to consider that the accused acted in anger rather than fear... The action of the victims, who he had dealt with before, so angered him — in the submission of the Crown — that he intentionally shot and killed them; that his action was unnecessary in the circumstances as the mere production of the gun would have been sufficient...

**GREENSPAN:** ***The trial judge completed his charge, and the jury retired to consider its verdict. The five hours that followed were, without doubt, the longest five hours in Scopelliti's life. And even though, unlike Mr. Scopelliti, I would be going home that night whatever the verdict, they were among the longest five hours in my life as well. There was nothing more I could do or say. Had I done, had I said everything that I could do and say on Antonio Scopelliti's behalf?***

*The jury returns to the courtroom.*

**REGISTRAR:** The accused will please stand. Members of the jury, have you considered your verdict?
**FOREMAN:** Yes, we have.
**REGISTRAR:** And what is your verdict?
**FOREMAN:** Not guilty.

**GREENSPAN:** ***It was not quite the last word. Tense months followed as the Crown appealed, but in the end the Ontario Court of Appeal unanimously upheld the jury's acquittal. Scopelliti was finally free. However, nothing would ever remove the tragedy of the two boys and their parents. We will never know what they wanted to do in that variety store five minutes before closing time, but there is no doubt that they made Scopelliti fear for his life. And the danger in bullying the weak and defenceless is that, once in a while, you may succeed in scaring them only too well.***

***Scopelliti was acquitted, but in the process he lost nearly everything for which he had worked for seven days a week and twelve hours a day for fifteen years. The Gold Star Trailer Camp is closed. He was never granted bail, so he had to spend over a year in jail, waiting for his trial. A year in jail is not much for killing two human beings, but it is a grave punishment for a person found entirely innocent by his peers.***

# Producer's Notes

I happened to be in Greenspan's office on the day he was retained to defend Antonio Scopelliti, the shopkeeper who was eventually acquitted of murder in the shooting death of two teenage boys in Orillia. On that day acquittal seemed very distant even as a possibility. Though the original charge of first-degree — that is, planned and deliberate — murder appeared to be wholly unjustified on the facts of the case (and was reduced to second-degree murder by Judge Montgomery after a preliminary hearing) Scopelliti did admit firing the shots that killed the two teenagers in his shop. Greenspan was troubled and saddened by the tragic case — as, he felt, would be the jury. Violent death, especially of young people, always cries out for a finding of guilt, at least in some degree.

But sane and peaceful shopkeepers don't normally shoot their customers, and there wasn't a hint of violence or instability in Scopelliti's past. No explanation made better sense than Scopelliti's own, namely that he shot the boys in self-defence because he had reason to think that they were going to rob and harm him.

This was the conclusion the jury reached after a difficult and suspenseful trial, and therefore the case became a good illustration of the right of self-defence. Our society, while increasingly accepting and excusing violence of all types, has become rather intolerant of citizens defending themselves or their property. I have always found this puzzling. There have been many recent cases in which people, after escorting a trespasser from their property or warding off a would-be rapist, found themselves charged with pointing a firearm or being in the illegal possession of Mace. With ordinary men and women being more and more at the mercy of burglars, muggers, rioters, terrorists, and other bullies, it was important, I felt, to include a case in our series where a jury's verdict reaffirms the legal right of self-defence.

At the same time I had a deep sense of regret over the untimely death of the two youngsters who came from decent, law-abiding families and, but for this incident, might well have grown up to be decent citizens themselves. We tried to reflect this sense of regret in the script, the production, and in Greenspan's commentary.

Antonio Scopelliti was portrayed by Harvey Atkin, the exceptionally gifted character actor, whose work is well known to radio and television audiences in this country as well as in the United States. He deservedly was nominated for an ACTRA Award for best radio actor for this performance.

The role of Greenspan in the script was performed, as always, by superstar Al Waxman. His work, along with the performance of Jim Morris as the Crown attorney, Eric House as Mr. Justice Saunders, and Ken James as Sergeant Hough, contributed to the production itself being nominated for the best radio program at the fourteenth annual ACTRA Awards. The excellent support of Jim Henshaw, David Ferry, Jayne Eastwood, Peggy Mahon, Dixie Seatle, Roger Dunn, Geza Kovacs, and Celestino De Juliius proved once again that there are no small roles in any production. On the other side of the glass in the control room, the same thing was reaffirmed by the work of production assistant Nancy McIlveen.

G.J.

# Snow Job

*Guy Gavriel Kay*

## The Cast

Commentary by Edward L. Greenspan, Q.C.

| | |
|---|---|
| **VICTOR AMATO** | Geoffrey Bowes |
| **MR. SIMONS** for the defence | Ray Stancer |
| **MR. KENNEDY** for the Crown | Neil Munro |
| **JUDGE McGIVERN** | Henry Ramer |
| **CONSTABLE GARY GODWIN** | Michael Hogan |

With the support of (in alphabetical order): Mellany Brown, Lawrence Dane, Ron Hartmann, Jim Henshaw, Mary Long, Arch McDonell, Frank Perry, Ken Pogue, Booth Savage, Paul Soles, and Marian Waldman

## Scene 1 / Inside a Moving Car, Nighttime, A Vancouver Residential Area, September 1977

**AMATO** (*tensely*): Okay. Just pull over and stop, just up there.
**LANGVIN** (*calmly*): Before the driveway?
**AMATO:** Yeah, anywhere along here. Just park the car.
**LANGVIN:** She live over here, Victor?
**AMATO:** No. A couple blocks away.
**LANGVIN:** What? So, what are we doing...
**AMATO:** Don, listen to me. We do this my way, or we don't do it at all. I just don't want you meeting her. She's got a kid. I... I don't want her to get any more involved than she is. You understand?
**LANGVIN:** Yeah, okay. But Victor ——
**AMATO:** No buts, Don. I want you to give me the money here and I'll go get the stuff for you.
**LANGVIN:** Up front? You want me to front the money?
**AMATO:** Don, if you don't like it we can go home now.
**LANGVIN:** It's just not the way I like to do business. But... I trust you. I trust you.
**AMATO:** ... sixty, eighty, hundred. All right. The deal is a hundred bucks for a gram of coke, right?
**LANGVIN:** That's the deal.
**AMATO:** All right. I'll be right back. You... you just stay here.
**LANGVIN:** I ain't going nowhere, Victor.

*Soon Amato returns to the car.*

**LANGVIN:** Welcome back. You get the snow?
**AMATO** (*a little breathless*): Yeah, yeah I got it.
**LANGVIN:** Where?
**AMATO:** In my pocket.

**LANGVIN:** Well, why don't you give it to me, Victor?
**AMATO:** Right here?
**LANGVIN** (*laughs*): Where would you prefer? For God's sake, Victor, take it easy. My spoon and I've been waiting a long time, you know that.
**AMATO:** Okay.

*Amato hands Langvin a plastic bag.*

**LANGVIN** (*snorting some of the cocaine*): Ahh. Ahh. Oh, God. Long time. That's good stuff. Victor, I'm very happy with this. You want?
**AMATO:** No. No, I don't. I... I just want to get back to my car. Can we go?
**LANGVIN:** Sure. No problem. (*Sniffs*) This is good, good stuff, Victor. I could ski in this snow all winter. (*Laughs*)
**AMATO:** Ah, Don, I told you. This was a favour. A one-shot deal. I don't ——
**LANGVIN:** Oh, by the way. I meant to tell you. My old man's got a line on a couple of new cars coming in from overseas. Class machines, he says. If you're interested, we could drive out to Surrey as soon as they're in. You want to take a look? I'll call you.
**AMATO:** Yeah, yeah sure, Don. You know I'd like to see the cars. Sure, call me. But not about this stuff, Don, you just call me about the cars.
**LANGVIN:** Sure, Victor. No problem. No problem at all.

**GREENSPAN:** ***A hundred dollars for a gram of cocaine. A small transaction by any standards, let alone those of the high-powered drug world of Vancouver where this deal took place in September 1977. What Victor Amato, a twenty-six-year-old hairdresser, didn't know was that Don Langvin, his new friend, a man with a very expensive cocaine habit, also happened to be a paid police informer — a tool in the RCMP's on-going war against drugs in Vancouver. Amato was to be involved in two more transactions. He and his supplier, a former girlfriend named June Lee, were to stand trial before a judge sitting alone in the B.C. Provincial Court. It was, in many ways, a very small matter. Why then are we examining it on "The Scales of Justice"? Because every person in that provincial courtroom knew that the case was not going to stop there, and before the Amato case was over, it would have changed the law in this country, leaving the Supreme Court***

***of Canada as sharply divided as it had ever been in its long history.***

***My name is Edward Greenspan, and the story you are about to hear has been reconstructed from the transcripts of the trial in the British Columbia Provincial Court, and the judgments in the B.C. Court of Appeal and the Supreme Court of Canada.***

***In June 1977 the RCMP were escalating their war on the drug dealers of Vancouver. When the Amato case ended up in court, Victor Amato's lawyer, Sid Simons, put his client on the stand to tell the story of how he got caught up in that war...***

## Scene 2 / In Court

**SIMONS:** Mr. Amato, where were you employed in June 1977?

**AMATO:** A hairdressing salon called Crimpers, in North Vancouver. I'd been there...ah, seven months.

**SIMONS:** And who was the manager of this shop?

**AMATO:** He was a fellow named André.

**SIMONS:** Now, in or around June 1977, did you have a conversation with this fellow André?

**AMATO:** Yes, I did. It was while I was working in the shop one day...

## Scene 3 / At Crimpers

**ANDRÉ:** Hey, Victor, got a minute?

**AMATO:** Yeah, I'm just finishing. Half a sec... Is that okay, ma'am?

**CUSTOMER:** Yes... Yes, fine. I like it.

**AMATO:** Great! Sue, at the front desk, will take care of... Oh, thank you ma'am. Thanks very much!

**CUSTOMER:** You're welcome.

**AMATO:** See you again!

**ANDRÉ:** You're good with the ladies, Victor. You're doing good work.

**AMATO:** Well, I've been at it for seven years. You learn. What's up?

**ANDRÉ:** Come on into the office for a second.

*They enter the office and close the door.*

**ANDRÉ:** I...ah, wanted to ask you a favour.

**AMATO:** Sure.

**ANDRÉ:** I got a good friend, named Don. He asked me to scout around for him for... Well, he's new in North Van, doesn't know many people, and he wants to score a little coke, ah, cocaine.
**AMATO:** Well, really, I don't know where I could get any. I don't know anything about it — I mean I don't understand why you're asking me...
**ANDRÉ:** Well, you know a lot of people, it looks like. He's...he's a good buddy of mine and he's been bugging me about this for awhile. And I told him I'd do some checking, you know...
**AMATO:** Yeah, sure. But I don't know anybody where I could get cocaine. Well, I'll keep my ears open if you like, but this is really, like, outside my...

## Scene 4 / In Court

**SIMONS:** Mr. Amato, until that time had you ever used cocaine?
**AMATO:** Never.
**SIMONS:** Had you ever trafficked in cocaine?
**AMATO:** Never.
**SIMONS:** Had you ever obtained any for anyone?
**AMATO:** Never.

**GREENSPAN:** ***Shortly after this conversation, Victor Amato left Crimpers and went to work for another salon in the same area, and very shortly after he got there, he received a phone call...***

## Scene 5 / At the New Salon

**RECEPTIONIST:** Victor, are you free? Phone call for you.
**AMATO:** Thanks... Hello.
**LANGVIN:** Victor Amato?
**AMATO:** That's me.
**LANGVIN:** Hi, Victor. My name's Don Langvin. I got...got your number there from André at Crimpers. He's a good buddy, an old friend of mine... I think he may have mentioned me to you?
**AMATO** (*guardedly*): Yeah, yeah he did, but listen I ——
**LANGVIN:** Victor, André spoke very highly of you. Said you were someone to be counted on. Y'see, I've only been in this part of

town for a little while. André's the only guy I know well, and well, I really badly want to score a gram of coke, and André says that ——

**AMATO:** For God's sake, I'm at work here! (*Lowers his voice*) Listen, André is just mistaken... He's mistaken if he told you I could help. I don't know the slightest thing about this kind of stuff. And frankly, well frankly, it seems stupid for us to be even having this conversation... I don't know you at all.

**LANGVIN:** I'm a friend of André's, for a couple of years now. But Victor, really, I just don't know where to turn. I don't know anyone in this area, and I'm just... I'm getting a little desperate to score a gram, if you want the honest truth.

**AMATO:** I don't want anything! I don't want to know about this. Listen, I'm sorry, I gotta get back to work. I'm sorry, I can't help you. Good-bye.

*Amato hangs up and then makes a call.*

**SUE:** Crimpers, can I help you?

**AMATO:** Sue, it's Victor. How ya doin'?

**SUE:** Good. How's life down the street?

**AMATO:** Fine. It's fine. Sue, is André around?

**SUE** (*laughs*): You don't want to talk to me anymore? Hold on, I'll call him. André, it's Victor Amato.

**ANDRE:** Victor, what's up? You ready to come crawling back? (*Laughs*)

**AMATO:** André, I just got a call from this friend of yours — Don Langvin. André, what is this? Who the hell is this guy?

**AMATO:** He called you? Yeah, I gave him your number, Victor, I hope you don't mind. Don's okay, I told you. He's one of the guys... We shoot pool every Sunday.

**GREENSPAN:** ***André was later to say that he put Don Langvin in touch with Victor Amato simply to get Langvin off his own back. It seems clear that André's involvement in this matter was quite innocuous, but it also became very clear that there was a lot he didn't know about his pool-playing friend, Don Langvin. Langvin's true role emerged in court, during Sid Simon's examination of RCMP Corporal James Tait...***

## Scene 6 / In Court

**SIMONS:** Don Langvin was acting as an RCMP informant, was he not?
**TAIT:** Yes.
**SIMONS:** And the function of an informant is to introduce the undercover policeman to persons who are trafficking?
**TAIT:** That is correct.
**SIMONS:** Not to make traffickers of them, then?
**TAIT:** That is correct.
**SIMONS:** And that would be a clear instruction you would give Langvin, wouldn't it?
**TAIT:** Yes.

**GREENSPAN:** ***This, as Amato's lawyer knew very well, was a critical issue. Simons pressed on...***

**SIMONS:** Was Langvin given an operative number?
**TAIT:** Yes, he was.
**SIMONS:** You knew that he was a user of cocaine?
**TAIT:** Yes.
**SIMONS:** While he was acting as your operative?
**TAIT:** Yes.
**SIMONS:** Do you know how much he was paid for his work on this operation?
**TAIT:** Yes.
**SIMONS:** How much?
**TAIT:** I really don't think that's relevant.
**SIMONS** (*sharply*): Well, perhaps His Honour will be the one to decide that, witness, and would you please answer the question unless His Honour tells you you needn't?
**TAIT:** Your Honour...
**CROWN:** Your Honour, the Crown objects to that question. Obviously this witness feels it's confidential police information and ——
**SIMONS:** All kinds of things are confidential police information ——
**JUDGE:** No, just a minute. Just a minute. Why are you objecting, Mr. Kennedy?
**CROWN:** Well, the witness seems to feel it's confidential information, which for some reason might be...
**JUDGE:** All right. Corporal, why is it confidential information?

**TAIT:** I just think that for the protection of future informants as little as possible should be divulged... However, if Your Honour directs me I will oblige and tell it...

**JUDGE:** All right. Tell me please.

**TAIT:** He received two hundred dollars a week.

**SIMONS:** Thank you. Where does he live now?

**TAIT:** I have no idea.

**SIMONS:** I see. Was one of the arrangements made with him that he would have the opportunity of relocating somewhere?

**TAIT:** Yes. For his safety, of course.

**SIMONS:** All right. And that's at government expense?

**TAIT:** No. He was given a final award, and what he did with it was up to him.

**SIMONS:** How much was he given?

**TAIT:** Ninety-five hundred dollars.

**SIMONS:** A fair moving bill, eh?

**TAIT:** Yes.

**SIMONS:** And you have no idea where he's living now?

**TAIT:** No, sir, I do not.

**SIMONS:** So, you couldn't, even without telling me the address, go serve a subpoena on him to come to court and testify?

**TAIT:** No, sir, I could not.

**SIMONS:** And who can?

**TAIT:** I know of no one who can.

**SIMONS:** You mean no one in Her Majesty's RCM Police knows the whereabouts of Donald Langvin?

**TAIT:** I don't believe so. I don't know, and know of no one who does.

**GREENSPAN:** ***And so, by the time the Amato case came to trial in 1978, Don Langvin was nowhere to be found, and this would have important consequences. Back in the summer of 1977, though, he was very much in the picture, as Amato told his lawyer, in court...***

**AMATO:** He must have called at least fifteen or twenty times. Most of the calls were at work during the day.

**SIMONS:** Had you ever asked him to call you?

**AMATO:** No. He said he was still looking for a gram of cocaine, and when I'd tell him I didn't know why he was calling me he'd change the subject, like, to cars. He said his dad imported these cars from England and that he had good deals on them, and if I ever needed a good buy I could count on him. He was more or less befriending me at this point.

**SIMONS:** And did you have any intention of obtaining cocaine for him?

**AMATO:** No, not at all. I was just... I was trying to be a friend with him because... He just seemed like a person I'd probably benefit from, and he just seemed like an all 'round nice guy on the phone. To me it... it didn't dawn on me...

**SIMONS:** All right. Did he ever come to your shop on any occasion?

**AMATO:** Yes, he did. It was some time in August.

## Scene 7 / At the Salon

**RECEPTIONIST:** Hi, can I help you?

**LANGVIN:** Oh, hi. Is Victor Amato here?

**RECEPTIONIST:** Yes, he is. Do you have an appointment?

**LANGVIN:** No, no. I just got my hair cut. No, I'm a friend of his.

**RECEPTIONIST:** Okay, just a sec, I'll get him. Victor!

**AMATO:** Yes? You want to see me?

**LANGVIN:** Victor? Hey, how ya doin'? I'm Don Langvin.

**AMATO** (*coolly*): Oh. Hi.

**LANGVIN:** Have you got time for a coffee? I figured... I figured you were right. I mean, it's crazy for us to just be talking on the phone... I mean, you didn't know me from a hole in the ground, right?

**AMATO:** Right.

**LANGVIN:** So I thought I'd cruise down here... I just got a new set of wheels from my dad anyhow... Grab you for a quick cup of coffee. What do you say?

**AMATO:** New wheels? Did you get that Rover you were talking about?

**LANGVIN:** Sure did. Parked right outside. Can you take half an hour?

**AMATO:** Yeah, yeah, I can. Just... ah, give me five minutes to finish someone. Okay?

## Scene 8 / In Court

**SIMONS:** Did you see his car?

**AMATO:** Yes, I did. It was a Rover. It's a very rare car; it was like an antique. We went inside the car and he was showing it to me — the wood panelling on it — and he was telling me about the deal his dad had got, and he said if I was interested I could count on him to see what he could find out for me.

**SIMONS:** And was there any further conversation about cocaine?

**AMATO:** Yes. He mentioned that he was still looking for a gram of cocaine at that time.

**SIMONS:** All right. And did you agree to see if you could find him some cocaine?

**AMATO:** I told him I would ask friends around and see if I could turn him on to someone.

**SIMONS:** All right. And did you ask around?

**AMATO:** Yes, I did.

**SIMONS:** Why were you willing, at this time, to do this?

**AMATO:** Well, because, like, he had been calling me every day for weeks, and, and I was...well, I was more or less trying to get a... a friendship happening with him.

**SIMONS:** All right. And who did you call?

**AMATO:** I called June Lee, who used to be my girlfriend, and we still kept in touch. See, I knew her brother was a heroin user, and I figured June could call his girlfriend — her brother was in jail at that time — and maybe his girlfriend could help us get a gram of cocaine for Don. So, about the middle of August, I called her...

## Scene 9 / At Amato's Home

**JUNE** (*on the telephone*): Hello?

**AMATO:** Hi, June, it's me. How are you doing?

**JUNE:** Hey, we're fine. What's happening?

**AMATO:** Ah, not a lot, actually. Just called to say hello.

**JUNE:** Oh. Well, how's work? The new job?

**AMATO:** Oh, work's fine... I...ah, I made a new friend...

**JUNE:** You're calling to tell me you've got a new lady?

**AMATO:** No, no, no, it's a guy.

**JUNE** (*mock shock*): Victor!

**AMATO:** What? Oh. (*Laughs*) No, no, it's nothing like that. You should know better.

**JUNE:** I *do* know better. (*Laughs*)

**AMATO:** No, he's a cool guy, and he may be useful too. His father's got a line on cars from overseas; he seems to know some interesting people. But, well, he's new in the area and, well, June, he's been on me all summer about trying to get a gram of cocaine.

**JUNE:** What? Victor, you?

**AMATO:** So, I thought maybe just this once as a favour you could call up Judy, you know, your brother's girlfriend, and maybe one of her friends could help out, 'cause, like, Don — that's my friend — he's... Well, he's really desperate to get this gram.

**JUNE:** Victor, why do you want to get involved with something like that for?

**AMATO:** I know, I know. But...well, he's really desperate. He's been on me so much and, like, I think if I do him this favour it could...it could really benefit me to have him as a friend.

**JUNE:** Oh, Victor. I don't like this at all. Now, why the hell should I get involved in this just so you can make a new friend?

**AMATO:** I know, I know, but, June, listen ——

**JUNE:** Listen, if you want to call me to talk and keep in touch, that's fine, that's good. But if you're just phoning to use me like this — well, don't bother! (*She hangs up.*)

**AMATO:** Oh, Christ.

## Scene 10/In Court

**SIMONS:** What happened next?

**AMATO:** I got back to Don and I told him I couldn't help him. And he said could I just keep trying, please — and he said he'd be keeping in touch.

**SIMONS:** And did he keep in touch?

**AMATO:** Oh yes, he just kept on phoning.

**SIMONS:** And did you again contact June Lee?

**AMATO:** Yes, I did. I had to make three or four calls.

**SIMONS:** And what was her response?

**AMATO:** Well, she kept asking me why she should stick her neck out for someone she didn't even know?
**SIMONS:** But eventually did she agree to help you?
**AMATO:** Yes, after I, I persisted for a while.
**SIMONS:** And what was arranged between yourself and Don?
**AMATO:** It was arranged that I meet him at the corner of Cassiar and Hastings. There was no way I was going to let him know where I was going to get his stuff because I wanted to protect June and her kid, so when we drove out to her area I made him park two or three blocks away from the house. He gave me a hundred dollars. I went to June's, picked up the gram of cocaine, I came back out, and I gave it to Don.

## Scene 11/Inside the Car

**LANGVIN** (*snorts cocaine*): Ah. Ahhh. Oh, God. Long time. That's good stuff. Victor, I am very happy with this. You want?
**AMATO:** No. No, I don't. I... I just want to get back to my car. Can we go?

**GREENSPAN:** ***And that, of course, was the transaction we heard at the beginning. In court, Sid Simons asked his client some important questions...***

## Scene 12/In Court

**SIMONS:** What happened to the hundred dollars?
**AMATO:** I gave it to June.
**SIMONS:** Did you make any profit of any kind on that incident?
**AMATO:** No.
**SIMONS:** Did you intend to?
**AMATO:** No.
**SIMONS:** Did you get any cocaine?
**AMATO:** No.
**SIMONS:** Did you intend to?
**AMATO:** No.

**GREENSPAN:** ***By the time the case came to trial, Don Langvin had, as we know, disappeared — with the RCMP's consent and financial support. As a consequence, there was no one to give evidence against Amato about this incident, and no charges were laid with respect to it. As we shall see, the situation was to change, very quickly...***

**SIMONS:** Mr. Amato, did you hear from Langvin again?
**AMATO:** Yes, I did. He came to my apartment a couple of days later.
**SIMONS:** And what was your discussion at that time?
**AMATO:** He said he was in the vicinity, and that he'd gotten my address from André and that he wanted to invite me to this party that was happening towards the end of the month, end of September, out in Surrey.
**SIMONS:** And who was going to be attending this party?
**AMATO:** He said he had some friends coming up from California.
**SIMONS:** All right. And was there any further conversation about cocaine?
**AMATO:** Yes. He asked if I could look into my source, if my source could get him half an ounce for this party, and I immediately said no.
**SIMONS:** Did you hear from him again?
**AMATO:** The next day. He called me at work... He said he needed a favour...

## Scene 13 / At the Salon

**LANGVIN** (*on the telephone*): So, Victor, really, I need this favour. I need it bad. Now, these guys are coming all the way from California for my party. They're gonna *expect* me to have snow for them. I just gotta get some.
**AMATO:** No way. Absolutely no way, Don. I only did it one time as a favour for you. Look, I don't know anything about dealing in cocaine and frankly the whole idea scares the hell out of me. I don't want to get involved, you understand? I'm a hairdresser — that's how I make my living and I'm happy to keep it that way. Now, I've got a client. Good-bye.

**GREENSPAN:** ***But this outburst did not deter Don Langvin, who seemed determined to earn the $200 a week the RCMP were paying him. He started calling Victor Amato on a daily basis at Amato's place of work.***

***If Amato refused to talk to him, he just called back. This went on all through September. On the 3rd of October Langvin increased the pressure a little more...***

## Scene 14/In Court

**AMATO:** On that day he came down to the shop and we went out back and sat in his car.

**SIMONS:** Was there any conversation about cocaine?

**AMATO:** Yes, there was. He said his friends were in town for the party. He said they were in town and waiting, and he begged me to do everything in my power to get him the half-ounce of cocaine that night.

**SIMONS:** All right. Did you agree then to do what you could?

**AMATO:** I said I'd call. I told him there were no promises but I said I'd call.

**SIMONS:** And did you call June Lee again?

**AMATO:** Yes, I did.

## Scene 15/At Amato's Home

**JUNE** (*answering the telephone*): Hello?

**AMATO:** Hi, June, it's me. What's happening?

**JUNE** (*not very friendly*): Not much.

**AMATO:** Me neither. Things are quiet. No real news... Except this guy, Don Langvin, he's asked me to do him another favour. He wants half an ounce of cocaine for this party he's ——

**JUNE:** Goddamn you, Victor. Screw off! (*She hangs up.*)

**AMATO:** Oh, shit. (*He dials June's number again.*)

**JUNE** (*on the telephone*): Victor, I don't like this one bit! I don't ——

**AMATO:** June, June, for God's sakes don't get so freaked out. Just cool down, for Chrissakes. Now listen, everything's cool. I know this guy, and these are good friends of his. They're up here for a party and they just want this half-ounce for the party they're having in Surrey.

**JUNE:** Victor, I...

**AMATO:** June, please, do me this last little favour. I promised him I'd try. I won't do it again. This will never happen again.

**JUNE:** Oh...

## Scene 16/In Court

**SIMONS:** Were you able to persuade her?
**AMATO:** After a few phone calls that day.
**SIMONS:** And what arrangements were made for that evening?
**AMATO:** I told Don to meet me in the Safeway parking lot at Cassiar and Hastings.
**SIMONS:** Was there any discussion about price?
**AMATO:** Yes, there was. I... I believe it was eleven hundred dollars for the half-ounce.
**SIMONS:** All right. Were you intending or expecting to make any profit from this transaction?
**AMATO:** No. I was just getting this price from June's friend and I just relayed it back to Don, and he said, "Well that sounds pretty fair to me."
**SIMONS:** All right. Who were you expecting to meet that night in the Safeway parking lot?
**AMATO:** Don.
**SIMONS:** Were you expecting anyone else?
**AMATO:** No, I wasn't.
**SIMONS:** And when you arrived there, what happened?
**AMATO:** When I arrived, there was no one there. I waited about fifteen minutes and then a car pulled up. I was expecting Don's Rover, but a beige Monza came instead. And I saw Don in the passenger seat, and he waved me to come over to their car, so I got out of mine and I walked over...

## Scene 17/In the Parking Lot

**LANGVIN:** Victor, good man. Come on. Get in.
**AMATO** (*furious*): Who the... Who the *fuck* is this guy? For Chrissake, Don ——
**LANGVIN** (*interrupting, soothing*): Hey... It's okay, it's okay. Now, cool down, Victor. I want you to meet my best friend, Gary. Gary, this is Victor.
**GARY GODWIN:** How ya doin', man?
**AMATO:** Son of a bitch, Don. Goddam it, what are you bringing other people in for? You said this would be between me and you — and no one else. Well, there's no way... There's just... just no way this is gonna happen now.

**LANGVIN:** Victor, he's my best friend, will you just ——

**AMATO** (*interrupting*): Look, I don't care. How do I know who this guy is? Don, I was doing this as a favour, a personal favour for you, and now you've changed the...the whole context of this by bringing in someone else. What the hell are you doing to me?

**LANGVIN:** Victor, for God's sakes just cool it. Hey... I've known Gary for a very long time. He's cool, he really is, I guarantee it.

**GARY:** Hey, Victor, I understand why you're jumpy. But you don't have to be. I've been in this business three years. I'm not heat. I'm not a cop.

**AMATO:** Oh, Jesus Christ!

**GARY:** Jeez, I've known Don well for years, Victor. We met in Europe years ago, running stuff across the borders.

**LANGVIN:** It's true, Victor. Years ago.

**GARY:** And then we were friends for a long time in Edmonton before Don came out here. I mean, there's really, honestly, nothing for you to be afraid of.

**GREENSPAN:** ***I want to stop here for a minute. There is an issue that needs to be discussed, and in order to do so, we should know a little more about the man Don Langvin introduced as his best friend, Gary. Eventually everyone did learn more — at the trial of Victor Amato, as the Crown attorney called his star witness...***

## Scene 18 / In Court

**CROWN:** Would you state your name and rank for the record?

**GARY:** My name is Gary William Godwin. G-O-D-W-I-N. I'm a constable for the Royal Canadian Mounted Police.

**CROWN:** Constable, what were your duties on October 3, 1977?

**GARY:** I was acting in an undercover capacity at that time.

**CROWN:** And what was the purpose of this?

**GARY:** Attempting to buy illicit drugs, mainly cocaine, and to gather information.

**CROWN:** Would you please tell the Court what your appearance was at this time?

**GARY:** Well, at that time I had longer hair, down past my ears...ah, not quite to my shoulders. I had mutton chops which were cut out in the middle, and a centre-piece beard in the middle, here.

**CROWN:** Who knew you were a police constable at this time?
**GARY:** Only my cover team and...ah, Don Langvin.

**GREENSPAN:** ***Godwin's presence in the car on October 3, and his activities from this point on, take us to the heart of the Amato case. The issue is entrapment. Sid Simon's defence of Amato was based on the contention that his client was an honest citizen who had been lured — entrapped — by the RCMP into becoming a criminal. The crime, he would argue, had been created by the state. In the United States, entrapment had long been an accepted defence. Car dealer John De Lorean had been acquitted because of it. In England the courts had always refused to accept the defence. Before Amato — which was to become the test case — the Canadian position on the issue had never been formally decided by the Supreme Court. As we return to the story it is important to consider events in the light of one central question: How far should the police be allowed to go? In court, Sid Simons continued his examination of his client...***

**SIMONS:** Had you ever met this Gary before?
**AMATO:** No.
**SIMONS:** All right. What happened from there?
**AMATO:** Well...ah, they...they finally talked me into not worrying about them being cops or anything, and then Gary says, "Don't worry, if you're worried about the girl, we don't have to meet her at all." So, I...I was given eleven hundred dollars by Gary and he said for me to leave my car keys with him, in case, but Don said, "Oh, that's not necessary. I know where he lives and where he works." Um, and at that time I was so confused and so scared, I just...I didn't know what to do. So I just took the money and I went and met June at another place in her car. And we drove to her house, and I waited there with her daughter, while June went out to get the cocaine. And about a half-hour later she came back to the house...

## Scene 19/At June's House

**JUNE:** Okay. Here it is. Take it and get it out of here. It's been weighed. It's all there. Take it back to this great new friend of yours. And, Victor?
**AMATO:** Yes, June?
**JUNE:** Don't ever bother calling me about this sort of thing again.

## Scene 20/In Court

**SIMONS:** Mr. Amato, did you receive any money for this transaction?
**AMATO:** None. It was never discussed.
**SIMONS:** Did you receive any cocaine?
**AMATO:** None. Never.
**SIMONS:** Was there any discussion about that?
**AMATO:** Yes, there was. It happened when I got back to the car with the half-ounce of cocaine...

## Scene 21/In the Car

**AMATO:** All right. Here it is. She says it's been weighed. Now you got what you want. And that's it. This is the last time. I'm not a dealer. I did this as a favour for you, Don. I'm not making anything out of this —
**GARY:** You're not? Well, we can fix that.
**AMATO:** No, no, no. You don't understand ——
**GARY:** Don, Victor should get a cut from this. Should we give him an end? Half a gram to cover his end?
**LANGVIN:** Sure, sure, that's only fair ——
**AMATO:** No, you don't understand. I don't *want* anything. I'm trying to get the point across that this will never happen again. This is... It's just too heavy for me. I don't need this.

**GREENSPAN:** ***However culpable he may or may not have been, Victor Amato was certainly not very decisive. There*** **was** ***to be another transaction, but this one, as we shall see, came after pressure that made the earlier stress seem almost trivial. Don Langvin dropped out of the picture at this point, never to surface again. From now on it was RCMP Constable Gary Godwin applying the pressure. We should note that Godwin's account of that last transaction was quite different from Amato's. Among other things, he said that Victor Amato asked for and received a half a gram of cocaine as his share or "end" of the transaction. In due course we shall see what ruling the trial judge made on this issue of credibility. The prelude to the third transaction was another call to Amato's place of work...***

## Scene 22 / At the Salon

**GARY** (*on the telephone*): Victor, it's Gary. Look, I'm very pleased with what went down the other night. Ah, I'd like to have a steady source here in Vancouver —

**AMATO:** Oh Christ, will you just...*no*!

**GARY** (*smoothly*): Just think about it, Victor. Just tell your people we want three ounces for six thousand dollars. If you know anything about cocaine you'll know it's a good price.

**AMATO:** I don't know anything about...about it. I have no idea who the hell you are. I am not interested. (*Amato hangs up.*)

**GREENSPAN:** ***Victor Amato may have been indecisive, but Gary Godwin was very, very persistent. A few days later he called again. Amato said he was busy. Godwin called right back. He called seven or eight times that day, Amato was to tell the court, and in the end he left a long-distance number for Amato to reach him — collect. Godwin was to deny that this happened, so Amato's account of it assumed some importance during the trial...***

## Scene 23 / In Court

**SIMONS:** So, he left a number for you to call?

**AMATO:** Yes, it was long-distance to the Interior...to the Okanagan.

**SIMONS:** All right. Did you make a call to that number?

**AMATO:** Yes, at the end of the day. I said... I said, "Look, you know, I don't know you at all. I'm not going through with what you want."

**SIMONS:** When you made this call...ah, who did you first speak to? Gary? Or someone else?

**AMATO:** An Oriental girl.

**SIMONS:** How could you tell?

**AMATO:** Well, by her accent. She had sort of a broken Oriental accent.

**SIMONS:** And what was said between you and her?

**AMATO:** I just asked for Gary, and she said he was in the washroom, and she asked me to hold on while she went to get him.

**SIMONS:** All right. And did he come to the phone?

**AMATO:** Yes, he did.

**GREENSPAN:** ***This minor exchange, just one more phone call in a case with so many, actually had real importance, because Constable Gary Godwin denied in Court Victor Amato's account of his having pursued Amato with seven or eight calls a day, with long-distance phone calls, and with other tactics we'll learn about shortly. In essence, this aspect of the case revolved around the credibility of Amato and Godwin, and when Godwin took the stand, Sid Simons zeroed in on this long-distance call...***

**SIMONS:** Constable, during your days off in early October, had you been in the Okanagan?

**CROWN:** I wonder what relevance that has, Your Honour?

**SIMONS:** Patience might demonstrate it to my friend.

**CROWN:** I suggest what this man does on his days off is hardly relevant to this trial.

**JUDGE:** Well, he did say he wasn't working. I don't imagine it is relevant, Mr. Simons.

**SIMONS:** If I didn't think it was relevant I wouldn't ask it, Your Honour. I'm not on a fishing trip.

**JUDGE:** Witness, do you remember where you were?

**GARY:** Yes, Your Honour, I do.

**SIMONS:** Was it in the Okanagan?

**GARY:** With all due respect I'd rather not answer that question, Your Honour.

**JUDGE** (*impatient*): Well, will somebody tell me why not?

**CROWN:** It's possible he was involved in another investigation...of ah, some sort...

**SIMONS:** Perhaps if I ask the next question this will clear itself up, Your Honour...

**JUDGE:** Well, Mr. Simons, if you know something, ask a question...

**SIMONS:** Did you phone Amato from the Okanagan area between the 3rd and the 11th of October and leave him a number at which to call you, and did he subsequently call you back at that number?

**GARY:** Ah, not to the best of my recollection. At...at least, I don't have that in my notes.

**SIMONS:** You have no recollection of this?

**GARY:** I do not, no. Not at this time.

**SIMONS:** Did you have anyone answering the telephone wherever you were who spoke English with difficulty and who appeared to be of Oriental background from the sound of her voice?

**GARY:** Ah, the place... the place I stay might very well have had that, yes.

**SIMONS:** And where would this be?

**GARY:** Well, I... I would rather not... It was in Rutland.

**SIMONS:** So this isn't some figment of my imagination. There *was* such a person at Rutland during that period?

**GARY:** Yes, there was.

**SIMONS:** Was she a police person?

**GARY:** No... She was a friend of mine.

**SIMONS:** And she was visiting you in Rutland in October 1977?

**GARY:** Well, at the time she was... oh, well, she... she would have visited me at that time, yes.

**SIMONS:** Well, can you imagine, Constable, how I would know about this, how I would know about this woman, if that phone call from Victor Amato did not take place? Can you offer any explanation, other than psychic inspiration on my part?

**GARY:** I cannot. I... I'm sorry, but I do not recall the phone call. I... I do not have it in my notes.

**GREENSPAN:** ***Very effective cross-examination. It did indeed seem obvious that for Amato to know about Godwin's Rutland phone number and his Oriental friend, that phone call must have taken place. Godwin may simply have forgotten about the call, but this would cast serious doubts on his memory, and even more important, on his police notes. Policemen, unlike most witnesses make notes at the time of an incident and are allowed to refresh their memories in Court by referring to them. If those notes are shown to be selective and incomplete, they are not only much reduced in value, they also become dangerously unfair. The fairness or appropriateness of the police conduct was, of course, at the centre of the Amato case, and nowhere was this issue more clearly revealed than in the incident Amato described next...***

**SIMONS:** All right, Mr. Amato, what happened after this call to the interior?

**AMATO:** A few days later, on October 12, he called me at work again. He called about eight times. I kept refusing to go to the phone. And then finally he left a message.

**SIMONS:** All right. And what was the message?

**AMATO:** He left his phone number in Vancouver and asked me to call him that night or he'd be in first thing in the morning to see me.

**SIMONS:** And did you want him coming to the shop to see you?
**AMATO:** Not at all.
**SIMONS:** So, did you call him back?
**AMATO:** Yes, I did.

## Scene 24 / At Amato's Home

**GARY** (*on the telephone*): Gary here.
**AMATO** (*very agitated*): It's Victor Amato.
**GARY:** Victor, Hi! Hey, man, listen I've got a ——
**AMATO:** No, no, no! You listen to me. You're to stop calling me, man! I'm not answering your calls because I don't want anything to do with you. I'm... I'm washing my hands of you. I don't trust you. I don't want any part of this. Okay? So just forget it! [*Amato hangs up and then counts to himself.*] One... two... three... four... five... [*The phone rings.*]
**AMATO:** Jesus Christ! I knew it! [*He picks up the phone.*] What are you trying to do? Don't you understand ——
**GARY:** Cool it, Victor! Don't hang up on me. This is very important. I have some people in town and I have to... answer to these people, and they're expecting to get this three ounces tonight.
**AMATO** (*explodes*): What? There's no possible way that's going to happen.
**GARY:** Well, these people are going to want to know why I brought them into town when there's no deal that's going to happen.
**AMATO:** Well, that's... that's your problem! I told you from the start this wasn't going to go on any more.
**GARY:** Well, can you... can you do me a favour? Can you give me the girl's number and I'll do it myself. I'll keep you out of it.
**AMATO:** No! Absolutely not. That's one of the reasons I'm not carrying this any further — I don't want her getting involved anymore.
**GARY:** Jesus. Look, Victor, you gotta understand, I am in a jam here, a real one. Now, please... please don't hang up on me. Can I meet you somewhere? Just for a coffee. I won't get you involved... Can we just talk for ten minutes? Please. I'm really... really on the spot. Now, I'll meet you anywhere you like.
**AMATO:** Denny's on Marine Drive in half an hour.

# Scene 25 / At the Coffee Shop

**GARY** (*calling*): Victor! I'm over here.

**AMATO:** Hi, Gary.

**GARY:** God, am I glad you're here. I'm in such a jam with these guys, I can't tell you.

**WAITRESS:** You want menus?

**AMATO:** Ah, no, just a coffee.

**GARY:** Same here.

**AMATO:** Look, Gary, you may be in a jam, but I don't know what it has to do with me. I mean, I'm sorry, but it was Don who got me into this, just to do him a favour, and all of a sudden I'm left with someone I don't even know and frankly I'm... I'm very scared, I just don't trust... I don't know *what* to think.

**GARY:** I know. I understand. These guys I'm talking about, they're in town now, but I didn't bring 'em here because I know how you feel.

**AMATO:** Gary, the amount of money you're talking, I mean, this is crazy. This is way beyond ——

**GARY:** Don't worry about that. Don't... don't get uptight about the amount. I'm very careful, I... I don't screw around and [*He pats his jacket pocket.*] I always deal with guns.

**AMATO:** Guns. Oh, for God's sakes what ——

**GARY:** Hey, Victor, I'm just trying to tell you there's nothing to worry about. It's just that I'm in this jam with these three guys. They're big dealers, and I called them into town, and they're expecting to do a deal tonight.

**AMATO:** Gary, I'm a hairdresser! I don't want ——

**GARY:** Look, just do me this favour. If, like, we don't do the deal tonight, these guys are gonna be coming down to see you tomorrow.

**AMATO:** What?

**GARY:** I mean, I *told* you this was a jam.

**AMATO:** They... They'll be coming to the shop?

**GARY:** I'm afraid so. These are big dealers, Victor.

**AMATO:** Well, ah, I'll... I'll give her a call and see what I can get arranged.

**GREENSPAN:** ***It is perhaps unnecessary for me to point out that none of what Constable Gary Godwin was saying here was true. From this point events proceeded to a rapid and perhaps predictable conclusion.***

*Amato made two phone calls to June Lee and persuaded her to obtain the cocaine for Godwin. About 11:00 that night a deal was made for two and a half ounces of cocaine for $4,900. Godwin refused to give Amato the money in advance, as he had done the last time, and so he succeeded in being taken to June Lee's house and meeting her when the deal was made. Once more, Amato said, he received no money and no cocaine for the transaction. This was the last deal. Shortly thereafter Amato and Lee were arrested and charged with trafficking in narcotics. It should be noted that when he was called to the stand, Constable Godwin painted a very different picture of Victor Amato. His version of that last conversation at Denny's restaurant was based on his notes. These notes, which we have already had occasion to consider, were filed as an exhibit in the trial...*

**GARY** (*reading*): Notes started approximately 1:15 a.m., 13 October 1977. Victor called me at approximately 7:00 p.m., 12 October 1977 and advised me to meet him at Denny's restaurant. I told him I would have to talk to him before we did anything tonight and...he agreed we'd talk...

**GARY:** Yeah, listen Victor, the reason I want to talk to you is because I want three ounces of coke. Can your connection do this? Like, I have some people in, eh, my people, and I told them I could do three ounces tonight.

**AMATO:** Ah...I'll have to call the broad about three ounces. Maybe we'll have to do it tomorrow. Is that okay?

**GARY:** No, no, no. They're leaving...they're leaving tomorrow morning, eh, like, I need it tonight.

**AMATO:** Well, I'll phone her and see what she can do.

**GARY** (*reading*): Victor and I had further general drug conversation and then Victor went to phone. He went to the back where the pay phones were. He then reappeared, saying he would go elsewhere to make his call. I went to the pay phones and placed a call to Constable Bennett, advising him of our conversation to date. Victor returned approximately ten minutes later and we moved to another booth...

**AMATO:** Yeah, she said she could probably put it together tonight.

**GARY:** Good, what does she want for three ounces?

**AMATO:** Sixty-one hundred.

**GARY:** That's pretty high. What will the quality be like?

**AMATO:** Same as last time, if not better, but never worse.

**GARY:** Well, I'll offer... No, no, on the other hand I'd better call my friends. I'll be right back.

**AMATO:** Okay.

**GARY:** I left Victor and went to the pay phone right next to us and called Constable Bennett. I discussed price with him and we agreed on $5,700. I returned to the table with Victor. I told him this price. He then went to the pay phone and called. He returned and sat down with me.

**AMATO:** She says fifty-nine hundred — Well, it's better than the last stuff, but she can't go any lower or she gets no end herself.

**GARY:** Well, fifty-nine hundred is a little steep. I don't know if they'll go for it.

**GARY:** The following conversation was recalled when I was reviewing my notes at 10:00 a.m., 13 October 1977.

**AMATO:** What about my end?

**GARY:** Well, if you can do it tonight?

**AMATO:** Like, it's the same as last time, eh? She's not taking care of my end.

**GARY:** Yeah, well, how does two grams sound? As long as you take it out before. I... I don't want to be fucking around with the stuff in the car.

**AMATO:** Yeah, that's okay.

**GREENSPAN:** ***This was Godwin's version of events. If, in fact, it had been accepted, the Amato case wouldn't even merit a footnote in Canadian legal history. But the fact is, it was* not *accepted. Before rendering his verdict in the case, the trial judge made the following critical ruling:***

**JUDGE:** The evidence tendered by the Crown would lead one to believe that the accused was ready, willing, and able to traffic in cocaine with a member of the RCMP acting in an undercover capacity. The evidence tendered by the defence would lead one to believe that the accused did, in fact, traffic cocaine but that he was forced to do so due to the pressure applied by an informer and by an undercover officer. In the present case, the Crown was unable to produce the witness who originally arranged for Constable Godwin to meet the accused, Amato. His evidence would have been extremely useful to me. He could have corroborated the evidence of the Crown or he could have corroborated the evidence of the defence. I believe he should have been called by the Crown. His absence has restricted the defence from making a full answer to the charge. For that reason, I am prepared to assume that my findings of fact ought to be made on the basis of the evidence tendered by the defence.

**GREENSPAN:** ***This was an essential and a fascinating ruling, for many reasons. The legal impact of what the judge had done was enormous; it turned the Amato trial into an absolutely perfect test case for the defence of entrapment in Canada. In effect it said as follows: Victor Amato, I believe everything you have told me. I must now decide if that allows you to avail yourself of the defence of entrapment. And on that issue, Judge McGivern rendered the following judgement:***

**JUDGE:** The defence submits that the actions of the undercover officer, as well as the actions of the paid informer, amount to entrapment and therefore the accused should be acquitted. In order to raise the defence of entrapment there must be evidence that the police had instigated the crime and had they not done so, the accused would not have been involved in the transaction. The instigation must, of course, go beyond mere solicitation or decoy work. The accused was, in my opinion, actively solicited to participate in an activity which he knew to be unlawful. I am satisfied, however, that the evidence falls far short of the evidence required at law to establish the defence of entrapment. The evidence amounts to no more than persistent solicitation to persuade the accused to engage in the trafficking of cocaine. I find the accused guilty as charged.

**GREENSPAN:** ***And so, the trial judge seemed to be of the view that entrapment*** **was** ***a possible defence in Canada, but that this case did not represent a police-instigated crime, merely a case of acceptable police solicitation. Amato was convicted. So, too, was June Lee, who had, it appears, also been involved in a completely different trafficking incident shortly after this one. She ended up being sentenced to two years less one day for all of the offences for which she was charged. With respect to Amato, the trial judge agreed with Sid Simon's submission that the police solicitation was very relevant in sentencing, and he did not impose a jail sentence. Amato was fined three thousand dollars and***

***placed on probation for two years. A sentence which clearly reflected the judge's negative view of the police behaviour in this case. Nonetheless, Amato now had a criminal record, and the British Columbia Court of Appeal soon had a major case on their hands. They made short, unanimous work of it. Mr. Justice Taggert ruled as follows...***

## Scene 26 / In Appeal Court

**TAGGERT:** I am not persuaded that the evidence to which we have been referred by counsel for the appellant does other than support the conclusion reached by the trial judge. Be that as it may, I think we are precluded by previous judgements in this Court and in the Ontario Court of Appeal where the view was expressed that there *is* no defence of entrapment. I think we ought to follow this view until such time as the matter is definitely settled by the Supreme Court of Canada...

**GREENSPAN:** ***As clear an invitation to the Supreme Court as could possibly be given. Mr. Justice Seaton, in his concurring judgement, was even more forceful...***

**SEATON:** I agree that the appeal should be dismissed. I wish to add this: I do not come reluctantly to the conclusion that there is no such thing as a defence of entrapment. I favour the English approach to this over the approach in the United States. In my view the court should try the accused, not the police. I do not accept entrapment, as such, to be a defence.

**GREENSPAN:** ***To no one's surprise, the Supreme Court of Canada granted Sid Simons leave to take the matter up to Ottawa. On August 9, 1982, Canada's highest court handed down judgement. Their ruling represented perhaps the most balanced division of opinion in the long history of the Supreme Court. Mr. Justice Dickson wrote one opinion, concurred in by three other judges...***

# Scene 27 / In the Supreme Court

**DICKSON:** I am of the opinion that on the facts of this case, the defence of entrapment, assuming it to be available under Canadian law, does not arise. The four British Columbia judges before whom the matter has come have been unanimous in concluding this. It does not seem to me to fall to this Court to retry the case and arrive at different findings. I would dismiss the appeal.

**GREENSPAN:** ***In short, these four judges refused to address the larger issue of whether entrapment*** **did** ***apply in Canada. Mr. Justice Estey, whose reasoning was also concurred in by three other judges, including Chief Justice Laskin, took an entirely different approach. In a lengthy, careful decision he considered the issue of entrapment as a whole . . .***

**ESTEY:** The proponents of this defence generally seek to advance it as something necessary to bring fairness or fundamental justice into criminal law. In my respectful view the true issue is the avoidance of the improper invocation by the state of the judicial process where the accused has been ensnared by the police force in order to bring about an offence. The repugnance which must be felt by the Court on being implicated in a process so shameful on the part of the state cannot be dissipated by the registration of a conviction and then the imposition thereafter of even a minimum sentence. I'm of the view that it is open to this Court to recognize a defence of entrapment and to give effect to it in proper cases. The conduct of the police in this case, in my view, clearly gives rise to entrapment. It is the plain fact that the drug trafficking which occurred was promoted by the police at a time when they had no reason to suspect, let alone believe, that the accused was in any way related to such activity. The cumulative effect of such behaviour by the police would, in my view, be viewed by the community as shocking and outrageous. For all of these reasons I would recognize the defence of entrapment and apply it to the case before us. I would allow the appeal, set aside the conviction, and direct a stay of prosecution.

**GREENSPAN:** ***And so four judges had avoided the larger issue and confirmed Amato's conviction, and four others had recognized entrapment and overturned that conviction. The scales had never been more precisely balanced. The final decision lay in the hands of the ninth justice, Mr. Justice Ritchie . . .***

**RITCHIE:** Although there is no authoritative judgement in Canada on the issue of entrapment, the weight of authority is to the effect that in a case where the crime in question would not have been committed save for the "calculated inveigling or persistent importuning" of the police, then the defence of entrapment may be established.

**GREENSPAN:** ***And so, quite simply, Mr. Justice Ritchie accepted the existence of the defence in Canada, which meant that five of the nine judges had . . . Entrapment, as of this moment, became a recognized defence in this country.***

***But what about the Amato case itself? What about Victor Amato? Did this case display the factors required for that defence?***

**RITCHIE:** Whether the activities of the police can be said to amount to the "calculated inveigling or persistent importuning" required must depend on the facts of each case. In the present case, although drug transactions were suggested to Amato by an *agent provocateur*, this is not in itself enough to invoke the defence of entrapment. In my view it is only where police tactics leave no room for the formation of independent criminal intent by the accused that the question of entrapment arises. I would dismiss the appeal.

**GREENSPAN:** ***And so, Mr. Justice Ritchie had crossed to the other side of the fence and joined the four judges who upheld Amato's conviction . . . Where does that leave us? Well, it certainly leaves Victor Amato with a criminal record — something I find profoundly disturbing and unfair. If the outrageous circumstances of this case do not amount to entrapment, I'm not honestly sure what facts will. On the other hand, I think something very positive did emerge from the Amato case. By that narrow five-to-four margin, the Supreme Court, in my opinion, sent out a signal to the courts of this country: that the defence of entrapment is available now in Canada. That may not be of much use to Victor Amato, but I would suggest it is of very great importance to the rest of us.***

# Producer's Notes

Guy Gavriel Kay undertook the scripting of the case of Vancouver hairdresser Victor Amato, whose trial for drug trafficking raised the question of whether or not the defence of entrapment is available to an accused person in Canada.

The Amato case did not completely resolve the issue. However, the case illuminated not only what the law is in this country, but, more important, what it ought to be.

The Vancouver trial of Victor Amato put certain police practices on trial as well. Few people question the necessity for undercover agents or decoys — say, an officer in civilian clothes walking in a park at night to catch muggers or rapists — but was there a need for the police to launch active investigations into the potential or "predisposition" of ordinary citizens for crime? The trial forced us to ask if we really wanted the authorities to tempt, cajole, and perhaps even pressure us to break the law just to test our moral fibre. It questioned whether this was not a wasteful and arrogant use of law-enforcement resources. It asked if it was not self-serving for the police to engineer an offence simply to solve it more easily. It made us wonder if any useful social purpose is served by the artificial creation of crime. How was punishing a hairdresser for something he would never have done except for police pressure going to reduce the problem of self-motivated pushers peddling narcotics in the streets? Did we start conscripting people to break the law because we have run out of volunteer criminals?

Fine, low-key performances by Geoffrey Bowes as Victor Amato and Michael Hogan as RCMP undercover policeman Gary Godwin brought the issues into sharp focus. As in many previous roles, Ray Stancer drew on his own experience as a real-life litigation lawyer for the courtroom battle between Amato's defence attorney and the prosecutor, the latter played with a fine sense of timing and drama by Neil Munro. Equally convincing was Henry Ramer in the role of Judge McGivern. Actor-director Ron Hartmann, prominent TV actor and film director Lawrence Dane, and Stratford veteran Ken Pogue excelled in supporting roles.

"The Scales of Justice" has long benefited from the willingness of major talent to perform in minor parts. In reality there are no minor parts in a production; while an actor is in front of the microphone, whether for a single line or for fifteen pages, he or she is the sole link between the show and the audience. One false note can ruin a play and one well-delivered word can make it memorable. The late Marian Waldman, a popular and prolific broadcast performer and writer both during and after radio's Golden Age, knew this well. In this, her last performance, she played the small role of a customer in a hairdressing salon and brought to it the same devotion she had brought to her many leading roles throughout her long career.

G.J.

# The Extradition of Cathy Smith

*Jack Batten*

## The Cast

Commentary by Edward L. Greenspan, Q.C.

| | |
|---|---|
| **CATHY SMITH** | Chapelle Jaffe |
| **JOHN BELUSHI** | Neil Munro |
| **MR. BRIAN GREENSPAN** for the defence | Saul Rubinek |
| **MR. COOMARASWAMY** for the Crown | Paul Soles |

With the support of (in alphabetical order): John Bayliss, George Buza, Alan Fawcett, Jim Henshaw, Michael Kirby, Paul Kligman, Roy Krost, Sean McCann, James Morris, Michael J. Reynolds, Angelo Rizacos, Booth Savage, Chuck Shamata, Ray Stancer, and John Stocker

## Scene 1 / In a Restaurant / Back Room

**JOHN BELUSHI** (*urgency in his voice*): Move your asses, you guys. I gotta do a hit. Come on, in here.

*They enter a back room and close the door.*

**CATHY SMITH:** This is kind of public, John.
**BELUSHI:** It's the owner's office. I know the guy. Nobody's gonna come in. Ah, Nelson can lean against the door if it's bugging you.
**NELSON LYON:** Just your friendly neighbourhood watchdog.
**BELUSHI:** Yeah, you'll get your goodies, man. You'll get 'em. Now. (*To Cathy*) Come on, Cathy, fix the stuff.
**SMITH:** It's the third time tonight. Hm...No, what am I saying, it's the fourth. That's getting heavy.
**BELUSHI:** Yeah, well, my bread paid for it. Right?
**SMITH:** You want me to stop being mother caution, okay, I'll stop.
**BELUSHI:** Eh, now, shoot me first, then Nelson.
**NELSON:** It's your stuff, man.
**BELUSHI:** Ah...Okay.
**SMITH:** Roll your sleeve up higher, John. I can't do everything.
**BELUSHI:** Yeah, all right.
**NELSON:** You haven't been doing bad so far.
**BELUSHI** (*sucking in and exhaling a long stream of breath*): Oh Jesus, Cathy. Man, that's fantastic.

**GREENSPAN:** ***In the early-morning hours of Friday, March 5, 1982, in a back room of a small private club in Hollywood, California, three people were injecting themselves with drugs. Within ten hours, one of the three would be dead of acute cocaine and heroin intoxication. He was John Belushi, the well-known comedian and movie actor. A year later, another member of the trio, Cathy Smith, would be accused of administering***

*the injections that killed Belushi. Cathy Smith is a Canadian, and shortly after Belushi's death, before the State of California indicted her on a charge of murder, she returned to live in Toronto. The U.S. government, on behalf of the State of California, requested her extradition from Canada to stand trial on the charge. The proceedings under the Canadian Extradition Act lasted almost two years. They shaped the fate of Cathy Smith, and, in a broader sense, they brought under unprecedented examination fundamental rights that Canadian citizens have been guaranteed by our Charter of Rights.*

*My name is Edward Greenspan, and the story you are about to hear is reconstructed from transcripts and judgements in the District Court of the Judicial District of York, the Supreme Court of Ontario, and the Ontario Court of Appeal, and from the trial notes of Cathy Smith's counsel, my brother, Brian Greenspan.*

*Cathy Smith belonged to the first rock-and-roll generation. She was born in 1947 to an unwed mother and grew up as the adopted daughter of a cement salesman and his wife in Burlington, a peaceful suburban community west of Toronto. But Cathy's early life was far from stable. She became a rebel and a loner. And in her mid-teens, she found an outlet for the emotional turmoil she was experiencing in the music of her generation. Elvis Presley, Rick Nelson, and other singers and bands seemed to speak directly to her, as they did to many teenagers of the early 1960s. But in Cathy's case, the music and the lifestyle that went with it became the central focus of her own life when a friend introduced her to the drummer in a rock band that was playing at a club in nearby Hamilton. The drummer's name was Levon Helm and the band was called Levon and the Hawks.*

## Scene 2 / In The Grange, 1960s

**SMITH** (*giggling*): Drummers, y'know, they're my favourite.
**LEVON HELM:** Well now, Cathy honey, that makes me feel real nice.
**SMITH:** I guess it's because drumming is so *physical*. You can *feel* it when a drummer plays.
**LEVON:** It's a lot of work, drummin'.
**SMITH:** You know what, Levon? I like it the way you play fast and talk real slow. (*She giggles.*)
**LEVON:** Everybody talks real slow where I come from down in Arkansas.

**SMITH:** Ah, I never been farther than Toronto.
**LEVON:** How old're you anyway, Cathy?
**SMITH:** How old do you think I am? Go on, take a guess.
**LEVON:** That dress with the slit up the back you got on there, all that real smart makeup, you could be most any age.
**SMITH:** Maybe I am any age.
**LEVON:** You're a very mature young lady, you know that?
**SMITH:** Some people think so.
**LEVON:** We got rooms at the motel down the way, the band and me, and we're gonna party after the last set. You like to come along? We got somethin' to drink, somethin' to smoke. It'll be real nice.
**SMITH:** Well, yeah, I like to party any time.
**LEVON:** Ah... Tell me somethin' else, Cathy. You like to cuddle when you sleep?

**GREENSPAN:** ***Cathy Smith became a groupie. Only sixteen, she began to hang out with Levon and the Hawks. The group eventually grew wealthy and famous under another name, The Band, one of the most critically praised rock groups of the day. As for Cathy, she was left with a poignant reminder of her first contact with rock music — a pregnancy. She gave birth to Levon Helm's daughter and put the child into adoption. But her fascination with the music world didn't fade. In the late 1960s, living in Toronto and working as a part-time waitress at the Riverboat, the city's leading folk club, she became the lover of another prominent musician, Gordon Lightfoot.***

## Scene 3 / In Lightfoot's Apartment

*Lightfoot is strumming a guitar and humming to himself, working out the chords for a new song.*

**SMITH:** These are the best times, Gordie, just the two of us.
**LIGHTFOOT** (*half listening*): Mm-hmm.
**SMITH:** I like it best when we're alone here, way up high in the apartment, up over the whole city, over everything.
**LIGHTFOOT:** I like it, too, Cathy.
**SMITH:** At night like this, that's when it's most peaceful, like there's nothing else in the world except you and me and all those lights out there.

**LIGHTFOOT:** Yeah, now if this song'd come right, things would be perfect.
**SMITH:** It'll come right. Your songs always do.
**LIGHTFOOT:** What's that you're sewing?
**SMITH:** I'm putting some beads on the shoulder of your new jacket. See, they sparkle in the lights. They'll look great when you're up there on the stage.
**LIGHTFOOT:** You know something, Cathy. You *understand*. I mean, some women, they're along for the ride and the money. But you — you understand the music and you understand the life.
**SMITH:** Maybe that's how come things are working for us.
**LIGHTFOOT:** That — and the great times in bed.
**SMITH:** It's weird. Sometimes I think about us — red wine, young love, the snow outside and everything — and I think what our life is, is a Gordie Lightfoot song.

**GREENSPAN:** ***Cathy Smith's song wasn't destined to become a standard. She lived with Lightfoot for almost four years, and at the beginning their relationship had the glow of romance and glamour. But the glow gradually faded, and romance and glamour gave way to jealousy and bitterness.***

***After Cathy and Lightfoot broke up, she worked on a singing career of her own. She was attracted by the sense of family she felt around the musicians, and she found herself increasingly drawn into their way of life. She drank heavily, she used soft drugs, and she sniffed cocaine. By the spring of 1978, almost without realizing where she was headed, she began to slip into a fondness for hard drugs. She was living at the time in a mansion in Hollywood with Keith Richards and other members of the Rolling Stones and their entourage.***

## Scene 4 / A Hollywood Mansion

**SMITH:** The way I look at it, Keith, maybe I'm screwed up and I don't care.
**KEITH RICHARDS:** Are we talking heroin here?
**SMITH:** What else?
**RICHARDS:** Well, there's nothing like it, is there?
**SMITH:** Hm... When I really started to get into it, when we were all in Paris and you guys were cutting the album, I used to take the

great stuff that Moroccan roadie had. Do you remember that guy? Anyway, I took his heroin, which was dynamite, and about every ten minutes, it seemed like, I'd have to run into the can and throw up. But I couldn't *not* take it, you understand?

**RICHARDS:** Cathy, you're talkin' to someone who knows.

**SMITH:** I couldn't stop because there's no goddamn high in the whole world like a heroin high...And after a while, it got even better because I stopped all the throwing up.

**RICHARDS:** You gotta watch it, Cathy. It costs. Look at me, I was busted by the cops in Toronto for possession. Had to go through lawyers, courts, and all that other shit. Ah...no more.

**SMITH:** You got off the charge.

**RICHARDS:** Yeah, more or less.

**SMITH:** Yeah, but, out here, heroin, coke, they're like part of the party scene. I mean, everybody does drugs. It's a very *social* thing.

**RICHARDS:** A person like me, in this business, I can go anywhere, not just bloody Hollywood, and people'll try to lay drugs on me. It's the fans. God bless them. They think they're doing me a favour.

**SMITH:** They can do me a favour any day they want. (*She laughs.*) I'm beginning to think I need heroin. And it isn't just to get feeling good. It's...it's to stop feeling bad. You know what I'm talking about?

**RICHARDS:** You're addicted to the stuff.

**SMITH:** You think so?

**RICHARDS:** Takes one to know one.

**SMITH:** Oh...Jesus, I'm a junkie.

**GREENSPAN:** ***For the following three years, Cathy Smith couldn't escape the Hollywood drug life. She scrambled for money, and almost all of it went into supporting her drug habit. And, in early March 1982, when a friend invited her to join a party with John Belushi, a party that promised money to buy drugs, Cathy was glad to accept. Belushi had plenty of money. He found his first national fame as one of the resident players on the immensely popular "Saturday Night Live" on NBC television. Belushi's comedy was brash and outrageous, a style that he used in creating the character Bluto in*** **Animal House,** ***a 1978 movie that became the biggest money-making comedy in Hollywood history. Another Belushi film,*** **The Blues Brothers,** ***was also a major***

***success, but after a couple of movies that hadn't attracted much attention at the box office, Belushi was in Hollywood in March 1982 in an effort to get his career back on track. Cathy Smith joined him for the party that started on Monday, March 1. With changing personnel and at different locations, the party was only beginning to wind down in the early hours of March 5 at the private club on Sunset Boulevard.***

***After Cathy, Belushi, and the third member of their group, Nelson Lyon, had injected themselves with drugs at the club, they drove a few blocks farther up Sunset Boulevard to a hotel called the Château Marmont. Belushi was registered in bungalow three at the back of the hotel...***

## Scene 5/In Bungalow Three

**BELUSHI** (*coughing, rasping*): I feel rotten. I think...Jeez, I'm gonna be sick.

**SMITH:** Don't do it in here. This place's enough of a mess already.

**BELUSHI** (*leaving the room*): Don't get on my case. I'm going to the can.

**NELSON:** John's been down all night. He's usually a lot of laughs, the cut-up at the party.

**SMITH:** What'd you expect, the guy's hardly been to bed for, like, five days.

**NELSON:** I've never seen anybody do so many drugs.

**SMITH:** You think so? You've only been around half the time. (*Raising voice*) Are you all right, John?

**BELUSHI** (*returning*): I ate all this greasy food earlier on, I guess.

**NELSON:** I'm wasted, man. I gotta get home to my old lady.

**BELUSHI:** Ah, so split.

**SMITH:** Go out on Sunset and a cab'll come by.

**NELSON:** Hm...Thanks for the party, John. You, too, Cathy.

*Nelson leaves.*

**SMITH:** You want me to leave?

**BELUSHI:** Well...Shoot me up again, you and me both.

**SMITH:** John, you ought to catch some sleep, like seriously.

**BELUSHI** (*growing angry*): Cathy, do like I say. I want a hit.

**SMITH:** Okay, all right, but afterwards, I'm putting you to bed.
**BELUSHI:** Yeah...

*Cathy sets up equipment and prepares the hits.*

**SMITH:** Some for you, some for me. Knot the belt around your arm.
**BELUSHI:** Yeah, yeah... That's very nice. That's nice.
**SMITH** (*with irony*): A person could get used to it.
**BELUSHI:** I need something to make me feel good. And I get so screwed over out here. I'm just...the studios, the agents — everybody's dealing me in the wrong goddamn projects.
**SMITH:** I'll tuck you into bed.
**BELUSHI:** Well, now, don't go. Ah, yeah...I wanna talk. I got all these projects, ya know, all these scripts, and none of these movies people want me to make are worth shit. I could go down the tubes...I don't feel any respect for the material. Yeah, not since I made *The Blues Brothers*...

*Later that day.*

**SMITH:** John, we've been talking, like, three hours or something.
**BELUSHI:** Yeah, maybe I'll sleep a while. And turn up the thermostat, will ya? I feel weird, like I got a chill.
**SMITH:** I'll be out in the livingroom. Call me if you want anything. (*Calling from other room*) Is there some paper around here to write on? (*To self*) What a junk pile. There's got to be a piece of note paper...Okay, now. (*Writes*): "Dear Bernie. I'm not too late in writing, huh? Sorry about that. I was considering coming back to Toronto and see what's shaking up there. I sure wished I had the money to lease a store. Pay somebody a percentage to run it. Whatever, I must get out of L.A. soon. It's driving me to an early death, what with all my self-abuse. I'm such a sucker for a good time. Ho, ho, ho, ho."

*Belushi begins choking and coughing in the other room.*

**SMITH** (*calling to him*): Hey, John, you want a glass of water?
**BELUSHI** (*from bedroom*): Yes...It's just my lungs or something. Don't leave.

**SMITH** (*entering bedroom*): Nobody's leaving, John. I'm gonna order from room service. You want a coffee?
**BELUSHI** (*in a small voice*): I just don't want to be alone.
**SMITH** (*into telephone*): Room service? I'd like one continental breakfast for bungalow three. But make the toast whole wheat and send up some strawberry jam...
**SMITH** (*raising voice*): John, you asleep? It's ten o'clock already. I gotta go out.

*Belushi is snoring softly.*

**SMITH** (*in a softer voice*): Yeah, you're asleep. (*Almost a whisper*) See you later, man.

*Later. There is loud knocking at the door.*

**BILL WALLACE:** Hey John, open the door. It's me, Bill. Come on, it's noon. (*To self*) What the hell, I'll use my own key. John, you in bed or what? Ah hell, John, get up. We're already late for the meeting. (*Growing insistent*) Hey, wake up. (*Puzzled*) John. John... Oh no, you dumb son of a bitch. John, you dumb son of a bitch.

**GREENSPAN:** ***Bill Wallace worked for John Belushi as a physical-fitness trainer. When he found his employer collapsed on the bed, he called for assistance. Within a few minutes the Los Angeles Police and a team of paramedics hurried to the Château Marmont. They were too late. John Belushi was dead. Lieutenant Randolph Mancini of the Hollywood Division of the L.A. Police Department took charge of the investigation at the hotel and Dr. Ronald Kornblum, Acting Medical Examiner for the County of Los Angeles, was summoned to examine John Belushi's body...***

**MANCINI:** It's back here in the bedroom, Doctor. You heard who it is, haven't you?
**KORNBLUM:** Yeah, I can see the headlines now.
**MANCINI:** It looks like he OD'd himself.
**KORNBLUM:** Hmm, well, those are fresh needle marks in his arms. I don't see any long history of needle use, though. Maybe he was a novice. Your people turn up any drugs around here?

**MANCINI:** Well, there was some powder over there on the dresser. Two kinds, we think — heroin and cocaine.
**KORNBLUM:** Ah, I can't give you anything definite on cause of death until I do the autopsy. Tomorrow probably.
**MANCINI:** The funny thing is we haven't found any of the paraphernalia for shooting the stuff. No needles, no spoon. Just a couple of paper bindles with powder traces on them and this belt.
**KORNBLUM:** Looped to about the size that'd fit around this dead man's arm.
**MANCINI:** Yeah, it's a woman's belt.

## Scene 6 / Inside a Car

**SMITH** (*humming to herself, stops abruptly*): A cop. What the hell is this?

*Cathy rolls down the window.*

**SMITH:** What is it, officer?
**OFFICER:** Ah, this is a one-way street, ma'am, and it isn't your way.
**SMITH:** Oh yeah sorry, officer. It's just a habit. Like, we always turn down here because it's a shortcut into the Château.
**OFFICER:** Is this car yours?
**SMITH:** It's a friend's. He's staying at the Château.
**OFFICER:** What's this friend's name?
**SMITH:** John Belushi. What's happening?
**OFFICER:** You mind telling me what that is in the top of the purse there?
**SMITH:** Ah... Those things aren't mine either. They're a syringe and other stuff.
**OFFICER:** You want to get out of the car, ma'am, and bring your purse.

**GREENSPAN:** ***Cathy Smith was taken to the Hollywood Station of the Los Angeles Police Department where Richard Iddings, a homicide detective, questioned her. To Cathy's surprise, Detective Iddings was agreeable and sympathetic...***

## Scene 7 / In an Office at the Police Station

**IDDINGS:** Ah, I'm going to tape this conversation, Miss Smith, but I want to make it clear that these are strictly routine questions about what looks like an accidental drug overdose, all right?

**SMITH:** What is this all about? I mean, whose drug overdose?

**IDDINGS:** I'm sorry. John Belushi's. I'm afraid he's dead.

**SMITH:** John? Oh my God, no. Not John. He was alive when I left this morning.

**IDDINGS:** Well... Let's back up a bit on this. Now, you tell me, have you been shooting heroin?

**SMITH:** I used to. Like, I went through detox last year.

**IDDINGS:** You mind if I look at your arms?

**SMITH:** There's a lot of discolouration there.

**IDDINGS:** These seem like fresh needle marks. Are you sure you haven't been shooting?

**SMITH:** Well, I did a few days ago, Tuesday. I shot cocaine.

**IDDINGS:** Okay, I'd like to look in your purse if you have no objections.

**SMITH:** There's a syringe and a needle and spoon in there that belonged to John.

**IDDINGS:** Would you like to tell me about it?

**SMITH** (*in a rush of words*): I didn't want the maid to find them. John was asleep at the Château and I was leaving, so I took them. It was just to protect him. He, he... was into shooting cocaine, and these last few days, he kept calling me to come over. He'd just gotten into shooting, him and Nelson Lyon. They... they were new to it, and John, well, he was a good guy, and I took the stuff so he wouldn't get hurt.

**IDDINGS:** You're being very candid, Miss Smith. I tell you what, I'm going to keep these things — the syringe and spoon. Ah, then you won't have to worry.

**SMITH:** Worry?

**IDDINGS** (*laughing*): Yeah, about the maid finding them.

**SMITH:** Oh, yeah. Right.

**IDDINGS:** Yeah... Do you want to rest in here for a while before you go home? The press is swarming around outside.

**SMITH:** That's all you want? I can... I can leave?

**IDDINGS:** No problem. Have a good day, Miss Smith.

**SMITH:** For once in my life, my God, for once I get a break.

**GREENSPAN:** ***Cathy Smith had lied to Detective Iddings when she denied using heroin. In any case, the Hollywood police did not seem interested in pursuing an investigation into all the circumstances of John Belushi's death. Perhaps they were satisfied that Belushi had died of a self-administered overdose of drugs. Whatever their motivation, the Hollywood police decided there was nothing in the autopsy of Dr. Ronald Kornblum to cause them to change their minds...***

## Scene 8 / In the Coroner's Office

**KORNBLUM** (*talking into a dictation machine*): Let's see, in the Belushi matter, I place the time of death at between 10:00 a.m. and 12:00 noon on March 5, 1982, and I determine that the cause of death is the result of acute cocaine and heroin intoxication. I base that on several factors. There are extensive needle marks on both arms, the most recent being within four hours or less of the actual time of death. There is cocaine throughout the body, and there is morphine, which is the chemical breakdown of heroin, present in the body's blood and bile.

**GREENSPAN:** ***The police in Los Angeles showed no further interest in Cathy Smith, but the California media pursued her for her version of John Belushi's death. Cathy returned to Toronto to escape the press, but she did not remain altogether silent. In mid-June 1982, two reporters from Florida, Larry Haley and Tony Brenna, came to Toronto and checked into the Sheraton Hotel. Over the following ten days, for up to twelve hours a day, Haley and Brenna talked to Cathy Smith in their hotel room about John Belushi's death. The newspaper that employed the two reporters paid Cathy $15,000 for the ten days of interviews. The newspaper was the*** **National Enquirer.**

## Scene 9 / In a Hotel Room

**TONY BRENNA:** The material you're giving us is excellent, Cathy. But bear with Larry and me for a few more details. Just to confirm.

**LARRY HALEY:** How's your Courvoisier, Cathy? Are you happy?

**SMITH** (*slurring slightly*): I'm doing okay. Let's finish. This place is making me a little crazy.

**TONY:** All right, you said you were doing drugs with John for the best part of a week.

**SMITH:** I hung out with him for most of the whole five days he was out there in Hollywood, and any time that he shot anything while I was around, I did it for him.

**LARRY:** You say John might have shot himself up, but there was some point where you took over the shooting for him?

**SMITH:** Like, it got to the situation where he couldn't even hold the needle up to his arm. He was right out of it. That was part of the reason I handled the shooting.

**TONY:** And when did it end?

**SMITH:** Hm... Three-thirty in the morning on the Friday. That's when I shot up John for the last time. You know what I think? I think John had a death wish.

**GREENSPAN:** *The* **National Enquirer** *is a tabloid weekly with a circulation of 6.5 million in North America. The issue of June 29, 1982, carried a copyright article that purported to tell in Cathy Smith's own words the story of John Belushi's last days and of Smith's role in his death. None of the* **Enquirer's** *audience read the issue with more interest than Michael Montagna and Richard J. Chrystie. Montagna and Chrystie were deputy district attorneys for the County of Los Angeles.*

## Scene 10/In the DA's Office

**MONTAGNA:** Have you seen this thing, Dick?

**CHRYSTIE:** Yea... Are you kidding? Right now, it's more popular around the office than Joe Wambaugh's new book.

**MONTAGNA** (*reading*): "I killed John Belushi. I didn't mean to —— but I was responsible for his death."

**CHRYSTIE:** Do you believe it?

**MONTAGNA:** I'm sure as hell not going to ignore it.

**CHRYSTIE:** Yeah, the people over at the Hollywood Station let the thing go as a self-administered overdose.

**MONTAGNA:** According to this article, the Smith woman did all or most of the injecting.

**CHRYSTIE:** You could probably get her under the Health and Safety Code, furnishing and administering a controlled substance and so on and so forth. That's a felony.

**MONTAGNA:** I think we can go for more.
**CHRYSTIE:** What more?
**MONTAGNA:** Murder. The Penal Code defines murder as the unlawful killing of a human being with malice aforethought. All right, the case law says malice is implied where the death results from an act involving a high degree of probability that it *will* result in death when the act is done for a base anti-social purpose and with a wanton disregard for life.
**CHRYSTIE:** And what the Smith woman did ought to put her in the category of implied malice.
**MONTAGNA:** She's already told the *Enquirer* she stuck the needles in Belushi's arms and we've got the autopsy report that says Belushi died of too much heroin and cocaine.
**CHRYSTIE:** No question, Mike, reopen the investigation.

**GREENSPAN:** ***Deputy District Attorney Michael Montagna put together his case against Cathy Smith and took it before a Grand Jury in Los Angeles.***

***On March 15, 1983, slightly over a year after John Belushi's death, the Los Angeles Grand Jury handed down an indictment charging Cathy Smith with thirteen counts of administering cocaine and heroin in violation of the Health and Safety Code of California and one count of murder under the California Penal Code.***

***In Toronto, Cathy Smith retained a lawyer. The lawyer was my brother, Brian Greenspan...***

## Scene 11 / In a Law Office

**SMITH:** Every American newspaper I look at, there's my name in the headlines.
**BRIAN GREENSPAN:** Uh-huh. The L.A. press is making a witch hunt out of this.
**SMITH:** You don't need to tell me who the witch is they're hunting — "Cathy Smith, the killer of John Belushi."
**BRIAN:** Yeah. At least nobody can quote you any more. Please keep it that way, Cathy. No talking to reporters. All right? And as for the legal side of things, well, just leave that to the people in this office.
**SMITH:** I'm charged with murder, which is ridiculous. But now what? What happens next?

**BRIAN:** The U.S. government, on behalf of the State of California, will go before our courts, right here in Toronto, okay? And they'll ask the judge to order you extradited back to Los Angeles for trial on the murder count and the thirteen drug counts.

**SMITH:** And you're going to fight the extradition.

**BRIAN:** Of course I am. But I have to warn you, Cathy, I'm fighting with one hand tied behind my back.

**SMITH:** Oh *God.*

**BRIAN:** Or maybe it's fighting with a blindfold over my eyes. Anyway, the point is this, Cathy: Now, you see, I don't know exactly what evidence the DA down in Los Angeles put before the Grand Jury. By law, Grand Jury proceedings are secret, you see. All I know about the case against you is what I've read in a couple of dozen affidavits that the counsel for the United States has filed with the court up here as the basis for his extradition request.

**SMITH:** These affidavits, they aren't any good?

**BRIAN:** Well, second best as far as we're concerned. The affidavits were sworn by the people who appeared before the Grand Jury and they're a kind of précis of what the people told the Grand Jury. They don't give us the whole story.

**SMITH:** Tell me the truth. It looks bad, right?

**BRIAN:** Every case looks tough at the beginning.

**GREENSPAN:** ***The United States began its extradition proceedings in the middle of June 1983 in the Courthouse on University Avenue in Toronto. The presiding judge was Judge Stephen Borins of the District Court of the Judicial District of York. Ari Coomaraswamy, a Canadian federal Crown attorney, represented the United States of America...***

## Scene 12 / In Court

**ARI COOMARASWAMY:** Your Honour, on behalf of the demanding state, I propose to put in evidence twenty-seven affidavits in support of the request for extradition of the alleged fugitive, Catherine Evelyn Smith. But I understand that my friend has a preliminary objection to these affidavits.

**JUDGE:** Go ahead, Mr. Greenspan.

**BRIAN:** Ah, not with respect to all twenty-seven affidavits, Your Honour. A mere nine.

**JUDGE:** Which nine are we talking about?

**BRIAN:** The affidavit of Dr. Ronald Kornblum. That's one, Your Honour. Dr. Kornblum performed the autopsy on John Belushi, and I submit that his affidavit is equivocal on the cause of Belushi's death. The affidavit of Nelson Lyon is another. Mr. Lyon was present when many of the alleged drug injections took place, and in my view, his affidavit contains misleading statements.

**JUDGE:** Let's suppose you're correct in your submission, Mr. Greenspan. How do you propose to cure the problem?

**BRIAN:** By cross-examination, Your Honour. The nine affidavits should not be admitted in evidence against Miss Smith until Your Honour permits me to cross-examine the deponents to the affidavits.

**GREENSPAN:** ***In arguing for the right to cross-examine Dr. Kornblum, Nelson Lyon, and the seven other deponents on their affidavits, Brian Greenspan was arguing against a long-established practice. In most courtroom proceedings, witnesses give their evidence* viva voce, *in person and in court, and opposing counsel have the right to cross-examine them on their testimony. But the Canadian Extradition Act provides that in proceedings under it, the foreign state asking for extradition of a fugitive person may introduce evidence by way of affidavits taken in the foreign jurisdiction. Brian Greenspan was asking Judge Borins to overturn the established procedure...***

**BRIAN:** Your Honour, I submit that the 1982 Charter of Rights has radically changed the situation we face in extradition proceedings.

**JUDGE:** The Charter's been raised as a defence in one or two other extradition proceedings in the past year.

**BRIAN:** Unsuccessfully, I'm aware of that, Your Honour.

**JUDGE:** Do you have an argument to distinguish those cases?

**BRIAN:** I'm relying on sections 7 and 11 of the Charter, Your Honour. Section 7 guarantees that no one will be deprived of his liberty except in accordance with the principles of fundamental justice. And Section 11 says that any person charged with an offence is presumed innocent until he's proven guilty in a fair and public hearing. Now, Your Honour, both these notions — a fair hearing and fundamental justice — demand the right to cross-examine on affidavits in an extradition hearing under the situation that Miss Smith faces.

**JUDGE:** What do you say to that, Mr. Coomaraswamy?

**COOMARASWAMY:** Yes, all we're deciding in this court, Your Honour, is whether the affidavits show there is sufficient evidence to send Miss Smith back to California. A court down there will determine her guilt or innocence. That is the stage, in *California*, where Miss Smith's counsel will properly have the chance to cross-examine Dr. Kornblum and these other people.

**BRIAN:** But if I can't cross-examine now, *before* extradition, then Miss Smith's Charter rights are infringed.

**JUDGE:** Mr. Greenspan, I don't have much difficulty being persuaded that the right to cross-examine is a principle of fundamental justice.

**BRIAN:** That's my point, Your Honour.

**JUDGE:** But another section of the Charter gives me trouble.

**BRIAN:** You're referring to section 1.

**JUDGE:** Exactly. Section 1 tells us that the rights and freedoms set out in sections 7, 11, and all the other sections of the Charter are subject to such reasonable limits as can be demonstrably justified in a free and democratic society. Aren't these proceedings against Miss Smith an instance where section 1 should be applied?

**BRIAN:** I submit not, Your Honour.

**JUDGE:** After all, as Mr. Coomaraswamy pointed out, this court isn't dealing with Miss Smith's guilt or innocence.

**BRIAN:** The question is this, Your Honour —— how far are we going to permit section 1 to go in infringing on Miss Smith's rights under the Charter? When does it stop?

**GREENSPAN:** ***Judge Borins reserved judgment to consider counsel's arguments. When Court resumed he made the following ruling...***

**JUDGE:** I appreciate counsel's submission that there's always a risk that a Canadian citizen might be extradited to face trial in a foreign state on the basis of affidavit evidence which might have been exposed as false by cross-examination. But that situation would be exceedingly rare. I must hold in these proceedings that admitting the affidavits in evidence without cross-examination of the deponents is a reasonable limit on Miss Smith's rights under the Charter.

**GREENSPAN:** ***Brian Greenspan appealed Judge Borins' decision on this fundamental constitutional question to the Supreme Court of Ontario and then to the Ontario Court of Appeal. The appeal process stretched over several months, and while it proceeded, the actual extradition hearing before Judge Borins was adjourned. During the same period, Brian Greenspan was carrying on a series of friendly telephone discussions with Michael Montagna, the Los Angeles assistant district attorney who had charge of Cathy Smith's case in California. Greenspan was looking for a plea negotiation. He believed in the correctness of his arguments in court on behalf of Cathy Smith, but he faced the very real probability that she would eventually be extradited to California. He was seeking to ensure that she would be sent there under the best possible circumstances. Late in 1983, he flew to California, and on December 28, he met in the Los Angeles district attorney's office with Michael Montagna.***

## Scene 13 / In the DA's Office

**BRIAN:** What I'm telling you, Mike, is how you can get Cathy back to California.

**MONTAGNA:** The sooner, the better. You wouldn't believe the pressure down here. All kind of press and other people asking what's taking so long to put this woman on trial. It's already almost a year already since the Grand Jury's indictment.

**BRIAN:** I'm not going to send her back on a murder charge.

**MONTAGNA:** We've put together a lot of evidence against her, Brian.

**BRIAN:** Well I'm prepared to concede from what I've read in the affidavits that you're got *prima facie* evidence for a criminal charge.

**MONTAGNA:** Yeah — *but*?

**BRIAN:** But it is not a murder charge.

**MONTAGNA:** I'll go this far, Brian, I've never taken the position she killed Belushi intentionally.

**BRIAN:** Well, that gives us plenty of room to move around. Now, what about scaling the charge down from murder?

**MONTAGNA:** How far down?

**BRIAN:** Involuntary manslaughter. From what I know of your evidence, the facts may constitute a charge of involuntary manslaughter.

**MONTAGNA:** Will she come back and plead guilty to that in our court?

**BRIAN:** Mike, I'm only Cathy's Canadian extradition counsel. I can't tell you how she'll plead.

**MONTAGNA:** Yeah, I appreciate that. She'll have a local attorney acting for her down here. It's his decision at that point.

**BRIAN:** That's right. I'll go this far — if you switch the charge to involuntary manslaughter, the odds are you'll never see a trial.

**MONTAGNA:** You think she'll plead?

**BRIAN:** I'm only talking about the odds.

**MONTAGNA:** How about the thirteen drug counts?

**BRIAN:** Thirteen is much too much.

**MONTAGNA:** Would you accept three?

**BRIAN:** If you're offering three, we might accept three.

**MONTAGNA:** All right, you realize if she comes back and pleads to one charge of involuntary manslaughter and three drug counts, she could do two, three years in prison?

**BRIAN:** Or she could do no time depending on how the judge feels, on what Cathy's attorney says, and on a few other things.

**MONTAGNA:** Here's what I'll do. I'll send up a new requisition for extradition to the people in Toronto. I'll drop the murder and the thirteen drug charges and change it to involuntary manslaughter and three counts of administering drugs.

**BRIAN:** And I'll recommend to Cathy that she return voluntarily to California.

**MONTAGNA:** That takes a lot of heat off my office. But, look, there's one thing.

**BRIAN:** Which is?

**MONTAGNA:** Before this arrangement goes through, I need approval from upstairs, from my district attorney.

**BRIAN:** But you're recommending the deal?

**MONTAGNA:** Brian, my strongest recommendation.

**GREENSPAN:** ***Brian Greenspan returned home with an excellent deal for his client. Instead of facing a murder trial and a possible life term in prison, Cathy Smith had a choice of pleading guilty to a less serious charge with the chance of no prison time. But over the following several weeks, Michael Montagna was unable to confirm the deal.***

***Brian Greenspan was caught in a dilemma. Without final approval of the arrangement he'd arrived at with Montagna, he had to continue the fight against Cathy Smith's extradition. His appeal on Judge Borins' refusal to allow cross-examination on the nine affidavits was turned down by the Ontario Supreme Court and then by the Court of Appeal. It was late March 1984. Greenspan applied for leave to appeal to the Supreme Court of Canada on the affidavit question. Two days before the application was scheduled to be heard in Ottawa, Michael Montagna telephoned from Los Angeles.***

## Scene 14/In a Law Office

**MONTAGNA** (*on the telephone*): Brian, this call is one of those good news–bad news things.

**BRIAN:** Mike, I've been waiting four months for confirmation of our arrangement. That's about all the bad news I can stand.

**MONTAGNA:** The trouble is my DA down here, Bob Philibosian. I can't get approval on the changes in charges out of him.

**BRIAN:** What's his objection?

**MONTAGNA:** If you ask me, it's politics. Philibosian's coming up for re-election in June and no DA can appear to be going soft on a drug case, at election time anyway, especially a case that's as high-profile as this one.

**BRIAN:** So give me the good news.

**MONTAGNA:** The man Philibosian's running against, a guy named Ira Reiner, I know I can get the okay on our arrangement from him.

**BRIAN:** What're Reiner's chances of beating Philibosian?

**MONTAGNA:** Pretty strong. But this gets us back into the bad-news area. See, even if Reiner wins, he doesn't take office for six months. Philibosian stays on the job until January 1, 1985.

**BRIAN:** Well, that shouldn't be a problem. Philibosian'd be a lame-duck DA. Why should he care what the voters think after they've voted him out?

**MONTAGNA:** You don't know the man. Small c conservative Republican, and a person like Cathy Smith, she's the opposite of everything he stands for.

**BRIAN:** I get you.

**MONTAGNA:** No matter what, I can't see Philibosian approving the deal.

**BRIAN:** Well... That leaves us waiting on this potentially new DA, what's-his-name, Reiner.

**MONTAGNA:** Keep the case before the courts until January. Then if Reiner gets in, we close the deal on the involuntary manslaughter and you send Smith back here.

**BRIAN:** I got at least another year of arguments and appeals as long as you don't oppose her continuing to remain on bail.

**MONTAGNA:** You're gonna need that time. But we're gonna have to... continue formally opposing the bail. However, the opposition won't be strenuous.

**BRIAN:** And what if Philibosian gets back into office?

**MONTAGNA:** Ah, forget it, Brian. I've given you enough bad news for one call.

**GREENSPAN:** ***The Supreme Court of Canada turned down Greenspan's application for leave to appeal Judge Borins' ruling on the affidavit evidence and the extradition hearing was set to resume before Judge Borins in August 1984.***

***In June, Ira Reiner was elected district attorney of Los Angeles. Robert Philibosian would remain in office until January 1985 and he continued to refuse to approve the arrangements that Michael Montagna and Brian Greenspan had arrived at.***

***As if Greenspan didn't have enough complications to deal with, the journalist Bob Woodward gave him one more...***

## Scene 15 / In a Law Office

**BRIAN:** You're in print again, Cathy.

**SMITH:** Well, we knew it was coming, the Watergate guy's book.

**BRIAN:** Book? You were supposed to be interviewed for a series of articles, not for a national best-seller. (*Reading*) "*Wired: The Short Life and Fast Times of John Belushi*, by Bob Woodward." We got a very fat book here, Cathy.

**SMITH:** I thought it was going to be an article in my favour. I mean, he's got a very straight reputation, the guy who wrote the book that nailed Richard Nixon.

*Brian flips through the book.*

**BRIAN:** Yeah, well... here's what Woodward says happened when you were alone with Belushi at 3:00, 3:30, on the morning he died... (*Reading*) "John produced a little more coke from his pocket. Smith mixed it with some heroin for a speedball. She gave herself the first shot and then made one for John that had a tenth each of cocaine and heroin."

**SMITH:** That's not good, eh?

**BRIAN:** Not really, Cathy. But I'm going to try something...

## Scene 16 / In Court

**BRIAN:** Your Honour, I propose to enter as an exhibit a work ostensibly of non-fiction entitled *Wired* by Robert Woodward.

**JUDGE:** Yes... I'm aware of the book.

**BRIAN:** My argument is that passages in this book allege that Miss Smith is guilty of the very acts that the State of California has accused her of committing. Your Honour, *Wired* is a national best-seller in the United States and the immense publicity its allegations have received make it impossible for Miss Smith to have a fair and impartial trial.

**JUDGE:** Isn't the trial court in California in a better position to make a decision about the book's impact on an impartial trial?

**BRIAN:** It has equal validity at this stage, Your Honour. My submission is that the book has undermined the principles of fundamental justice by announcing to all of North America a verdict of guilty on the matters that are just now coming before Your Honour to decide. The only remedy is for you to quash the warrant for Miss Smith's extradition.

**JUDGE:** Well, Mr. Greenspan, as I read the present law of extradition, it's for the California court ultimately to decide whether the book has taken away Miss Smith's chances of a fair trial. I must hold against your motion to quash the extradition warrant.

**GREENSPAN:** ***With Judge Borins' ruling, Ari Coomaraswamy at last began an outline of the U.S. government's case against Cathy Smith. Mr. Coomaraswamy suggested to the Court that the affidavit evidence led to an inescapable conclusion...***

**COOMARASWAMY:** Your Honour, we have Miss Smith's admission to the *National Enquirer* reporters that Mr. Belushi received some twenty-four injections of drugs in the last thirty hours of his life and that she was responsible for administering most or many of the injections. We have evidence that she was alone with Mr. Belushi in the last hours of his life. We have Dr. Kornblum's report that Mr. Belushi died of drug injections that were administered in the hours shortly before his death. Your Honour, I suggest it is open to a California jury to find that Miss Smith is guilty under California law of Mr. Belushi's murder. And I submit that is sufficient for you to order her extradition.

**GREENSPAN:** ***Brian Greenspan spent little of the court's time in disputing Mr. Coomaraswamy's interpretation of the affidavit evidence. Instead, he presented an argument to Judge Borins based on the comparison of the definitions of murder under the California Penal Code and the Canadian Criminal Code. In California, the act which Cathy Smith was alleged to have committed, that is, administering drugs in a reckless manner, fell into a category of murder. But such an act would not be considered murder in Canada unless Cathy Smith*** **meant** ***to cause bodily harm that she knew was likely to cause death. Brian Greenspan argued that since she had no such intention, her act did not constitute murder under the Canadian Criminal Code...***

**BRIAN:** The point I'm leading to, Your Honour, is that if it's murder in California but it isn't murder in Canada, then the Extradition Act does not apply.

**JUDGE:** I think you're putting an interpretation on the Act that may be too strict, Mr. Greenspan.

**BRIAN:** Ah, I'd argue it this way, Your Honour. If the offence charged in California is murder and if the acts that Miss Smith is alleged to have committed amount to a *prime facie* case of murder under our Code, then the Extradition Act can be invoked. Otherwise it has no application.

**JUDGE:** I take it that the key element to your argument is intent.

**BRIAN:** Well, it wouldn't be murder under our Code unless Miss Smith intended to kill Belushi when she injected him or intended to harm him.

**JUDGE:** I agree with you up to a certain limit. As I read the affidavits that Mr. Coomaraswamy has filed, I don't see any evidence from which a jury could decide that Miss Smith intended to kill or harm Mr. Belushi. But there's another point you haven't addressed, Mr. Greenspan.

**BRIAN:** Your Honour?

**JUDGE:** I think on the facts alleged against Miss Smith a *prima facie* case of manslaughter could be made out against her under our Criminal Code.

**BRIAN:** I can't dispute that, Your Honour.

**JUDGE:** So that at least we've got murder under the California Penal Code and we've got a *prime facie* case of manslaughter under the Canadian Criminal Code.

**BRIAN:** But I'd argue, Your Honour, that it must be murder under *both* codes before the Extradition Act comes into effect.

**JUDGE:** I think you're making an interpretation of the Act that's too narrow, Mr. Greenspan. It's enough, as I see it, that the conduct alleged against Miss Smith would constitute *any* criminal offence under Canadian law. You and I have agreed that her acts would amount to a *prima facie* case of manslaughter in Canada. That, in my view, satisfies the requirements of the Extradition Act.

**GREENSPAN:** ***The circumstances may well have satisfied the requirements of the Extradition Act. The larger question, though, is whether any fair-minded Canadian would be satisfied with the situation in which a citizen could be extradited for murder on facts that everyone agreed could never amount to murder in this country. Brian Greenspan appealed the decision to the Supreme Court of Ontario. The appeal was dismissed. Greenspan went the next step and appealed to the Ontario Court of Appeal. That hearing was scheduled for the last week in January 1985.***

***A few days before he was to go to the Court of Appeal, however, Brian Greenspan received another telephone call from Michael Montagna...***

## Scene 17 / In a Law Office

**MONTAGNA** (*on the telephone*): Brian, the deal's on. Tell Smith to pack her bags.

**BRIAN:** Wait a minute. Are you saying the new DA's given his okay on the terms you and I've been talking about for the last year?

**MONTAGNA:** Ira Reiner. Yeah, right, he's in favour, absolutely. The only thing Ira insists on is we announce the deal from down here. We're the guys who go public first.

**BRIAN:** Ah, Mike, Cathy will want reassurance she's going back on involuntary manslaughter and three drug counts.

**MONTAGNA:** Tell her sure, of course, that's the condition we accept. Who's going to represent Smith when she gets down here?

**BRIAN** (*with irony*): Oh, I think you might know the man I've retained. Howard Weitzman.

**MONTAGNA:** *Know* him? Are you kidding? He blew us out of the water on the De Lorean prosecution.

**BRIAN:** All right now. If you want to make the announcement on our deal first, that's fine with me, Mike. But the timing is important. I don't want Cathy to spend any time in jail up here before your people take her back to Los Angeles.

**MONTAGNA:** No sweat on that. We announce down here and your woman's on the plane for L.A. the same night.

**BRIAN:** Okay, I think the whole thing's locked in.

**MONTAGNA:** Nice doing business with you, Brian.

*Telephone hung up.*

**BRIAN:** Betty, ask Cathy to come in.

**SMITH:** It's all over?

**BRIAN:** Well, the part up here is over. The part in Los Angeles is just starting.

**SMITH:** What about this guy Weitzman? He's good?

**BRIAN:** Everybody knows about him these days because he's the one that got an acquittal for John De Lorean in a high-profile drug case. Now, but the reason De Lorean hired him in the first place, Cathy, was because Howard already had a reputation as a fantastic defence attorney.

**SMITH:** Hm. So I'm going back.

**BRIAN:** You fly back next Monday evening.

**SMITH:** Hm... The last time I was in L.A., I was a junkie and free. Now I'm clean and maybe I'm going to jail.

**GREENSPAN:** ***On January 22, 1985, Cathy Smith appeared with her California attorney, Howard Weitzman, before Superior Court Judge Robert Devich in Los Angeles. As soon as Cathy Smith had personally entered the jurisdiction of the California courts, something significant to her defence took place. By California law, the Grand Jury proceedings which had been secret up until that point, now became available to Cathy Smith's lawyers for the first time. Howard Weitzman spent several days reading a transcript of the proceedings. When he finished, he telephoned Brian Greenspan...***

# Scene 18 / In Weitzman's Office

**WEITZMAN** (*on the telephone*): Brian, I've got no choice. I'm gonna back out of the deal you made with Montagna.

**BRIAN:** Now, wait, wait... Wait a minute, Howard. Back up and tell me what you're talking about.

**WEITZMAN:** We don't need to go for involuntary manslaughter. Let them put Cathy on trial for murder. I can beat it.

**BRIAN:** Ah, ha! What do you know that I don't?

**WEITZMAN:** That's the whole point. I know plenty you didn't know when you were doing the extradition. It's all in the Grand Jury proceedings.

**BRIAN:** Like what? Give me a taste.

**WEITZMAN:** Listen to this. The guy who did the autopsy, Kornblum, he's testifying. (*Reading*) "*Question:* Dr. Kornblum, did the 3:30 injection cause death? *Answer:* No." How d'you like that, Brian?

**BRIAN:** Cathy hasn't admitted she gave Belushi any injections after 3:30.

**WEITZMAN:** Right. There's *no* evidence she had anything to do with the drugs from 3:30 until she left around 10:00 that morning.

**BRIAN:** You see, that admission of Kornblum's, that's the kind of thing I would have found out if the courts up here had allowed me to cross-examine on the affidavits.

**WEITZMAN:** Sure... and there's even a small hint in here that maybe somebody else, a third person, might have gone to Belushi's bungalow after Cathy left.

**BRIAN:** Ha... That's strong stuff.

**WEITZMAN:** So, what's your position on this?

**BRIAN:** You do what's in Cathy's best interests.

**WEITZMAN:** I thought you'd see it that way.

**BRIAN:** If you want to repudiate the deal I made with Mike Montagna, you go right ahead. The deal was made on the basis of what I knew and the assumption that what I knew was factually accurate and it isn't.

**WEITZMAN:** Brian, I'm getting into my well-known fighting stance.

**BRIAN:** How's Cathy taking all of this?

**WEITZMAN:** Patiently.

**BRIAN:** Hmph. Well, that's something she's learned a lot about these last three years.

GREENSPAN: ***In the light of these developments, had Judge Borins decided to allow cross-examination on the affidavit evidence, it is my view that Cathy Smith would never have been extradited to California on either murder or manslaughter. The law is wrong. And this case shows the need for fundamental legislative change by Parliament.***

***Weitzman backed out of the arrangement. Montagna reinstated the original murder count and the thirteen counts of administering drugs. The stage seemed set for a dramatic trial that would inevitably attract intense media and public attention. But that trial lay many months away, perhaps as much as a year.***

***Cathy Smith, on bail in Hollywood, appeared to have found a different life. She lived quietly with a friend. She found a job. And she avoided her old acquaintances.***

SMITH (*reading*): "After John Belushi's death, my life changed completely — both for better and for worse. The best part is I've discovered what life is like without drugs and I like it. The worst part is not knowing what will happen to me. The prospect of prison frightens me and I wonder how I'd survive. I've broken my heroin habit for good and that counts for something. It took John's death to shake me awake. But I dearly wish that both of us had done it differently."

# Producer's Notes

The death of popular TV comedian and film star John Belushi from an overdose of drugs became one of the most widely discussed events in 1982. The way Belushi lived and died seemed to many people to be symbolic of our times, serving as a comment on the lifestyle and preoccupations of an entire generation.

Belushi died in California. His death became relevant to our program when authorities in Los Angeles charged a Canadian woman, Cathy Smith, with murder in connection with Belushi's death. The extradition of Cathy Smith raised many intriguing legal questions.

It is, of course, the business of the courts to determine what the law *is* in Canada — that is, what procedures are or are not lawful or what kind of acts do or do not amount to a crime. But it is the business of every citizen to think about what the law should be. For instance, do we want to surrender Canadians to foreign jurisdictions without first enabling them to challenge the evidence against them through cross-examination of witnesses in the same way they could if a charge were brought against them in this country? Do we want to surrender them at all if the acts of which they are accused would amount only to a much less serious crime (or no crime) in Canada? Should we surrender them if the penalty they face in the foreign jurisdiction is far graver than the penalty they would face here for the same offence? Should we take another look at the "included" crimes in some of our extradition treaties, and at the level of proof we require before granting extradition?

Cathy Smith's hearing raised many of these issues in the context of one of the most sensational cases of the decade. When, in the end, her lawyer, Brian Greenspan, allowed Smith to return to California voluntarily in exchange for a significant reduction of the charges against her, the case also provided room for an examination of the plea-bargaining process and the practice of overcharging defendants for tactical or political reasons. In another twist, when Smith's American counsel, the well-known California lawyer Howard Weitzman (whose successful entrapment defence led to the acquittal of the automaker John De Lorean) decided to repudiate the plea-bargain because the evidence against Smith, which her Canadian counsel had been precluded from testing, indicated to him that his client should not be committed to trial on the charges against her in any case, the validity and fairness of our extradition process became even more questionable.

The writer and lawyer Jack Batten, whose biography of the great Canadian lawyer J. J. Robinette has been a recent bestseller, prepared a concise script which reflected the intricacies of Cathy Smith's case with accuracy and dramatic flair. The portrayal of Smith combined restraint with a fine feeling for nuance in the performance of the young actress Chapelle Jaffe. Defence counsel Brian Greenspan's courtroom style was stylishly rendered by Saul Rubinek.

The brief roles of famous show-business personalities were performed with gusto as well as much attention to authentic detail by Neil Munro (John Belushi), George Buza (Levon Helm), Booth Savage (Gordon Lightfoot), and Roy Krost — an award-winning film producer in his more usual incarnation — as rock star Keith Richards. Lightfoot's guitar was played by the musician (and CBC Radio Drama's former executive producer) Paul Mills.

A final irony: the probable expectation of defence attorney Howard Weitzman that the original charge against Cathy Smith would be dismissed before trial did not materialize. As I'm writing these notes, Smith has been ordered to stand trial in California for the murder of John Belushi.

G.J.

# John Down's Body

*Guy Gavriel Kay*

**The Cast**

Commentary by Edward L. Greenspan, Q.C.

| | |
|---|---|
| **KATIE HARPER** | Jayne Eastwood |
| **SANDY HARPER** | Frank Perry |
| **MR. WOLCH** for the defence | Saul Rubinek |
| **MR. DANGERFIELD** for the Crown | Lawrence Dane |

With the support of (in alphabetical order): Harvey Atkin, Pixie Bigelow, David Calderisi, Michelle Claire, Eve Crawford, Alan Fawcett, Rosalind Goldsmith, Nicky Guadagni, Kay Hawtrey, Bill Lynn, Arch McDonell, Frank Moore, James Morris, Ken Pogue, Michael J. Reynolds, Chuck Shamata, Ruth Springford, Ray Stancer, John Stocker, and Joe Ziegler

## Scene 1 / Inside a Car, Winnipeg, June 1959

**PATTERSON:** Hurry up, Katie, we're going to be late... A housecoat? A nurse going to work in a housecoat? No, don't tell me. I know what happened: You stayed up drinking last night and you're calling in sick. Am I right, Katie?

**KATIE** (*walking up*): John was killed last night.

**PATTERSON:** What? In a car accident?

**KATIE:** No, he fell out through the bedroom window. The police have already been here.

**PATTERSON:** Oh gosh. Katie, what happened?

**GREENSPAN:** ***"Katie, what happened?" The question was first asked of twenty-six-year-old Winnipeg nurse Katie Down on the morning of June 2, 1959. It was a question that would not receive a final answer from the courts until 1983. The intervening years would see one of the most bizarre murder investigations and two of the most dramatic trials in Canadian history.***

***My name is Edward Greenspan, and the story you are about to hear is based on the trial transcripts, the documents filed in the Manitoba Court of Appeal, and interviews with some of the main participants in the case.***

***Twenty-eight-year-old Constable Cletus A'Hearne had been the first officer on the scene at about 1:45 a.m. on June 2. A'Hearne arranged for photographs of John Down's naked body and for an autopsy. A'Hearne then went next door at about 2:00 a.m. to the house of neighbours named Sadler. Katie Down was waiting there for him...***

## Scene 2 / At the Sadler House

**A'HEARNE:** Ma'am, I know this is difficult, but can you help me a bit with what happened here?

**KATIE:** Yeah, all right. I have two children. My little girl was sleeping with him. When I went up to bed I took her and put her in her own room. Then later — when the baby woke up — I noticed that John was missing.

**A'HEARNE:** What did you think?

**KATIE:** Well, I don't know. I mean, I don't know what I thought. I don't even know why I went outside. I saw him there and I ran to get a coat and covered him up and then... I just ran over here.

**GREENSPAN:** ***Two days later Constable A'Hearne had another, much longer interview with John Down's young widow and she gave him a remarkably frank signed statement.***

**KATIE:** I met John Down at Saskatoon in 1955. I was nursing at the North Battleford Hospital at the time. I was two months pregnant when we got married. We didn't get along too well from the beginning of our marriage.

I noticed that he was always troubled in his mind, such as mentioning knowing important people when I knew he didn't. And he couldn't seem to relax and he was very restless. I've known him to walk in his sleep only once since we were married. This was about six months ago.

**GREENSPAN:** ***These latter comments, implying suicide or sleepwalking, did not sit well with Constable A'Hearne when he wrote his report...***

## Scene 3 / At the Police Station

**A'HEARNE:** Suicide did not appear to be the answer to this man's death due to the manner and the short distance of the fall, and sleepwalking appeared doubtful for the same reason, as he did not appear to have fallen on his head.

**GREENSPAN:** ***John Down was buried in Newfoundland, where his***

***family lived. Katie Down first met her in-laws at her husband's funeral. And then, on June 24, the Coroner's Inquest took place in Winnipeg and a Dr. Strawbridge gave the following evidence...***

**STRAWBRIDGE:** The organs of the deceased were sent to the RCMP laboratory at Regina. I got a preliminary report yesterday, by telephone. There was a significant concentration of barbiturate found in the blood, which got into the liver. While it is impossible to *say* that this was a lethal concentration, this concentration of 50 micrograms in most any barbiturate, would in fact be sufficient to cause death... without any other factor.

**GREENSPAN:** ***It will be seen how much controversy this caused twenty years later. But in the meantime, where did all this leave young Constable A'Hearne?***

**A'HEARNE** (*reading and typing*): There would seem to be suspicion towards Mrs. Down, but so far this suspicion cannot be supported by facts.

**GREENSPAN:** ***And so Constable A'Hearne laid no charges and continued to investigate through the summer. He did have one more conversation with Katie Down. Again, she spoke with remarkable frankness to the young officer, and this time she discussed the man she was now involved with...***

**KATIE:** Ah, Sandy Harper used to work with me and drove me home from work a few times. I never had sexual relations with him but we'd stop for a beer and he would drive me home. After John's death I started associating with Sandy Harper and have had sexual relations with him. Granted, I do miss my husband and it was nice when he was there but I never loved him and I find it hard to know how I feel.

**GREENSPAN:** ***Harper's name had come up before, but A'Hearne had been unable to find and interview the man. Six months later he finally did find Sandy Harper, though it didn't do him much good...***

# Scene 4 / On the Porch of the Harper Home

**SANDY** (*answering the door*): Yeah?

**A'HEARNE:** Are you Sandy Harper?

**SANDY:** Uh-huh.

**A'HEARNE:** I'm Constable A'Hearne of the RCMP —

**SANDY:** What do you want?

**A'HEARNE:** I'm here in connection with the death of Mr. John Down last June 2, and I wonder if you could help me with some information?

**SANDY** (*angry*): Christ! I... I don't know nothing. I... I got nothing to say. Nothing!

**A'HEARNE** (*soothing*): I see, all right. Ah, you do know Katie Down, I gather?

**SANDY:** Course I know her. My wife's divorcing me and Katie's co-respondent. What are you guys... What are you...

**A'HEARNE:** Mr. Harper, I understand you received a telephone call from Mrs. Down on the night of John Down's death. Is that true?

**SANDY** (*very upset*): Jesus, Jesus! [*He bangs the wall.*] You goddamn cops! I told you I got nothing to say. I don't remember nothin'. Maybe I did, maybe I didn't... Listen, you get outta here now! You get your ass off this porch or I swear by Christ I'll throw you off...

**GREENSPAN:** ***A'Hearne would later testify that Sandy Harper seemed so close to violence that he terminated the interview at that point.***

***The file on John Down's death was closed, and it remained closed for a very long time.***

***In 1960, Sandy Harper and his wife, Rose, were divorced. Four days later, forty-year-old Sandy and Katie Down were married. They bought a house in Winnipeg and settled in. They had a baby girl, Sherry, to join Katie's two daughters by John Down. The years passed. The two older girls grew up and left home. Katie and Sandy stayed together, although the whispers about his drinking problem grew, and many friends of bright, friendly Katie Harper wondered aloud about her union to this man who seemed clearly to be an alcoholic, and perhaps even a violent one. It was not until almost seventeen years had passed that some answers emerged... The case came to life again on a***

***December evening in 1975, and it was Katie herself who revived it during a conversation at the apartment of a man named Doug Shelmerdine, who was her daughter Daphne's common-law husband...***

## Scene 5 / In the Shelmerdine Apartment

**DOUG:** Katie, ya want a joint?

**KATIE:** Oh, Doug, you know I don't do that stuff.

**DOUG:** Oh, why not? Come on. Do you good, wind you down. You're so uptight, you're wired.

**KATIE:** Mmm.

**DOUG:** Jesus, Katie... Look at you.

**KATIE:** Oh... Must I?

**DOUG:** How many times do I have to say it? Or Daphne? Leave him, Katie, get outta there. That bastard is a drunken, useless, dangerous... What the hell are you staying there for anyway?

**KATIE** (*placatingly*): Oh, Doug. I know, I know. Please... just drop it. Okay?

**DOUG:** No, I won't. I wanna know. Now, why do you put up with that goddamned alcoholic? Why, Katie? Why?

**KATIE:** Doug please, I can't ——

**DOUG:** You can! Now, tell me? Why are you there? Why don't you leave him? Why?

**KATIE:** Because Sandy killed my husband in 1959 and I watched him do it, that's why! And he told me... he told me what to tell the police and I did it... and I've been living in fear... ever since. Ever since then.

**DOUG:** No shit? That's unreal. That is unreal! But, Katie, it's okay... it's okay. I can help. I can. I know some cops. I can get you help right now...

**GREENSPAN:** ***Douglas Shelmerdine did indeed know some cops. By a bizarre coincidence Shelmerdine had moved from the wrong side of the law to the dark side of the law: he happened to be a paid police informer — a fact about which Katie knew absolutely nothing. Shelmerdine wasted little time, and in February 1976 a meeting was arranged in his apartment between Katie and Constable Raymond Thibeau of the RCMP.***

**THIBEAU:** All right, Mrs. Harper. Tell me about it.

**KATIE** (*quite calm*): Ah, well... there isn't much to tell, really. My husband, John Down, went to bed early on the night of June 1. Late that night Sandy Harper came over to our house. And he wanted to... well, he made a pass at me, and I said, "No way; my husband's sleeping upstairs." And he said, "Well, I'll fix that." So, he went upstairs, and I went up a few moments later and I saw him bent over John's bed and he was smothering him with a pillow. He forced me to make love after that... I mean he as much as raped me. Then he went back up and lifted John out of the bed and put him through the window so that he fell on the grass beside the house. He threatened me and my children if I ever said a word... I mean, I was absolutely terrified, and I did what he told me.

**THIBEAU:** I see, I see... All right, Mrs. Harper, I'm going to get moving on this right away. We'll be in touch. Very soon.

**GREENSPAN:** ***A week later Thibeau and another officer named Cameron had a long interview with Katie, and this one was taped...***

## Scene 6 / In an Office at the Police Station

**THIBEAU:** You've got three children?

**KATIE:** Yes, I do.

**CAMERON:** Are two from your... ah, first ——

**KATIE:** Two from the first marriage, yes. Sherry is his.

**CAMERON:** I see. How old is Sherry now?

**KATIE:** She's fourteen. And... you know all of the kids have been, you know, I mean really terrified of him, especially when he's been drinking, because, I mean, one minute he's fine then the next minute...

**THIBEAU:** I see. I see. Over the years has he threatened you again?

**KATIE:** Yes, he has. I mean there's always been... you know, little sly remarks from him. But four years ago he really did threaten us with a gun and... ah, he was... he was going to kill all of us, but we managed to stop him... and after, Kathy went into hysterics and that was the night she told me he'd been molesting her since she was ten years old.

**CAMERON:** Okay, okay, Katie. Go back now to... ah, 1959. Why did you move in with him after something like this, when you knew he was a murderer?

**KATIE:** Because I was afraid not to. And I was afraid for my kids.

**CAMERON:** Okay, but why did you marry him?

**KATIE:** Well, it didn't really make much difference at that point.

**THIBEAU:** Ah... Katie there was some mention of your husband having taken some pills, some sleeping pills, back then. Do you have any idea where they came from?

**KATIE:** I've no idea. And... ah, you know the autopsy back then said it was barbiturates, you know, and it didn't show he'd been smothered and I sat there and thought... well, Jesus Murphy, if it didn't show up on the autopsy report no one'll ever believe me.

**THIBEAU** (*to Cameron*): Okay?

**CAMERON:** Okay. I think...

**GREENSPAN:** ***But then the police made a somewhat curious demand. They said they would go no further with the case unless Katie took a lie detector test and six days later she was introduced to Sergeant Charles Koppang, the examiner...***

**KOPPANG:** Okay. Okay... Well, Katie, it looks fine. It looks just fine.

**KATIE:** Good. That's ——

**KOPPANG** (*quickly*): Except for two questions, ah, Katie. There's two areas where I don't think you've told me the complete truth.

**KATIE** (*subdued*): Which? What areas?

**KOPPANG:** Ah, well the first is when I asked if you gave sodium amytal to John... and the second is when I asked if you deliberately helped anyone in any way to kill John... Everything else is okay, but... ah, there were reactions to these two areas, and I wonder if you want to explain them.

**KATIE** (*quietly*): Yeah, okay, I guess I do. I can explain.

**KOPPANG** (*formal*): Do you want to have any further conversation with Sergeant Cameron and Constable Thibeau about this?

**KATIE:** Yes, all right. I wouldn't mind.

*In another room in the police station.*

**THIBEAU:** Go ahead, Katie, slowly, because I'm writing this down.

**KATIE:** Well,... it ah, all started jokingly, you know. I must have had an argument with my husband or something. I said something to Sandy to the effect that I wished my husband was dead, I mean, we all say these things, some time or another. And Sandy said I'll do away with him for you, and I said okay, not taking him serious, but he must have been I guess... Well, one evening my husband was tired and wanted to sleep so I gave him three sleeping pills. And he went to bed. Around 11:00 or 11:30 Sandy came over and he made sexual advances towards me, and I said, look, just no way, my husband was asleep. And then Sandy went upstairs. He made me go with him. Then he took the pillow and smothered John. He also made me lift his legs to get him over to the window when we slid him out. I will never forget the thud as long as I live when he hit the sidewalk. Sandy told me what to say...All these years and these threats...I just know that I have lived in sheer hell for years.

**THIBEAU:** All right, Katie, will you sign that?

**KATIE:** Yes, yes...ah, yes, I'll sign it.

**GREENSPAN:** ***The rest of Katie's story checked out on the lie detector. So, as of March 1, 1976, the police had this story. Were charges laid at last? Not yet. It was not until October 14, 1977, more than eighteen years after John Down died, that a charge of murder was laid — a first-degree murder charge against Katie Harper alone. Sandy was not charged or tried. Why? Well, despite all their investigation, the police were still unable to make a case against him beyond what Katie herself had said — and they must have decided that she was simply not enough to build a prosecution on, especially since they had evidently decided that she was a murderer herself. It was Lawrence Greenberg, Q.C. who was defending Katie when her trial began in Winnipeg in September 1978. The very effective George Dangerfield was the Crown attorney in charge of the case. The Crown began with some medical evidence. Dr. Strawbridge, the man who had said in 1959 that there was a lethal quantity of barbiturate in John Down's body, now had a different view...***

## Scene 7 / In Court

**CROWN:** Doctor, can you make any comment about the level of drug found in the deceased's body?

**STRAWBRIDGE:** Well, this is what one would normally term a reasonably high therapeutic level. This concentration is not unusual in a therapeutic sense...

**GREENSPAN:** ***So what had been a lethal dose of sodium amytal — a very common sleeping pill in the pre-Valium days of 1959 — was now described as being within the normal therapeutic range. And there would be more to come on this question.***

***A number of the Downs' neighbours testified for the Crown...***

**CROWN:** Now, Mrs. Sadler, some weeks before he died, do you recall whether John Down had an operation?
**SADLER:** Yes, I do.
**CROWN:** And during the time he was in hospital, what, if anything, did you see at the Down home?
**SADLER:** I saw a man come down the stairs.
**CROWN:** Yes. What time was this?
**SADLER:** About 7:30 in the morning.
**CROWN:** Do you recall how he was dressed?
**SADLER:** He had no shirt on.
**CROWN:** Now, did you ever see that man again?
**SADLER:** Yes. After the funeral.
**CROWN:** Were you introduced to him?
**SADLER:** Yes. I was.
**CROWN:** And what name did he go by?
**SADLER:** Sandy. Harper. Sandy Harper.

**GREENSPAN:** ***What Mrs. Sadler saw from her kitchen window was, if true, of some significance because Katie had always denied having an affair with Sandy Harper before her husband's death.***

***Margaret Marshall, the wife of a good friend of John Down's, also testified for the Crown...***

**CROWN:** Mrs. Marshall, I understand that a short time after the funeral Katie and her children came to stay with you?
**MARSHALL:** Yes.
**CROWN:** Now, were there any instances involving you and Katie?
**MARSHALL:** Well, right away she was receiving phone calls from a man named Mr. Harper. And then...and then one night she and I were walking...

## Scene 8 / On the Street at Night

**KATIE:** Ah, it's a nice night. Warm for June, isn't it?

**MARSHALL:** It is, I guess... Katie, ah... you know, Katie, there's a lot of rumours going around...

**KATIE:** What kind of rumours?

**MARSHALL:** Well, I'm hearing... People have been saying that John didn't die accidentally.

**KATIE:** Well, if John did die accidentally nobody'll ever be able to prove it...

**GREENSPAN:** ***Mrs. Marshall's evidence was extremely confusing; in fact, it was hard to understand why the Crown had called her at all. But, in another strange twist to the case, she was to offer a different, much more incriminating version of the story later on.***

***The keys to Dangerfield's case were, of course, Katie's own statements. And it was here that the Harper trial became unique. First,* voir dire *was held with the jury absent, in order for the judge to determine the voluntariness of Katie's statements. George Dangerfield stood up and announced very clearly just what he wanted admitted...***

**CROWN:** I intend to offer in evidence the taped recording of the interview with Cameron and Thibeau, and their final brief interview with her. Also, if Your Lordship permits, what took place in her interview with Koppang. Not what she said to him, but just what happened, and that after the polygraph test he took her back to the officers. Just so the jury will understand that five-hour gap in time.

**GREENSPAN:** ***Despite strenuous efforts on the defence's part, the judge ruled both of Katie's statements to be voluntary. The jury returned, and the Crown called Thibeau and Cameron to lead the evidence of her statements and to play the tape. He then called Koppang as his last witness for ten minutes only, merely to explain what he had done with Katie for the time they were together. But then, Lawrence Greenberg got up to cross-examine...***

**GREENBERG:** Sergeant, just to clear this up, did you ever read the last statement Katie gave Cameron and Thibeau?

**KOPPANG:** Yes, I did.

**GREENBERG:** And did this match up with what she had told you?

**KOPPANG:** Ah, pretty well, yes.

**GREENBERG:** Okay, and you didn't write down your conversation with her after your test was over, did you?

**KOPPANG:** I don't believe I did, no.

**GREENBERG:** So, what you're going from, then, is the best of what you recollect was said to you two years ago?

**KOPPANG:** Yes.

**GREENSPAN:** ***The stage was set. Koppang was the last witness for the Crown. Greenberg had already indicated that he was calling no evidence for the defence, so the trial was, at this point, over. Or it could have been. Except that under the pressure of events, the very senior Crown attorney thought he saw an opening, and he made a mistake: he got up to re-examine his last witness...***

**CROWN:** Ah, just before you step down, Sergeant...when Mr. Greenberg asked you if Mrs. Harper's last statement was the same as what she had told you, you said, quote, "Pretty well the same," end quote. Now what...in which way did it differ?

**KOPPANG:** Well...ah, she told them (*reading*), quote, "One evening my husband was tired and wanted to sleep so I gave him three sleeping pills," end quote. The difference is that she had advised me that, yes, she gave him three sleeping pills in his coffee without him knowing it.

**CROWN:** I see. Thank you. That's the case for the Crown, My Lord.

**GREENSPAN:** ***And the trial proceeded to counsel's addresses to the jury — but the fatal damage was done. By leading evidence of what Katie had stated to Koppang, and after specifically saying he would not lead such evidence, Dangerfield had made an irreversible slip. Koppang's improper testimony was enormously prejudicial to Katie; without this evidence of secret drugging, the jury would have found it very hard to find planning and premeditation. But, in the upshot, they did find them: Katie Harper was convicted of first-degree murder and sentenced to life imprisonment.***

***Two and a half years later, though, the Supreme Court of Canada took only eight minutes to unanimously order a new trial based on the error that had occurred on the last question of an otherwise straightforward trial.***

***Katie had been in jail for those two and a half years, but now she was released again. The case wasn't over yet, and before the new trial***

***began, some new characters came into the picture; Sandy Harper's first wife, Rose, and his daughter Sandra…***

## Scene 9/In Rose Harper's Apartment

**SANDRA:** I can't stand it, Mom, I just can't stand it! Have you seen last week's *Maclean's*?

**ROSE:** Sandra, calm yourself. That is no state of mind for a Sunday before church.

**SANDRA:** But, Mom, they're doing it again! The articles in *Maclean's* — they're impli-implicating Dad again, the same way they were two years ago: they're saying he was involved in k-killing John Down with Katie!

**ROSE:** Oh dear. I thought we were past that by now.

**SANDRA:** Well, we're not, because there's going to be a new trial and it'll all be news again and I-just-can't-stand-it!

**ROSE:** Sandra, be quiet…Call your father. I think we should talk to him. Yes, for the good of his soul it's time for us to talk to him.

*Later.*

**ROSE:** Good morning, Alexander. Come in. How are you?

**SANDY:** Mornin', Rose, ah…A Happy New Year to you…Bit late…[*He laughs.*]

**SANDRA:** Dad! Have you seen last week's *Maclean's*! They're connecting you to John Down's death again.

**SANDY:** Oh. Is it…Is that what this is about?

**ROSE:** Alexander, sit down. You gave me a hint a long time ago. I want the whole story now.

**SANDRA:** Please, Dad.

**SANDY** (*after a pause*): I got a call from Katie that night. I…I went over to the house. Went upstairs. He was…He was almost gone.

**SANDRA:** What do you mean?

**SANDY:** He was drugged. I…I went to put a pillow over his face and I…I couldn't do it. I…I just couldn't do it. I went back down and I told her. I said she could do what she had to do but I wasn't going to kill anybody. So, sh…she went upstairs and…and did…what she had to do. And then later I went up and helped her throw the body out the window.

**SANDRA:** Oh, Dad. Dad. Is that what happened?
**SANDY:** Yeah, yeah. That's what happened.
**ROSE:** Alexander, God has been with you today. But now you must go on. You must tell this to the police. Will you?
**SANDY:** Yes, Rose. All right, Rose.

**GREENSPAN:** ***It wasn't that simple though, because after sleeping on the question and consulting a lawyer, David Margolis, Sandy decided that he didn't want to give the police a statement after all. So what happened? His daughter Sandra did instead. And so, when the second trial began in Winnipeg on February 1, 1982, Sandy and Katie Harper were sitting side by side in the prisoner's box.***

***Katie's lawyer now was the very talented, aggressive Hersh Wolch, and Sandy was represented by the equally experienced David Margolis. George Dangerfield once more headed up the prosecution...***

## Scene 10 / In Court

**CROWN:** Members of the jury, you have just heard the charge against these defendants. The nature of the allegation against them, that which the Crown sets out to prove, is that they killed John Bruce Down by a massive overdose of a sleeping drug followed by suffocation when he was unconscious from the drug. They then put his body through the second-floor window...

**GREENSPAN:** ***A massive overdose of drugs. Once more the issue arose: How did John Down die? And once more there was an utterly bizarre twist to this issue. Dangerfield called William Radych, the RCMP chemist who had done the original blood analysis of the barbiturate levels in John Down's body in 1959. Now Radych sprang a surprise on everyone, especially the Crown attorney...***

**CROWN:** Now, this week, Mr. Radych, I understand you had occasion to review your 1959 calculations?
**RADYCH:** Um, yes. And I...ah, I noticed that I had made a...well, a mathematical error back then, so I...ah, I have to correct my initial figures.
**CROWN:** And what did you correct them to, please?

**RADYCH:** The blood was found to contain 1.2 milligrams of alcohol...er, no, not alcohol, I mean amobarbital per 100 millilitres of blood.

**CROWN:** All right. So we're absolutely clear on this, you reviewed your 1959 calculations...

**RADYCH:** Yes, and I, uh, got 2 milligrams back then instead of 1.2 because I, uh...well, I multiplied by the wrong number.

**CROWN** (*unhappily*): Thank you.

**GREENSPAN:** ***An unbelievable turn of events. This was now the third set of figures as to the presence of drugs in John Down's body, and Hersh Wolch had something to say in the absence of the jury...***

**WOLCH:** My Lord, I want to make a motion that the charges against my client be dismissed, because of what happened this afternoon. I want to point out that the history of this matter is that my client went through a preliminary hearing, a trial, was convicted, and spent two and a half years in prison and the major thrust of the Crown case against her was the evidence of excessive barbiturates in the system. Now, frankly, My Lord, I'm frightened at how close we've come to having a case concluded on evidence we now learn was significantly wrong.

**GREENSPAN:** ***Mr. Justice Guy Kroft refused Wolch's motion. In the midst of all this extreme tension there was one moment of high comedy. The two accused were, of course, sitting beside each other in the prisoner's box, as far apart as possible. Then, one day, as everyone returned to court after the lunch break...***

**KATIE:** Oh, my God, he's drunk! Mr. Wolch! Someone! He's rotten drunk! I won't sit beside him! I won't! Get him away from me! You...

**WOLCH:** All right, Katie, all right. Katie, it's okay. Mr. Margolis, I think your client is somewhat...

**MARGOLIS:** I can see that. Sandy, what the hell are you doing? Do you want your bail revoked?

**KATIE:** Will you get him away from me!

**MARGOLIS:** Give him some coffee, quick. Before the judge comes back in. Jesus, Sandy!

**DANGERFIELD:** Well, well. A tipsy client, David?

**MARGOLIS:** Christ!

**CLERK:** Here's the coffee. Mr. Harper, drink this.

**SANDY:** Coffee! Y'want me t'drink coffee wi' *her*...here? Do you think I'm *crazy*? I won't touch it. I...I won't drink a drop 'less she tastes it first!

**GREENSPAN:** ***Sandy's bail was indeed revoked despite his having the best one-liner of the trial.***

***The case against Katie Harper was almost exactly what it had been four years before at the first trial. Mrs. Marshall, the woman Katie lived with for a few weeks after John's death, repeated her disturbing exchange with Katie...***

**MARSHALL:** We were walking home one evening and I told her that people are saying that she did something to him, to her husband. And she said, "Well, they'll never be able to prove it."

**GREENSPAN:** ***But this was a* very *different phrasing from the last trial, and Hersh Wolch jumped on it...***

**WOLCH:** Mrs. Marshall, you do agree that you testified at a hearing four years ago?

**MARSHALL:** Yes, I did.

**WOLCH:** And you know what you said then?

**MARSHALL:** Well, I was so mixed up at the time that...ah...

**WOLCH:** Well, let us review it. You were asked, quote, "Did she make any comment?" end quote, and you answered, quote, "She told me that if John did die accidentally, that nobody would ever be able to prove it," end quote. Now do you agree you said that last time?

**MARSHALL:** Yes, because I remember being questioned by the press after. Everyone was jumping on me for saying it that way. I just mixed up my words probably. I've thought about that conversation many, many times.

**WOLCH:** But clearly your memory does not get better after four more years?

**MARSHALL** (*defiantly*): Maybe it does.

**WOLCH:** Maybe it does?

**MARSHALL:** Maybe.

**WOLCH:** So, perhaps we'll wait another four years and we'll get even closer to the accurate ——

**CROWN:** Objection! There's no need to belittle the witness. I submit that sarcastic remarks ——

**WOLCH:** Well, did you say it that way once or more than once?

**MARSHALL:** I don't remember.

**WOLCH:** Well, the transcript has you saying it that way at page 371 and then again, quite a bit later, exactly the same at page 386.

**MARSHALL:** Well, I erred if I said it that way.

**WOLCH:** Twice?

**MARSHALL:** Well, I was nervous.

**WOLCH:** And you're not nervous now?

**MARSHALL:** No. But I'm telling the truth now.

**WOLCH:** You weren't telling the truth then?

**MARSHALL:** Yes, I was.

**WOLCH:** Well, you say the press jumped on you back then?

**MARSHALL:** Yes, because of the error I made.

**WOLCH:** Because of the error you made?

**MARSHALL:** Well, they said it was an error.

**WOLCH:** The press told you you'd given wrong evidence? I'm just asking how could the press know what your right evidence was or your wrong evidence?

**MARSHALL:** I don't know.

**GREENSPAN:** ***A good cross-examination, and a necessary one, because there is no question that Marshall's version of the dialogue was much more incriminating this time around.***

***But what about the case against Sandy Harper? The Crown did call his daughter, Sandra, to testify to what her father had told her, but that statement certainly did not incriminate him in murder, only of helping Katie push a dead body out a window, which indeed was what David Margolis' defence was. But the Crown had more, and they got it, ironically enough, from two of the other children of Sandy and Rose Harper...***

**CROWN:** Mr. Harper, how old are you now?

**NORMAN:** Thirty-eight.

**CROWN:** And you are the son of Sandy Harper?

**NORMAN:** Yes.

**CROWN:** I wonder if I can take you back to when you were fifteen, in 1959. I understand that something happened that has remained with you all these years?

**NORMAN:** Yes. Ah, I was... I was in bed at night, sleeping, and then... I... ah, I woke up. I heard... I heard this... this shouting from downstairs.

## Scene 11 / In Norman Harper's Bedroom in 1959

**ROSE** (*from downstairs*): Alexander? What is it?

*Sandy is crying.*

**ROSE:** What is it?
**SANDY:** I... I... Oh God... I... I just... killed somebody. I killed someone...

## Scene 12 / In Court

**CROWN:** Go on. What else?
**NORMAN:** I didn't hear any more. I closed the door and, ah, that was the end of it.

**GREENSPAN:** ***But it wasn't, because there was another child, Denise, Sandy and Rose's oldest daughter; she was thirteen in 1959 and she, too, woke up that night...***

## Scene 13 / The Harper Home in 1959

**SANDY** (*crying*): Oh, Rose, Rose... I've done something terrible.
**ROSE:** Well, it couldn't be that terrible.
**SANDY** (*sobbing*): Oh God... We... we killed a man. We killed a man.

*Denise screams and begins to cry.*

**ROSE** (*sharply*): Denise! Go to bed, right now!

**GREENSPAN:** ***Both statements were very incriminating, and the second***

***one, Denise's version, was incriminating of both Sandy and Katie; this raises a critical issue, perhaps the most contentious legal point of the whole trial. In cases of this nature, it is a fundamental principle of Canadian law that a statement by one co-accused is evidence against that person only and*** **not** ***against the other co-accused. This made for an incredibly complex evidentiary situation and for motion after outraged motion by both defence lawyers for the trial to be stopped and the two accused tried separately...***

## Scene 14/In Court

**JUDGE:** Well, gentlemen, I am not dealing with this matter lightly, but when all is weighed and considered, it seems to me that in a case where the accused are alleged to have been inextricably interwoven in the commission of an offence, that fairness and justice are best served, notwithstanding the problems, in having a joint trial.

**GREENSPAN:** ***One way or another, it seemed, the fates of Katie and Sandy Harper were bound together now. The last key piece of Crown evidence against Sandy was, for a change, not from one of his children, but it was, yes, another statement. Staff Sergeant Stewart was called...***

**CROWN:** Staff Sergeant, if you might turn your attention to January 21, 1981.

**STEWART:** Yes, sir.

**CROWN:** I understand that prior to that time you had received certain information from Rose and Sandra Harper, and as a result of that you arranged for a meeting with Sandy Harper?

**STEWART:** That's correct. He was brought to our office by his lawyer, Mr. Margolis. He was given the police warning and advised that he might be charged with murder. He was asked if he wanted to give a statement to which he replied, quote, "No, sir, not at this time," end quote. The interview was terminated and then Mr. Margolis left the building, leaving Sandy Harper with us...

## Scene 15/In the Police Station in 1981

**GREENSPAN:** ***What followed is a recurring nightmare for all criminal lawyers with clients who talk too much...***

**STEWART:** Wash your hands please, Sandy. We've got to fingerprint you.

**SANDY** (*almost to himself*): I'm not running anymore. I've been running too long.

**GREENSPAN:** ***And that wasn't all. Despite his counsel's advice, Sandy kept talking in the police car all the way to the Winnipeg jail...***

## Scene 16/In the Police Car

**SANDY:** I've been running for nineteen years. Almost drank myself to death. Don't want to see her get off scot-free...

**STEWART:** Sandra told us you went there and he was almost done?

**SANDY:** Well, he was almost done, that's for sure. She done the job. I never killed a man in my life. I... I couldn't even kill an animal. She done the job herself. (*Mumbling*) Tired of runnin'... Too many lies...

**GREENSPAN:** ***There is no question that by 1982 Sandy Harper looked old beyond his sixty-two years — something which may have helped David Margolis, and which certainly hurt Hersh Wolch whose defence was that Katie had been terrified of this man. Not long after this, the Crown closed its case. Hersh Wolch rose to make an opening statement on behalf of Katie Harper...***

## Scene 17/In Court

**WOLCH:** Ladies and Gentlemen, I intend to show that Sandy Harper is, or at least was, a person of a vicious, cruel nature with totally no control, absolute lack of control in sexual matters.

**GREENSPAN:** ***With the jury out, Wolch told the judge that he wanted to lead evidence of Sandy's sexually abusing his step-daughter Kathy. Despite Margolis' objections, the judge admitted the evidence. So twenty-five-year-old Kathy testified, rather painfully, to having been abused in this way from the age of ten to fifteen. Then Katie and John Down's other daughter, Daphne, took the stand...***

**WOLCH:** Can you tell us a little more about your relationship with your mother?

**DAPHNE:** All the years with my mother were beautiful. She was... She was always there. She was more of a friend than I've ever had. She grew up with us is more what it was like. She always softened the blows.

**WOLCH:** All right, now, Daphne, do you recall an incident about two weeks ago, during this trial?

**DAPHNE:** Yes, it was after that man testified about making the mistake on the amount of drugs. My mother came home that evening after court and we all sat down...

## Scene 18 / In the Harper Home

**KATIE** (*weeping*): Oh... God how could they? How could they have done that to me?

**DAPHNE:** All right, Mom. It's all right.

**KATIE:** No, no... it's not... It's not all right. All those years... so many years. They said drug overdose and I... I knew... I knew it wasn't. It couldn't have been... But I couldn't say.... I just couldn't say...

**DAPHNE:** Oh, Mom, I know. Oh, Mom...

**KATIE:** And all that time... all that time he was wrong...

**GREENSPAN:** ***Then it was the turn of Sandy and Katie's daughter Sherry...***

## Scene 19 / In Court

**SHERRY:** My feelings for my Dad... it's... I don't know him as a father. I know him as someone to be frightened of.

**WOLCH:** In the course of your growing up, did you have occasion to see physical violence in your house?

**SHERRY:** There was one... ah, around Christmas time. He came home late. He'd been out... So, then he got a rifle he had behind the freezer. He was... He was going through the house like a madman. We were all trying to hold him down. He was knocking plants over and throwing things, and finally I stopped him...

Ya see, he only listened to me because I was the youngest. And then he turned towards the door and his voice went whiny and he was just like an animal and he said, "Just leave me alone. Just leave me alone or I'll... I'll shoot you and break you all in two"...

**GREENSPAN:** ***On cross-examination, David Margolis, acting for Sandy Harper, raised the obvious implication...***

**MARGOLIS:** Sherry, ah you're trying your best, I suggest to you, to make your mother look like a very nice lady and your father to look like a very bad man?

**SHERRY:** No. You know... No. I would love to... I would love to be able to love my father. I would love to be able to know what it's like to love a father. I'm sorry, but what you're saying just isn't true.

**GREENSPAN:** ***Before David Margolis could begin the evidence for Sandy Harper, George Dangerfield rose to his feet to make a request, a request that would take this already extraordinary case into the realm of the unbelievable...***

**CROWN:** My Lord, I...ah, I want to make a motion to re-open the Crown case and call fresh evidence.

**JUDGE:** What evidence, Mr. Dangerfield?

**CROWN:** The nature of the evidence is that of a witness about whom we only learned last week. She is a nun who moves about quite a bit in the course of her duties and we were only able to speak with her last night. She seems to have been a prison visitor and had a series of visits with Mrs. Harper, and Mrs. Harper said something to her that...ah, well...that is a confession in the view of the Crown.

**JUDGE:** Yes, yes, well...I suppose I'd better hear arguments from the three of you on this...

**GREENSPAN:** ***This was an utterly extraordinary situation: At the very end of a six-week trial, a trial taking place twenty-three years after the alleged murder, the Crown was seeking to lead evidence it claimed to have only uncovered that very week. And not just any piece of evidence, but an alleged confession to a murder! After hearing a very lengthy and heated argument Mr. Justice Kroft ruled that the Crown should be allowed to lead this evidence...***

**CROWN:** Sister, with which Order are you associated?

**SISTER:** I'm with the Sisters of Our Lady of Charity.

**CROWN:** And I understand that in your duties for your parish you had occasion to be at the Bardal Funeral Home and you met someone by the name of Katie Harper working there?

**SISTER:** Yes, on many occasions. She was of great assistance to us. She was certainly very good with the bereaved families.

**CROWN:** Now, I understand that Mrs. Harper found herself in... some difficulties and you learned that she was at the Portage Correctional Institute?

**SISTER:** Yes, that's correct.

**CROWN:** And you went out to visit her?

**SISTER:** Yes, four or five times.

**CROWN** (*carefully*): All right, now in discussing the events of 1959, what if anything did she tell you of her part?

**SISTER:** From what I remember of it, she always spoke that it was something that she and Sandy Harper had done together.

**CROWN:** And what did she say that led you to that conclusion?

**SISTER:** Well, she would have spoke about how it happened...ah, insofar as either drugs, smothering, out the window, um, and then you know...um, what led me to believe was...well, that I think I was kind of shocked.

**CROWN:** Did you see any indication of remorse?

**SISTER:** Well, I guess that's hard to say. But something that stayed with me was that she remarked that if she had to do it all over again she'd do the very same thing...

**CROWN:** Mr. Wolch?

**WOLCH:** Speaking in general terms, Sister, if someone is saying they're innocent of a crime, you wouldn't expect them to say I'm sorry for what I did. Isn't that true?

**SISTER:** Oh, no.

**WOLCH:** Now, Sister, I suggest to you that the line that sticks out for you is when Katie said "If I had to do it all over again, I would"?

**SISTER:** Yes.

**WOLCH:** Well, in the course of dealing with her did you come to appreciate her strong feeling towards her children?

**SISTER:** Yes, I did.

**WOLCH:** Well, I suggest that in the course of dealing with Katie you saw a letter from her to her children where she used that very same phrase in the context of protecting them over the years?

**SISTER:** Yes, I have.

**WOLCH:** If I had to do it all over again, I would?
**SISTER:** Yes, I've seen that.

**GREENSPAN:** *And that was the Sister's evidence. In my view it was vague, ambiguous, and highly prejudicial — not only in the way in which it came before the Court, but also in the way in which it was presented. The Sister should never have been allowed to testify that she got an* **impression** *that the crime had been done by both Sandy and Katie, or that she had an* **impression** *of no remorse.*

*There was only one witness called for Sandy Harper. This was his middle daughter, Pam. Her evidence was essentially that her father was not the vicious brute that Katie's children had said he was, and that from her observations, she did not think Katie had lived in fear of Sandy during their life together. And that, finally, ended the evidence. The Crown had no more late surprises to spring. Instead, it was time for the closing addresses. Hersh Wolch went first...*

**WOLCH:** Ladies and gentlemen, shortly after John Down died came the one thing that causes the whole problem: the inquest. And what is the cause of death at the inquest? Barbiturate poisoning. They didn't get the drug right, and they didn't get the amount right. And you heard Mr. Radych at trial here. He was wrong twice. But imagine what this did to Katie Harper? From that point on her position is absolutely hopeless. What does she do? Come forward and say to the police: Oh no, no, I... I saw Sandy Harper kill my husband. And they say: You're a nurse. He died by drug poisoning. What happens to her in that case? Literally, she gets hanged. Now, we aren't saying that she lived in a state of fear all those years because Sandy Harper kept her a prisoner; that would be ridiculous. We're saying that because of the inquest finding, she had nowhere to turn. She's been the victim of a set of circumstances that just boggle the mind. It is time that the person who killed John Down and ruined the lives of so many people was brought to justice, and he's before you at this very time. In the words of those who know her far better than I, Katie is a beautiful, caring, loving, compassionate human being. Justice will only be done if she is acquitted of this charge.

**MARGOLIS:** Ladies and gentlemen, we are not presenting my client, Mr. Harper, as a model of virtue. He himself admits he is not. But that does not make him a murderer. I submit to you that Katie Harper's first husband's demise was a very drastic one.

She chose for her second husband's demise a slightly more diplomatic way of getting him out of the picture: She was going to do it by accusing *him* of what *she* had done in 1959.

**CROWN:** The evidence here, ladies and gentlemen, is of these two people working hand in glove to kill John Down. We have two people entwined together and a husband who is hated by one and in the way of the other. Fear played absolutely no part in Katie Harper's actions, absolutely none. Imagine a man so rash as to go to another man's house and murder him right in front of his wife, and walk away with the threat that if you tell anyone I'll come and kill you? What possible hope could he have that such a threat would sustain him? How could such a threat hold her silent? It couldn't. It couldn't, because there wasn't any threat. Ladies and gentlemen, John Down was murdered on June 2, 1959, by two people who wanted him out of the way, who conceived a plan to murder and carried it out to its ghastly conclusion.

**GREENSPAN:** ***The jury in the second Harper trial deliberated for nine hours, before reaching their verdict. When they returned, they convicted Katie Harper of first-degree murder, and Sandy Harper of second-degree murder. Katie, they had decided, had planned John Down's murder in advance; Sandy had not been part of that plan, but had helped kill him that night.***

***And was that the end? Of course not. There was one last extraordinary twist to the strange case of John Down's death. Both Wolch and Margolis launched appeals to the Manitoba Court of Appeal. Judgement was delivered by Chief Justice Samuel Freedman, a very distinguished jurist near the end of a brilliant career...***

## Scene 20 / In Appeal Court

**FREEDMAN:** Many grounds of appeal have been raised before us. We have already given much time and effort to this case and would not shrink from the task of giving further time and effort if we felt it to be necessary. But we do not find it necessary, for in our view both appeals can be disposed of on one clear ground — namely, that the issue of manslaughter was not adequately dealt with in the charge to the jury. It is very much in the public interest that the Harper proceedings be brought to a just end. Taking that course, we would set aside the convictions and substitute in each case a conviction for manslaughter. We will now hear counsel on sentence.

**GREENSPAN:** ***There was shock and jubilation on the part of both defendants and their counsel. What had happened? Well, the fact is that the trial judge* had *charged the jury on manslaughter. And furthermore, there seems to be virtually no way that a double manslaughter was a possible verdict in the Harper case. Katie and Sandy had either killed John Down together, or one of them had: it wasn't a double manslaughter case. Why then had the distinguished Chief Justice ruled this way? It seems fair to speculate that he and his colleagues had seen the errors in that long trial and known that the verdict could not be upheld; at the same time, it must have seemed intolerable that this affair continue for yet a third go-around. Chief Justice Freedman seems to have decided to end the Harper saga once and for all. What about the sentence? Well, that's where the Court wrapped things up. A sentence in a normal domestic manslaughter case usually runs somewhere between three and five years...***

**FREEDMAN:** We will now hear counsel on sentence...

**WOLCH:** Well, My Lord, given the normal range of sentences in these cases, and bearing in mind that my client has already spent more than two and a half years in jail, then ——

**FREEDMAN:** Mr. Wolch, you aren't suggesting that we should let her walk out of here?

**WOLCH:** Ah, no, My Lord.

**GREENSPAN:** ***And in the end, this is what the Chief Justice said...***

**FREEDMAN:** Having heard the submission of counsel and keeping in mind the time spent in custody, we impose, in each case, a sentence of imprisonment for twenty years.

**GREENSPAN:** ***And that, quite effectively, ended the Harper case. The manslaughter ruling was, in law, just about as unjustifiable as the twenty-year sentence. If either side tried to appeal further, the other side had a lethal counter-appeal readied. The judges of the Court of Appeal withdrew, leaving a stupefied array of very senior lawyers to figure out what had just happened. And it was Hersh Wolch, trying to***

***explain it to the press, who had what is probably the definitive last word…***

**WOLCH:** I'm in shock. I don't think…I don't think anything could surprise me anymore after this. If…if John Down were to walk into this room right now, I don't think I'd even blink.

# Producer's Notes

John Down died in 1959. It was not until 1982 that the trial of the woman who had been Down's wife and of the man who had been her lover twenty-three years earlier — and later became her husband — began in Winnipeg. Katie and Sandy Harper were facing a charge of murder in connection with John Down's death.

The mills of justice grind almost as slowly as the mills of God (even if they do not grind anywhere as exceedingly fine) but for all that it is very rare for people to be put on trial for a crime after the passage of nearly a quarter of a century. The case of Katie and Sandy Harper, in addition to many other complex legal issues, raised the question of whether it is possible, even in theory, to uncover facts and arrive at a just result after such a long period.

Once again it was Guy Gavriel Kay who became attracted to the difficulties posed by the labyrinthine story of the Harpers, and he proceeded to unravel them with his customary enthusiasm and lucidity. The result was, I believe, one of the best scripts and productions of "The Scales of Justice".

Four actors stood out among the many first-rate performers in the exceptionally large cast. Jayne Eastwood's Katie Harper was a model of good character-portrayal. She proved once again that acting need not lack drama and intensity in being totally realistic. Frank Perry, possibly the most versatile actor among the regulars on "The Scales of Justice", rendered the difficult role of Sandy Harper with polished perfection. Lawrence Dane made every line count as Crown Attorney George Dangerfield. And Saul Rubinek, regarded by many as the most powerful and intelligent young actor in Canada, gave a great portrayal of defence lawyer Hersh Wolch.

The investigating officers played by Alan Fawcett, Jim Morris, Bill Lynn, and Chuck Shamata set a standard for the portrayal of policemen. The actresses Nicky Guadagni, Michelle Claire, Pixie

Bigelow, and Rosalind Goldsmith performed their smaller but very demanding roles as professionals do: while they were in front of the microphone, they were the stars of the show. So was Ruth Springford, in the role of Sandy Harper's first wife. And even in this company veteran actress Kay Hawtrey stood out with her portrayal of a nun, the prosecution's last surprise witness.

The sound was Derek Stubb's, the sound- and musical-effects Stephanie McKenna's, and credit for the superb cast belonged to Anne Weldon Tait and Cathryn Kester, two excellent casting directors whose recent departure from radio drama is public broadcasting's loss and private industry's gain. As usual, it was Edward L. Greenspan's commentary that tied one of the most puzzling cases of Canadian legal history into an instructive package.

G.J.

# The Thirty-Three-Thousand-Pound Trap

*William Deverell*

## The Cast

Commentary by Edward L. Greenspan, Q.C.

| | |
|---|---|
| **GARY SEXTON** | himself |
| **WILLIAM DEVERELL** | himself |
| **SPECIAL AGENT ERNIE STAPLES** | Chuck Shamata |
| **PADDY MURPHY** | Neil Munro |
| **BIG SID WARD** | Michael Hogan |

With the support of (in alphabetical order): Don Allison, David Bolt, Ian Deakin, Ken James, Paul Kligman, Sean McCann, James Morris, Frank Perry, Angelo Rizacos, Jack Scott, Paul Soles, Ray Stancer, John Stocker, and Marian Waldman

## Scene 1 / In Court

**JUDGE:** Gary Sexton, you're a smart young man, and you should have used your brains in a business other than marijuana smuggling. You and your friends brought into Newfoundland four thousand pounds of the drug, and I have to say you're a menace to the youth. Ten years in penitentiary.

**GARY** (*horrified*): Ten years! How in the name of God am I going to get through that?

**LAWYER:** Keep it down, Gary.

**COURT OFFICER:** Order in the court!

**GARY:** I can't do it. I won't do it.

**GREENSPAN:** ***Gary Sexton, the archetypal Newfoundland rowdyman, confounded prison authorities by becoming a model prisoner at Springhill Jail in Nova Scotia. There he formed a prison chapter of the Junior Chamber of Commerce and, on May 22, 1977, a year after his sentencing, he was released on a day pass to attend the national Jaycee convention in Halifax. Gary Sexton took the train to Halifax, registered, had a wonderful time, then flew to South America...***

## Scene 2 / Street in Colombia

**STREET DEALER:** Hey, meester, you like Colombian grass, coca, I connect you, real groovy, man.

**GARY:** You're a menace to the youth, my darlin' man.

**STREET DEALER:** You like meet my seester, maybe?

**GARY:** It's a civil day in Bogota, Paddy, b'y, a grand day to do a little business with Alfredo Gomez.

**PADDY:** He's not going to be happy. That four thousand pounds, he fronted it.

**GARY:** Alfredo is a businessman, b'y. In business, sometimes you win, sometimes you lose.

**GREENSPAN:** *Alfredo Gomez, padre to one of the seven Mafia families that controlled Colombia's major export industry (it is no longer coffee), did indeed seem to understand. Although the* RCMP *had seized four thousand pounds of Gomez's marijuana when Sexton's boys had tried to land it in Newfoundland, he welcomed Sexton and his Canadian friend, Paddy Murphy, with a warm Latin embrace. And he agreed to front them — no cash down — another thirty-three thousand pounds of Colombian gold.*

*And thus commenced the saga of a gang of Newfoundland rogues and the thirty-three-thousand-pound trap that was set for them. A saga that commenced in Bogota, Colombia, and ended in a courtroom in British Columbia one year later, with seventeen persons on trial. My name is Edward Greenspan, and in this episode of "The Scales of Justice" we will be looking at a police sting that was either brilliantly conceived or, as the defence lawyers argued, the most remarkable example of police entrapment in Canada's history. The story you are about to hear has been reconstructed from the transcripts of the trial in the County Court of British Columbia...*

*When the matter finally came to court some of the seventeen accused elected to be tried by a judge alone while others elected a judge and jury. As a result, there were two trials and six different lawyers involved. Since the issues were identical in both trials, we have condensed events in court into one trial. William Deverell, one of the defence lawyers, cross-examined the man who ended up being the Crown's principal witness — American Special Agent Ernie Staples...*

## Scene 3 / In Court

**DEVERELL:** Agent Staples, the name Alfredo Gomez appears in your files, does it not?
**STAPLES:** Yes, sir, that's the name on the file in this case.
**DEVERELL:** Is that a man who is suspected of being able to make marijuana available in large quantities?
**STAPLES:** Yes.
**DEVERELL:** He's an acquaintance of Nilo Batista, isn't he?
**STAPLES:** I believe so.

**GREENSPAN:** ***Alfredo Gomez. Nilo Batista. Although they never testified, their shadows were cast across the courtroom, and they are central to the story. The deal made was this: Gomez would supply the cargo, Batista the boat. They met with Sexton at the Acapulco Yacht Club in Mexico...***

## Scene 4/Cocktail Bar at the Yacht Club

**GOMEZ:** *Salud y dinero!* Health and wealth, the important things.
**GARY:** To the high seas.
**GOMEZ:** Nilo, you see he is not like the Americanos, an honest face. Gary comes from a country called Newfoundland.
**BATISTA:** But Newfoundland ees on the East Coast, no? My yacht, she ees in Costa Rica, on Pacific.
**GARY:** Then we'll take her to British Columbia.
**BATISTA:** And the fee? Forgeev, I sound like a, you say, mercenary.
**GARY:** I'm short. I'll have to make some phone calls. I'll have the money in two weeks.
**GOMEZ:** Eighty t'ousan', yes? And another hundred and fifty t'ousan' on delivery, which you will pay to my captain when the sheep arrive in Canada, *si*?
**GARY:** Your captain?
**BATISTA:** Oh, yes, I provide Captain Pierera, four crew.
**GARY:** Four crew? Uh, you don't mind if I send a couple of the b'ys along with them?
**BATISTA:** Ah, *si, si, bueno, bueno*.

**GREENSPAN:** ***Sexton and his friends back in Canada managed to put together the eighty-thousand-dollar down payment. And the amiable Nilo Batista found a way to enforce collection of the balance — and at the same time obtain an iron-clad guarantee that his hundred-and-ten-foot motor yacht would not be seized or he, his captain, or crew arrested by the authorities. At the trial, a U.S. narcotics agent in charge of the case, Phillip Vandiver, admitted to defence lawyers Sid Simons and William Deverell that Batista was, in official jargon, an OCI — Official Co-operating Individual.***

# Scene 5 / In Court

**VANDIVER:** Yes, he was registered as an OCI with the Drug Enforcement Administration.

**SIMONS:** Is there a vernacular for that position?

**VANDIVER:** There are various terms, sir.

**SIMONS:** What?

**VANDIVER:** One of them is "informant".

**SIMONS:** Yes. What are the others?

**VANDIVER:** Snitch.

**SIMONS:** Right. That is more familiar. Thank you.

**JUDGE 2:** Ah, Mr. Deverell?

**DEVERELL:** Ah, Mr. Batista had prior involvement as a drug smuggler, to your knowledge?

**VANDIVER:** Yes, sir, he did.

**DEVERELL:** He was not a typically penniless Mexican peasant?

**VANDIVER:** No, he was not.

**DEVERELL:** A man of means?

**VANDIVER:** Yes.

**DEVERELL:** And he had a shipping line of some kind?

**VANDIVER:** I understand he was the owner of various ships, but I'm not certain it was a shipping line.

**DEVERELL:** And he was a member of the Acapulco Yacht Club?

**VANDIVER:** Yes, sir.

**DEVERELL:** There's no question he had certain contacts in Colombia capable of supplying marijuana on a large scale?

**VANDIVER:** Yes.

**DEVERELL:** Where's Mr. Batista now? You see, the difficulty is we can't cross-examine him. Do you know where he is?

**VANDIVER:** Well, he was in Acapulco.

**DEVERELL:** Have you made any effort to have him here as a Crown witness?

**VANDIVER:** I don't believe he would appear, sir.

**GREENSPAN:** ***While Gary Sexton put a Canadian team together and arranged for two west-coast fishing boats to meet and off-load from Batista's mother ship, Batista dickered at the U.S. Embassy in Mexico City with members of the American Drug Enforcement Administration (the DEA) and the RCMP. Deverell asked agent Vandiver about the deal that was reached...***

**DEVERELL:** At that meeting the RCMP officers were made aware that Batista was a co-operating individual, is that right?
**VANDIVER:** Yes, sir, that is correct.
**DEVERELL:** And the arrangement was made that as long as Batista assisted the police he wouldn't be charged with any offence?
**VANDIVER:** Yes, sir, that is correct.
**DEVERELL:** And through the services of Batista a certain Captain Pierera came in contact with police authorities?
**VANDIVER:** Yes, sir, that is correct.
**DEVERELL:** And he became the captain of this vessel, the *Tournyn*, isn't that right?
**VANDIVER:** Yes, sir.
**DEVERELL:** And he was also assisting the DEA and indirectly the RCMP?
**VANDIVER:** Yes, sir.
**DEVERELL:** And it was arranged he would not be arrested?
**VANDIVER:** Yes, sir, that is correct.
**DEVERELL:** Is it fair to say that part and parcel of this deal with Batista and Pierera was that all the money they could get and all the money you could help them get they would keep?
**VANDIVER:** Yes, sir, that is correct.

**GREENSPAN:** ***Entrapment: The luring by a law officer of a person into the commission of a crime in order to prosecute him for it. That activity has historically been condemned by the courts of the United States. One need look no further back, for example, than the celebrated recent case of the State*** **versus** ***John De Lorean in which the car manufacturer was acquitted of cocaine dealing by reasons of police entrapment. But as far back as 1928, the eminent jurist Mr. Justice Brandeis of the U.S. Supreme Court said, in the Holmstead case:***

**BRANDEIS:** Our government is the potent, the omnipresent teacher. For good or ill, it teaches the whole people by example... If the government becomes a lawbreaker, it breeds contempt for the law; it invites every man to become a law unto himself; it invites anarchy.

**GREENSPAN:** ***The major problem the defence lawyers faced in the Sexton case, however, was that as of 1979 entrapment had*** **not** ***been recognized as a defence by Canadian courts. The British system of jurisprudence, the well-spring of our Common law, has historically***

*honoured the assumption that the accused should not lightly be allowed to put the conduct of the State in issue. Nevertheless, the defence in the Sexton trial determined to make this a test case of entrapment. But the problem was, how to fit the facts of the case to that defence. The Crown produced neither Gomez nor Batista as witnesses. The accused, anxious not to implicate friends, would decline to take the stand. To build a defence of entrapment, the defence had only one key player to work with. His name was Ernie Staples, an American undercover agent with a B.A. in physics and a master's degree in business administration, who had traded a lucrative career in electronics for the excitement and the danger of a job working the fringes of the drug underworld. On May 23, 1978, in Puntarenas, Costa Rica, aboard the* **Tournyn,** *Batista introduced him to Paddy Murphy, a seaman with a deep-sea ticket in navigation.*

## Scene 6 / Aboard the *Tournyn*

**BATISTA:** Thees ees very good amigo, Ernie. He weell look after all the details, insurance, so on. Ees my agent.

**PADDY:** That is fine. As long as you're not a DEA agent. (*He laughs.*) You look like one, you know.

**BATISTA:** Oh, no, no.

**PADDY:** Yeah, he does.

**STAPLES** (*also laughing*): So you're off to Colombia in what, a few days?

**PADDY:** Soon as I get equipped.

**STAPLES:** Why don't you just tell me what you need. You got it written down there?

**PADDY:** *Una lista de necesidades . . .*

*Paddy hands the list to Staples.*

**STAPLES:** World-band radio, nautical almanac, deep-sea charts. Let's see, you want charts for the British Columbia coast, Strait of Juan de Fuca to Queen Charlotte Sound.

**PADDY:** Yeah, that's right.

**STAPLES:** No problem. Well, who's going to be in charge of the cargo? You can sure get ripped in Colombia. You gotta make sure you get quality as well as quantity.

**PADDY:** Ah, yea, well, that's me, b'y. Ah, Ian and me — he's not here yet — we're going with the ship all the way, anchor to anchor.

**STAPLES:** Good. I'll feel better with some people on board we can trust.

**PADDY:** Yeah, right.

**STAPLES:** How much product you planning to carry?

**PADDY:** Ah, thirty-three thousand pounds.

**STAPLES** (*with a low whistle*): What's that going to set you back?

**PADDY:** Ah, we'll owe our Colombian friends six million. We aim t'make six million after that.

**BATISTA:** Hm. Not bad. Big money.

**STAPLES:** Where you fellows going to store it?

**PADDY:** Lower half-section. She'll carry all of that. She's a beat-up old piece of junk though, isn't she, for a luxury yacht? So, you fellows care to smoke a joint in the wheelhouse?

**STAPLES:** I think I'll take a rain check on that.

**GREENSPAN:** ***Twelve million dollars' worth of marijuana. It would be the largest and most valuable shipment of cannabis ever to enter Canadian waters. Delivering it would be Murphy and Ian and five unofficial police agents — Captain Pierera and his four crewmen. But in case these co-operating individuals proved unreliable, the authorities decided to bug the*** **Tournyn.** ***It was no ordinary bug. They used a Sat-Track transmitter which, when hidden on board the boat, would beam signals to a satellite of the National Aeronautics and Space Administration, the Nimbus-6. The messages would be dumped by ground command to a tracking station at Fairbanks, Alaska, relayed by microwave to the Goddard Space Flight Center at Greenbelt, Maryland, and ultimately passed on to Staff Sergeant Hawkes of the RCMP in Victoria.***

## Scene 7 / In Court

**DEVERELL:** Sergeant Hawkes, aboard the *Tournyn* was a satellite-tracking transmitter?

**HAWKES:** Yes, sir.

**DEVERELL:** Which was functioning from the point the *Tournyn* left Costa Rica, went down to Colombia, loaded up with marijuana, and came up to American waters, then Canadian waters?

**HAWKES:** That's correct.

**DEVERELL:** You knew where the *Tournyn* was every inch of the way upon the high seas?

**HAWKES:** No, I think we got two readings a day, one or two readings a day.

**GREENSPAN:** ***And so the course of the* Tournyn *was charted as she made her way south from Central America to the long, flat beaches of the Pacific coast of Colombia, where Senor Gomez's airplanes had unloaded the thirty-three thousand pounds. It was waiting there, on stilt platforms, in sixty-pound bales wrapped in plastic and burlap. But Captain Pierera refused to come closer than five miles to shore...***

## Scene 8 / Aboard the *Tournyn*

**PIERERA:** No, no, no, no, *señor*.

**PADDY:** Yes, well, that's fine, but how are we going to pick up the pot?

**PIERERA:** That is your business, *señor*, and mine is to keep the *Tournyn* safe. I am the captain; my ship and my life are one thing together.

**GREENSPAN:** ***So that night Paddy and Ian went ashore on a Zodiac, negotiated the use of a punga — a thirty-foot dugout canoe — loaded three thousand pounds of marijuana on board, jury-rigged a sail by ripping out the floorboards for a mast and lashing plastic to it, and promptly lost the wind.***

## Scene 9 / In the Dugout Canoe

**PADDY** (*frightened*): Jasus Almighty, Ian, b'y, the currents are taking us the wrong way.

**IAN** (*with urgency*): Paddle, will you just paddle like your life depended, me dear man.

**PADDY:** Well, where's the ship? I don't see her lights.

**IAN:** We're going out to sea. Sure, we'll be lost by the mornin'.

**PADDY** (*shouting*): I think we better jettison the cargo, b'y!

**IAN:** Not on your life. Thirty thousand lids of pot; it's worth a million dollars!

**PADDY** (*with authority*): Jettison the fuckin' cargo!

**GREENSPAN:** ***And fifty bales of marijuana went floating out to sea — never, as far as it is known, to be found again. When the searing tropical sun rose that morning, Paddy and Ian found the shore, the ship, and a bottle of Colombian rum. Somehow they persuaded Captain Pierera to bring the*** **Tournyn** ***closer to land, and the remaining fifteen tons were ferried out to the boat by the crew and loaded aboard. At Goddard Space Flight Center, a DEA agent wrote in his log: "June 5-6, one mile off Colombia coast. June 7, set sail north and left Colombian waters."***

***More harrowing experiences were yet to be endured...***

## Scene 10 / Aboard the *Tournyn*

**ANNOUNCER ON SHIP'S RADIO:** Winds eighty-five knots to one hundred knots at the centre, spreading outwards to fifty, the epicentre at eighty kilometres due west of Acapulco.

**IAN** (*excited*): It's a wonderful grand dorty hurricane, Paddy, and it's movin' right toward us! Look at the needle jorkin', old son.

**PADDY** (*shouting*): Captain! Captain! Let's get the hell to shore! Captain!

**IAN:** He don't hear you, Paddy. What's he doin', prayin'?

*The wind is screaming and there is a ripping noise and the sound of breaking glass.*

**IAN:** We're all dead. There goes the dinghies!

**PADDY:** Watch out for the flyin' glass, b'y!

**IAN:** Where the Jasus are we?

**PADDY:** Give me the sextant. I'll try to get a shot when we come out of the trough! Where's the captain?

**IAN:** They set up an altar down below. Wow... There goes the hatch cover!

**GREENSPAN:** ***Stripped of antennas and all but one dinghy, wood torn from the gunwales, food provisions ruined by the seawater taken on, the battered*** **Tournyn** ***fought Hurricane Carlotta for three days and three nights, using up her entire supply of fuel...***

**IAN:** See there, about eight miles abeam, it's called Guadeloupe Island. The pilot book says it's uninhabited.
**PADDY:** Inhabited or not, that's where *this* dumb Newfie gets off. The trip's over. I'm gonna set up house with the gannets and the seagulls, b'y... Ian, what am I seein'?
**IAN:** Dear Lard, it looks like a navy ship.

**GREENSPAN:** ***A Mexican destroyer to be exact. The pilot book was ten years out of date and Guadeloupe Island was now a Mexican naval base. While the crew collected abalone from the rocks, Captain Pierera took the dinghy in and negotiated with the commander. A few hours later he returned, towing four barrels of diesel fuel, enough to get them near the Mexican mainland, where Murphy went ashore at the town of Ensenada and telephoned Batista. Batista called Agent Staples. Staples called Paddy back at an Ensenada motel. At the trial, Deverell questioned Staples about the conversation...***

## Scene 11/In Court

**STAPLES:** I expressed surprise to Mr. Murphy that he was in Ensenada, Mexico, because the trip we had planned did not project a stop in Mexico.
**DEVERELL:** Well, you were aware there was a hurricane.
**STAPLES:** I was aware there was a hurricane and I was aware of their position from our monitoring, but Murphy was the one that told me it was a... rough ride, essentially.
**DEVERELL:** He told you they were out of fuel, out of food?
**STAPLES:** Yes.
**DEVERELL:** And he even had to pawn his watch for thirty dollars?
**STAPLES:** Yes.
**DEVERELL:** So obviously they were out of money?
**STAPLES:** Yes.

**GREENSPAN:** ***Defence counsel, Sid Simons, picked up that thread...***

**SIMONS:** What had he done with the thirty dollars he pawned his watch for?
**STAPLES:** Ah, I don't know.
**SIMONS:** If I suggested to you he managed to buy himself a bottle of

wine and two whores with the thirty dollars and said he was going to abandon the whole project, are you saying that this is the first time you heard of it?

**STAPLES:** I think I recall some version of this in a magazine article, but I never heard anything like this from Mr. Murphy.

**GREENSPAN:** ***A third defence lawyer, Peter Hart, pressed harder...***

**HART:** When the boat was floundering in the waters off the shore of Mexico, was there an indication that some marijuana had been thrown overboard?

**STAPLES:** As I recall, Mr. Murphy either directly or indirectly implied if they ran out of fuel they were about to consider the option of throwing it overboard.

**HART:** But that option didn't have to be considered because you people arrived and towed the boat, is that correct?

**STAPLES:** That's correct.

**GREENSPAN:** ***The implication was clear: if the government hadn't intervened, the whole expedition might have been abandoned. This would be central to the entrapment defence. As the boat lay dead in the water a mile off the Mexican coast, a U.S. customs undercover launch, bearing Batista, Ernie Staples, and other agents, came alongside and transferred two hundred gallons of fuel to the*** **Tournyn...**

**HART:** And then did you tow the *Tournyn*?

**STAPLES:** We...ah, we gave it a tow for half a mile, mile, to get its engines started.

**HART:** The *Tournyn* was in Mexican territorial waters?

**STAPLES:** Probably.

**HART:** One of your major concerns was that the Mexican authorities could seize this boat, is that correct? Batista, of course, was a resident of Mexico?

**STAPLES:** I don't know if this was a major concern; it was a possibility.

**HART:** Oh, come on, now, Agent Staples. It was a major concern. Now, let's be honest about it.

**STAPLES:** Well, yes. This was acknowledged as a possibility, yes.

**HART:** Batista stood to lose his boat and his investment, right?

**STAPLES:** I guess that would be the case from...ah, from his point of view.

**HART:** You wanted to get it out of there under the safety of your wing, if you like?
**STAPLES:** Yes.
**JUDGE:** Mr. Deverell.
**DEVERELL:** Agent Staples, one of the other DEA persons on board the undercover boat was Agent Caplano?
**STAPLES:** Yes.
**DEVERELL:** And what was his role?
**STAPLES:** Well, I represented his role as an associate of mine in San Diego who could help us get the things we needed in San Diego and try to do it in such a manner that the *Tournyn* wouldn't be intercepted by law-enforcement authorities.
**DEVERELL:** In other words, you represented that he was a crook.
**STAPLES:** Yes.

**GREENSPAN:** ***The suggestion was that certain officials could and would be bought off. The* Tournyn *was towed into San Diego harbour and dropped anchor there at two o'clock on the morning of July 3. Staples told Paddy and Ian to stay on board until he came back after daybreak...***

## Scene 12/Aboard the *Tournyn*

**PADDY:** Ian, you asleep?
**IAN:** No, b'y. You?
**PADDY:** No... Why are they so anxious for us to stay on board?
**IAN:** They said if we get busted, they can't fix that.
**PADDY:** No, no. Listen, old cock, they've been able to fix that.
**IAN:** Paddy, b'y, I told you, if these was cops, we'd already be in the joint... It's gettin' light.
**PADDY:** ...You can see some of the boats — Ian, do you think they fixed the American navy, too?
**IAN:** Why?
**PADDY:** Lard Jasus, that's a nuclear sub! And a destroyer. I mean, we're in some kind of naval compound, b'y.

**GREENSPAN:** ***At 10:00 a.m., Agent Staples and Batista came by, inspected the cargo — fifteen tons of marijuana in burlap sacks filled the staterooms and cabins of the lower deck — and discussed Murphy's***

***plans to off-load onto two Canadian fishing vessels near Sidney Inlet on West Vancouver Island, where Gary Sexton and his crew would be waiting. But without food or fuel the* Tournyn *couldn't embark from San Diego to continue her journey north. Deverell explored this with Agent Staples...***

## Scene 13 / In Court

**DEVERELL:** Now, where did the *Tournyn* fuel up?
**STAPLES:** At a fuel dock in San Diego.
**DEVERELL:** And money was advanced by the DEA to Batista to pay for the fuel?
**STAPLES:** Yes...ah, three thousand dollars.
**DEVERELL:** And also to pay for some food and other provisions?
**STAPLES:** Yes.
**DEVERELL:** U.S. taxpayers' money, is that correct?
**STAPLES:** That's correct.
**DEVERELL:** And without the assistance of the DEA, you will agree, the *Tournyn* would not have made it to Canada?
**STAPLES:** Yes, that's correct.
**DEVERELL:** And you were concerned that the *Tournyn* might never finish its proposed journey to Canada, weren't you?
**STAPLES:** Yes.
**DEVERELL:** And you wanted to do everything in your power to make sure it got up to Canada. I'm not putting that badly, am I?
**STAPLES:** Ah, I...I would phrase it differently.
**DEVERELL** (*impatiently*): I know you might like to phrase it differently but that's about right, isn't it?
**STAPLES:** I'm sure some of my actions assisted this to happen...that would be a more precise way of putting it.
**DEVERELL** (*wearily*): Witness, do you understand the question?
**STAPLES:** ...Maybe I don't. Ah, would you rephrase it please?
**DEVERELL:** That you did everything in your power to make sure the boat got up to Canada.
**STAPLES:** As a result of my activities I'm sure the journey to Canada was...ah, assisted.
**DEVERELL:** Agent Staples, had your agency wished to frustrate this venture, it could have been done before the *Tournyn* left Acapulco for Costa Rica?

**STAPLES:** Yes.

**DEVERELL:** And similarly from Costa Rica to Colombia, from Colombia to Mexico, from Mexico to San Diego, right to the West Coast of Vancouver Island?

**STAPLES:** Yes.

**DEVERELL:** And you resuscitated the boat with fuel and provisions and then you dispatched it northward?

**STAPLES:** Yes.

**DEVERELL:** And you are a person sworn to uphold the laws of the United States of America?

**STAPLES:** Yes, that's correct.

**GREENSPAN:** ***In the 1928 Holmstead case, Mr. Justice Oliver Wendell Holmes, one of the greatest jurists in the history of the United States of America, said:***

**OLIVER WENDELL HOLMES:** "We have to choose, and for my part I think it a less evil that some criminals should escape than that the government should play an ignoble part."

**GREENSPAN:** ***Had Paddy and Ian been arrested in the United States they might have availed themselves of the entrapment defence. But the DEA and the RCMP were aware that the courts of Canada had steadfastly refused to recognize it. Agent Staples denied that this was why the police assisted the* Tournyn *in its voyage north. The reason, he said, was that the police wished to further their investigation, and spread their net to catch Sexton, who was in a remote part of Vancouver Island getting ready for the landing. Part of his crew were with him and part were gathered at a Victoria hotel.***

***The RCMP, who were very much involved at this point, obtained a court order to wiretap some of the guests of that hotel, the Château Victoria.***

## Scene 14 / Hotel Room/Phone

**MALE VOICE** (*on the telephone*): Hello.

**WOMAN OPERATOR:** Is this room 405?

**MALE VOICE 1:** Yup.

**WOMAN OPERATOR:** One moment for long distance. Ah, two-eighty please, sir.

*Coins are dropped into a pay phone, seemingly forever.*

**MALE VOICE 1** (*laughing*): Is that it?

**WOMAN OPERATOR:** Go ahead.

**GARY:** That's it.

**MALE VOICE 1:** Hey, *que pasa*, Gary? (*Laughing*) What's happening up there?

**GARY:** It's 10-4, Eleanor.

**MALE VOICE 1:** Hey, is everything looking kosher?

**GARY:** Way better. Really good. (*Laughing*) Experience helps.

**MALE VOICE 1:** Hey, the boys woke me up last night. They came in at two-thirty...ah, then they went somewhere.

**GARY:** Oh, boy, they're gonna be in great shape, eh? They all in the kip now, are they?

**MALE VOICE 1:** Everything's groovy?

**GARY:** Yeah, I've got everyone else up here.

**MALE VOICE 1:** Is that right? They're already there? What about Big Sidney?

**GARY:** The way I got things now, I got him on the boats, too. I figure we're gonna have more men this year. So Sunday's the earliest now, is it?

**MALE VOICE 1:** Oh, yeah, as far as I know, the 21st.

**GARY:** Jasus, I got those guys left up here a long time.

**MALE VOICE 1** (*laughing*): How many of them are up there?

**GARY:** Ah, nine.

**MALE VOICE 1:** Lord Jesus, I don't know half of the people, do I?

**GARY:** You know everyone but two, and you would have met them, you know, like they worked last year. I've got the beefiest boys you ever did see. I've got an extra big boat and engine, you know, so anyone can go ashore. We're operating as smooth as hell.

**MALE VOICE 1:** Well, listen, what about the coin? How much we gotta give them?

**GARY:** I, well, a hundred and fifty.

**MALE VOICE 1:** Yeah, well, that's gonna have to be negotiable.

**GARY:** Yeah, we just haven't got it. I haven't got any.

**GREENSPAN:** ***Nilo Batista would have been displeased at this news. The hundred and fifty thousand dollars was to be given to his captain, cash on delivery, before the marijuana was off-loaded. Undercover Agent Staples made a recorded telephone call from RCMP headquarters in Vancouver to Sid Ward — Big Sidney — acting treasurer for the smugglers.***

## Scene 15 / In the RCMP Office/Phone

**STAPLES** (*on the telephone*): The boat owner is, ah, somewhat anxious about the money because, ah, the impression he got was that, ah, it might not all be forthcoming.

**SIDNEY:** Uh-huh.

**STAPLES:** Ah, so he is pretty much insisting that, ah, although he says everything can go exactly on schedule, ah...he would like to have the money, ah, before it goes.

**SIDNEY:** Uh-hum.

**STAPLES:** I think he's, ah, he's lost a fair degree of confidence, and, ah...so I think he would want all of it, although he might settle for a substantial portion of it.

**SIDNEY** (*despairing*): Well, we can't do that, we just can't do it.

**STAPLES:** Ah...well, I'm afraid he will quite likely call off the delivery. And, ah, you know the man, he's quite stubborn when he gets that way. Ah, if it's not forthcoming, then I think he'll hold off until it's, ah, forthcoming.

**SIDNEY:** Yeah, well, I need to talk to him, you know. I mean I can't do any better. We're at our wit's end. I mean if that man wants to get, you know, too small, he can get small, you know, I mean, goddamnit, man, I been in good faith, always in good faith you know.

**STAPLES:** Oh, okay, well, he would probably accept a hundred and another forty-five on delivery. I don't think that's an unreasonable request on his part, and, ah, delivery could go through without any further hitches, 'cause, ah, you know the boat is at sea, heading your way, and, ah, it's just a matter of you paying the money about three days early.

**SIDNEY:** Well, I don't know. I don't know. I've got a feeling about this...I'm gonna put this to my boys.

**STAPLES:** Okay.

**SIDNEY** (*growing animated*): We might just say, well, fuck it, you know we don't like to be held over the barrel, we're good, we're upright citizens, and we do things right, and we don't like to be treated like a bunch of...like we're being treated.

**STAPLES:** Okay, well, okay, but you see his point of view, of course.

**SIDNEY:** No, I don't really.

**GREENSPAN:** ***The next day there was a second telephone call, also from the Vancouver RCMP office...***

**STAPLES** (*on the telephone*): Well, if you don't mind my asking, ah, if you don't have it now, how are you going to have it in a few days when the boats get here?

**SIDNEY:** I'm just telling you we can get it, from people, but it's not ours to give. But once what's coming is ours, then what we have to give is ours to give. But until the other stuff is ours then what we have to give you is not ours to give.

**STAPLES:** Well, ah, I don't think we want the boat to go beyond our control until we have some good faith money, and, ah, I think this is the position the, ah, captain is instructed...

**SIDNEY:** Okay, okay, what are you gonna do if we don't come up with this good faith?

**STAPLES:** Ah, we'll tell the boat to turn around, and, ah...

**SIDNEY:** And what are you going to do with my friends on board? Eh?

**STAPLES:** Well, ah, ah, frankly, they're very mad at you, do you know that?

**SIDNEY** (*very angry*): Listen, you know if you want to play the forties game, you know we can play the forties game, I guess. But this is the 1970s, and I always thought it was a different world now.

**STAPLES:** It's not a matter of the forties, frankly. Ah...I think it's a matter of money.

**SIDNEY:** Listen, it's hard to talk right now, can you come here to talk to us? A phone is not the place to be talking.

**STAPLES:** Well, that's possible. You're in Vancouver somewhere, I assume, right? Ah, Paddy said there's generally a fair lot of, ah, heat in Vancouver, and, ah, maybe we could come to Seattle.

*There is a noise on the line.*

**STAPLES:** Hello?

**SIDNEY:** Yeah, I'm still here. It sounded like somebody hung up.

**STAPLES:** Well, ah, I'm in a hotel, so I don't know, maybe somebody screwed up. Ah, I think we're relatively cool so far, but let me call you back at a certain time. I'll call from a different phone.

**GREENSPAN:** ***That night, Sid Ward mulled the problem over with friends until the small hours. Agent Staples called in the morning, once again from the RCMP offices in Vancouver.***

**STAPLES** (*on the telephone*): So, what's happening?

**SIDNEY:** So, I'm gonna head your way.

**STAPLES:** Okay, why don't you, we're in Seattle. Ah...you got some bread with you?

**SIDNEY:** Yeah, we hope we have a hundred, I guess.

**STAPLES:** Okay, that would, ah, that would clear everything beautifully and, ah, you know the boat'll be in in a couple of days, and, ah ——

**SIDNEY:** Yeah, yeah, yeah, okay, I wanna see, I wanna see himself.

**STAPLES:** No problem. Hey, you know, there's really no problem with this thing, it's just a matter of you assuring ——

**SIDNEY** (*angrily*): Well, listen, we're willing to go along with you, but as far as we're concerned there is a problem, like, you know, we're being treated like a piece of shit, and we feel like one. We're gonna play the game 'cause you got all the cards, but you know, you know it is a problem.

**STAPLES:** Okay.

**SIDNEY:** So don't say it isn't.

**STAPLES:** Okay, I'll see you in Seattle, right, bye-bye.

## Scene 16/In Court

**GREENSPAN:** ***In court, lawyer Sidney Simons cross-examined on this issue...***

**SIMONS:** Okay, did you attend that night at the Washington Plaza Hotel in Seattle?

**STAPLES:** Yes, sir, I did. Shortly after midnight Mr. Batista and I met with Mr. Ward and we had a conversation.

**SIMONS:** And Batista walked away with a hundred thousand dollars in his pocket, is that correct?

**STAPLES:** Yes.

**SIMONS:** Now, you knew what those monies were intended for?

**STAPLES:** Yes.

**SIMONS:** For the transfer of an illicit cargo?

**STAMPLES:** Yes.

**SIMONS:** He was allowed to keep the money?

**STAPLES:** Yes.

**SIMONS:** In his role as a co-operating individual he was motivated undoubtedly by greed?

**STAPLES:** Well, I obviously can't say what was in his mind.

**SIMONS:** Well, you spent considerable time with him, were you not able to judge from your knowledge of human nature whether he appeared to have been motivated by greed as opposed to some deeply seated religious conviction that he should assist you?

**STAPLES:** I would say in this case the money was probably the interest.

**SIMONS:** Thank you.

**JUDGE:** Do you have something further, Mr. Deverell?

**DEVERELL:** You were in effect holding the shipment for ransom while helping Batista extort this money from them, would you agree?

**MACDONALD:** Objection. That question calls for an opinion.

**JUDGE:** The witness may be willing to adopt that description. It's up to him, I guess.

**DEVERELL:** He may very well agree he was holding the shipment for ransom in order to help Batista extort the money from Ward. Or would you?

**STAPLES:** I wouldn't use the term "extort" to characterize the activity.

**DEVERELL:** Extort means to wrest something from a reluctant person by intimidation, or — or abuse of authority, you understand that?

**STAPLES:** Yeah, but I don't look at it in that sense. I look at it in the sense that I look upon myself as a law-enforcement officer pursuing an investigation...ah, in an appropriate manner.

**DEVERELL:** Yeah, I suppose you have to. That's all I have, thank you.

**GREENSPAN:** ***And where, during these negotiations, was the* Tournyn *on its slow northward journey? In trouble. After leaving San Diego, the boat ran into another Force 10 gale, and a sea-cock blew out. Making three knots and taking on huge amounts of water, she made Shelter Cove, near Mendocino, California, just as her props began churning air. Five feet of water were pumped from her forward holds, and she moved on again. The Nimbus-6 satellite was still reporting her position, but — to be on the safe side — a U.S. Coast Guard HU-16 Albatross tracker airplane was added to the surveillance. It made nine eighteen-hour trips before the* Tournyn *crossed the U.S.-Canadian border on July 14, when a Canadian Air Force Argus aircraft out of Comox took over. Its Omega tracking system gave the operator a fix on the* Tournyn *every ten seconds.***

***Then the Canadian navy entered the picture. Rear Admiral Mike Martin, Commander Pacific Region, at the naval base in Esquimalt, provided two escort destroyers, the* Terra Nova *and the* Kootenay*, both***

***with complements of two hundred and thirty officers and men, a strike force armed with nine-millimetre pistols and 7.62 automatic rifles. That wasn't all: The RCMP threw in a helicopter, a Cessna seaplane, a dozen Inspector Class motor launches, and other police boats. Officers were helicoptered to mountain tops near Sidney Inlet and equipped with night-vision scopes. And everyone waited for the* Tournyn *to arrive. What they did not expect to arrive along with the* Tournyn *was fog: heavy, billowing blankets of fog behind which the* Tournyn *was off-loaded onto the Canadian fishing boats Gary Sexton had obtained—the* Weatherly *and the* Sunfish.**

## Scene 17 / On Deck

**GARY:** Paddy! Ian! That you? I can't make out a thing.
**PADDY:** A mausey night to be sure. Have a drap o'stuff, Gary. I saved a bottle of rum, b'y.
**GARY:** Paddy, you dorty old gawk, you made it!
**MALE VOICE 1:** Hey, they made it.
**VOICE 2:** Praise the Lard and pass the pot!
**VOICE 3:** Let's get it in the ground.
**GARY** (*calling*): Keep it to a low roar, you guys.
**PADDY:** Hey, Big Sid, how're you doin', man? You b'ys won't believe what we been through. Now, this here is Captain Pierera.
**PIERERA:** *Tienes el dinero, mi amigo?*
**SIDNEY:** Yeah, I got your *dinero* — forty-five, *cuarenta y cinco*. I should tell you to swim for it.
**VOICES:** "We's the b'ys that builds the boats. We's the b'ys that sails them..."

**GREENSPAN:** ***When police and naval officers boarded the* Tournyn *the next morning, all the marijuana was gone — and so were all the Newfoundlanders, including Paddy and Ian.***

***Agent Staples testified, in response to questions from lawyer Sid Simons, that he debriefed Captain Pierera...***

# Scene 18 / In Court

**STAPLES:** Agent Vandiver and I made sure that the captain was not in any dire straits and that the authorities were aware of the fact he was working with us, and he made some statement that we need fuel, and other than that, I guess we wished him a good trip back home.

**SIMONS:** And thanked him for his co-operation undoubtedly?

**STAPLES:** Ah, yes, probably.

**SIMONS** (*sarcastically*): No medals or celebrations?

**STAPLES:** No, no.

**SIMONS:** Did you observe this refuelling?

**STAPLES:** I sort of have a funny image of the *Tournyn* coming alongside one of the destroyers...

**GREENSPAN:** ***Refuelled, this time by the Canadian navy, the* Tournyn *chugged out of Canadian waters and returned to Mexico. The forty-five thousand dollars in cash remained safely with the captain. RCMP Staff Sergeant Hawkes was cross-examined by William Deverell...***

**DEVERELL:** No instructions were given to anyone to seize such money?

**HAWKES:** Not that I am aware of, no sir.

**DEVERELL:** The decision that was made not to arrest Captain Pierera or the crew members or detain the vessel — that was made by various high-ranking RCMP officials, in consultation with personnel in Ottawa.

**HAWKES:** Yes, sir.

**DEVERELL:** Well, do you know if it went up to the Department of the Solicitor-General?

**HAWKES:** No sir, I don't.

**GREENSPAN:** ***And what of the fifteen tons of marijuana? When the fog lifted, the* Weatherly *was spotted and given chase. Arrested on board were Paddy Murphy, Sid Ward, and seven other men. The cannabis was gone but most of it, all but two tons, was discovered stashed on Obstruction Island. Not far away, Gary Sexton and three others were taken into custody. The remaining two tons? During the night, the* Sunfish *had slipped away in the fog, and police found her scuttled a week later near Egmont, on the mainland, near the Sunshine Coast***

*Highway. Four thousand pounds of Colombian marijuana were gone. Through the combined efforts of the Drug Enforcement Administration, NASA, the U.S. Coast Guard, the RCMP, and the Canadian air force and navy, 3.2 million dollars' worth of marijuana — the street value according to RCMP experts — made it safely into the country. And so did Ian who had been Paddy's shipmate aboard the* **Tournyn.** *Several others from the landing party also escaped on the* **Sunfish.** *They have never been arrested to this day.*

*There is a final twist to the story. It lies in the evidence of RCMP analyst Murray Clark, in cross-examination by Deverell...*

**DEVERELL:** You did a qualitative analysis of the amount of THC from ten samples from the bales of marijuana?
**CLARK:** Yes.
**DEVERELL:** And THC is the intoxicating ingredient in cannabis?
**CLARK:** That's correct.
**DEVERELL:** And the analyses ranged from a low of 0.008 per cent to a top rating of 0.029 per cent?
**CLARK:** Yes.
**DEVERELL:** Well, it's very, very poor-quality marijuana?
**CLARK:** Yes.
**DEVERELL:** The THC content comes close to being negligible compared to other samples you've analysed?
**CLARK:** It is very low, yes.
**DEVERELL:** And most marijuana is in the order of a hundred times stronger than these exhibits?
**CLARK:** That's correct, yes.
**DEVERELL:** It's quite clear that marijuana which has a nil or almost nil intoxicating effect is really quite worthless?
**CLARK:** I would guess that, yes.
**DEVERELL:** Yeah, I suppose if you smoked a ton of it you might get something out of it.

**GREENSPAN:** *The Newfoundlanders had been burned. We are left to speculate why. Clearly, Alfredo Gomez had fronted them thirty-three thousand pounds of what is known in the drug trade as spinach — the nearly worthless outer leaves of the marijuana plant. Had he done so out of revenge over the loss of two tons a couple of years earlier in Newfoundland? There is another theory — one that was postulated by novelist Robert Harlow, author of a magazine article written about the case, entitled "The Great Canadian Dope Bust":*

**HARLOW:** But another explanation is possible — that from the beginning, Colombian, American, and Canadian narcotics agents orchestrated the whole venture from behind the scenes.

**GREENSPAN:** ***...and arranged to supply the smugglers with sixteen and a half tons of worthless marijuana in order to trap them into the commission of a crime. For that had to be the theory if defending counsel were to succeed in an argument that their clients were entitled to be acquitted by reason of police entrapment. Staff Sergeant Hawkes vehemently denied that the police set up the accused from the beginning — and without Alfredo Gomez or Nilo Batista available to give evidence, counsel had little ammunition to make the argument.***

***Gary Sexton represented himself throughout the trial and addressed the jury on his own behalf...***

**GARY:** We must rely on the testimonies of the two special agents of the DEA to be able to figure out what happened. Supposedly two or three Canadians initiated this agreement to import. But there would not have been anyone to conspire with if the DEA hadn't stepped in with their boat owner, his captain, his boat, his crew and, with all the available facts, it appears his marijuana as well. If you knew the marijuana was destined for the incinerator, wouldn't you deliver the lowest grade possible? If it was destined for the marketplace, certainly a higher grade would have arrived. Do the police forces of this country plan to play the role of host in other ventures of this nature? Whatever happened to crime prevention? The result of all this is to foster scepticism about the viability of the entire legal system and thereby weaken the bonds of shared attitudes that make it possible for society to function democratically. The use of the law to achieve ends for which it is not appropriate is, to borrow some lines from H.G. Wells, "Like a magnificent but painful hippopotamus, resolved at any cost upon picking up a pea that is hidden somewhere in the jungle. The hippopotamus may conceivably succeed in its quest, more likely it will fail. What is certain is, that in the attempt, it will knock down many innocent victims and will give up much of its dignity."

**GREENSPAN:** ***But in the end, the trial judge ruled as follows...***

**JUDGE:** The defence advanced was the defence of entrapment, and I propose to deal with it now in very simple terms: as the law is at present, the facts in the case at bar preclude the defence of entrapment being applied.

**GREENSPAN:** ***Indeed, as the law was then, the defence was not available in Canada, until August 9, 1982, when five of nine judges of the Supreme Court of Canada, in the case of Amato* versus *the Queen, held that no conviction may result where a crime is manufactured by the police under circumstances so shocking and outrageous as to bring the administration of justice into disrepute. But even that decision did not assist the Sexton group when the case was later argued before the British Columbia Court of Appeal. According to Mr. Justice Lambert...***

**JUSTICE LAMBERT:** The offences here were not instigated by the Drug Enforcement Administration or the Royal Canadian Mounted Police or their agents. There was nothing in the police conduct that ensnared the appellants in the commission of the offences. And I do not regard the assistance in making the introductions that led to the use of the *Tournyn* or the refitting in San Diego as shocking or outrageous by any standard that might be suitable for assessing shock or outrage.

**GREENSPAN:** ***Of seventeen persons arrested, two were discharged, four convicted of the lesser offence of possessing marijuana for the purpose of trafficking and sentenced to four years or less. The others were jailed for terms ranging from seven to ten years for importing, seven years being the minimum sentence required by law for that offence. Paddy Murphy and Sid Ward received ten-year sentences. And Gary Sexton, too, received a ten-year sentence but it was made concurrent with the ten years he was already serving on the east coast. Why? As it happened, two of the people arrested with him in British Columbia were involved in the earlier Newfoundland affair. They had never been convicted. One had jumped bail, and the other had never been arrested. They were convicted in British Columbia and sent back to Newfoundland to be tried. They were convicted and sentenced for the earlier smuggling incident. When they were then returned to British Columbia for sentencing on this matter, defence lawyers called into play sections of the Criminal Code that compelled concurrent sentences***

*in such a situation. Once the judge accepted this argument, it was considered unfair to Sexton to give him a consecutive sentence, causing him to serve twice as much time as his fellow offenders. As a result, the outrageously expensive international police sting resulted in Sexton's not receiving a single day of extra sentencing time.*

*The courts in Canada did not accept the entrapment defence in the Sexton case. But we are left to wonder, as we review the facts, whether Mr. Justice Brandeis was not entirely correct when he pointed out that entrapment situations breed contempt for the law. Gary Sexton served six years in jail. He is presently on parole in Victoria, British Columbia. His profession: actor. His most recent role: the role of Gary Sexton in this episode of "The Scales of Justice".*

# Producer's Notes

It is hardly surprising that some of the best writers (and performers) on our series are lawyers. In addition to Guy Gavriel Kay and Jack Batten, radio listeners have heard the work of such other lawyer-writers as Ray Stancer (who, in collaboration with his wife, re-examined the mysterious murder of Sir Harry Oakes) and the late Barbara Betcherman, whose excellent script on the Horvath matricide case, called "Hypnosis" is included in Volume 1 of *The Scales of Justice*. Outstanding among the performances have been those of J.J. Robinette, Q.C., the doyen of Canadian litigation lawyers, re-enacting his famous cross-examination of a witness in the 1947 Evelyn Dick case, and Senior Crown Attorney Stephen Leggett taking his own role in the notorious Toronto hit-and-run case that resulted in the death of dance instructor Judy Jordan.

West-coast lawyer and best-selling author William Deverell carried the tradition a step further in the Sexton case. He not only wrote the script but performed his own role as defence lawyer for Gary Sexton, one of the chief conspirators in what must rank as the most amusing drug-related case in Canada.

There is nothing intrinsically funny about smuggling drugs, of course. However, when a group of Newfoundlanders decided to follow in the footsteps of their rum-running ancestors by delivering 33,000 pounds of what they took to be the finest product of Columbia's marijuana fields to the shores of Vancouver Island, the ensuing caper could only be described as a comedy. The law-enforcement authorities — who tracked the smugglers by satellite and used naval vessels to refuel them only to lose them in the fog a few miles from their destination — played a role in the case only slightly less comic than the role of the conspirators.

There were many first-rate performances in what was probably the only more or less cheerful case we ever re-created on "The Scales of Justice", but Chuck Shamata's portrayal of U.S. Special Agent Ernie Staples rated an all-time best. Working with the smallest effects and the most delicate timing, Shamata rendered unforgettably the straight-laced and self-assured police officer testifying about slightly embarrassing events on the witness stand. Another outstanding performance came from Michael Hogan in the role of Big Sid, the treasurer of the Newfoundland smugglers. The happy rogues Paddy and Ian were played by Neil Munro and Ian Deakin to great effect.

In addition to Deverell, there was another person in the show re-creating his own role. It was none other than Deverell's client, the reformed-conspirator-turned-actor, Gary Sexton. The clear, pleasant voice and the easy, natural style he brought to his debut augured well for his success in his new profession.

G.J.

# Game Misconduct

*George Jonas*

## The Cast

Commentary by Edward L. Greenspan, Q.C.

| | |
|---|---|
| **PAUL SMITHERS** | Phil Akin |
| **MR. MALONEY** for the defence | Michael Tait |
| **MR. McGUIGAN** for the Crown | Frank Perry |
| **JUDGE SHAPIRO** | Henry Ramer |

With the support of (in alphabetical order): Mia Anderson, Harvey Atkin, Jim Carrey, Joy Coghill, Norma Dell'Agnese, Jon Granik, Tom Hauff, Bill Lynn, Angelo Rizacos, Jack Scott, Errol Slue, Ray Stancer, Dennis Strong, Sean Sullivan, and Leslie Yeo

## Scene 1 / Interview

**PAUL** (*to the interviewer*): If they send me to jail, I'll go to jail with class... I'm going to fight this until it can't be fought any longer. If I go to jail, I'll come out fighting.

## Scene 2 / At the Unitarian Church

*Two people are distributing handbills to those entering the church.*

**SPEAKER 1:** Okay, brother... Freedom for Paul Smithers... Framed-up and convicted for manslaughter for challenging some racist insults... Take one, brother...

**WOMAN 1:** Here, take one... Freedom for Paul Smithers... Convicted for manslaughter for challenging some racist insults... Freedom for Paul Smithers...

**SPEAKER 1:** All right, all right, settle down... settle down. All right, now you know why we're here. We're here to fight racism in Toronto... I'm a black man and I'm angry. I'm angry at the court's decision. This case is just another example of racism. I'm just sorry it took someone getting killed to bring you all out tonight. But, I'll tell you one thing: Don't just let it stop here.

**SPEAKER 2:** All right, all right, all right, all right. Now, you heard the brother... Now, I don't live here, but I'm angry too... I come from New York to urge the black community, and the white community, of Toronto to take a stand... to say we will not tolerate this kind of racism, this kind of legalized lynching... I want you to listen to Paul Smithers, listen to what Paul has got to say. Come on, Paul.

**PAUL:** Thanks... ah, I'm, like... ah, I'm confident we can get this... this conviction... ah, over... overturned, you know, by... by a higher court... If we can get enough people behind us... I'd like you all to come to court next Tuesday, to... to fill the court when they sentence me. Thank you.

*The crowd cheers wildly.*

**GREENSPAN:** ***These words were spoken in the spring of 1974. The meeting was organized by a group calling itself the Friends of Paul Smithers and it was attended by about two hundred people at the Unitarian Church on St. Clair Avenue in Toronto. The incident that gave rise to it was a court case following the death of one young boy in a fight with another: a very tragic but not uncommon occurrence. But the Smithers case was uncommon. Its reverberations filled the Canadian press in the mid 1970s, and even reached the pages of the*** **New York Times.** ***More importantly, the case resulted in one of the few recorded instances in which attempts were made, through political pressure, to influence the decision of a Canadian court.***

***My name is Edward Greenspan and the story that follows has been reconstructed from the trial transcripts of the Ontario County Court.***

***It was a cold Sunday, February 18, 1973. The hockey game that was about to begin at Mississauga's Cawthra Arena between the Cooksville and the Applewood Midgets, seemed to have been marked right from the start with the competitive and, unfortunately, not always sportsman-like spirit that infuses some teams in house-league hockey... Heading the attack for Applewood was sixteen-year-old Barrie Cobby, the best player for his team, the son of middle-class parents who came to Canada from England shortly after Barrie was born... The best player for the Cooksville team was Paul Smithers, also sixteen, also of middle-class parents. The two young athletes were similar in every respect, except one. Although Paul's mother was white, his father was a black Canadian, from Truro, Nova Scotia. Barrie and Paul had met each other on the ice before and, as they were the star players of their respective teams, there was a certain amount of rivalry between them. The game that Sunday was a rough game, as all witnesses would later agree in Court. There was some dispute, however, about which of the two boys got really rough with the other one first...***

# Scene 3 / In Court

**MARILYN:** He was, well, he was... He speared Barrie in the arm.
**CROWN:** Now, when you say he speared Barrie, you are referring to who?
**MARILYN:** Paul Smithers.
**CROWN:** And when you say speared, what do you mean by speared?
**MARILYN:** Took the end of the stick and pushed him.
**CROWN:** And did you observe this happen?
**MARILYN:** Yes.

**GREENSPAN:** ***But while Marilyn, Barrie's girlfriend, may have observed this, the referee of the game did not. The first misconduct for which the referee saw fit to assess a penalty, around ten minutes into the first period, was against Barrie Cobby for spearing Paul Smithers.***

# Scene 4 / At the Arena

*A whistle sounds.*

**REFEREE:** Okay, Cobby. Five minutes for spearing.
**BARRIE:** But I... It was that bastard...
**PAUL:** Yeah, you lousy goof...
**REFEREE:** Shut up, Smithers. Get going, Cobby.

**GREENSPAN:** ***Obeying the referee, Barrie went into the penalty box. The game continued, and within a minute Paul Smithers scored a goal against Barrie's team... Exuberant in triumph, Paul skated by the penalty box where Barrie was sitting...***

**PAUL:** All right...
**FAN:** Way to go Paul.
**PAUL:** Ha, ha, we scored! That'll show you.
**BARRIE:** Stupid, fucking coon...
**PAUL:** Yeah, you're a fucking goof yourself...
**BARRIE:** Dumb black bastard... They shouldn't even let you...

*Pandemonium breaks out among the players on the ice and on the bench. During the shouting and name-calling, the words "fucking nigger" are used once or twice.*

**COACH:** Hey, fellows. Quit the name-calling, eh, stick to hockey!

**GREENSPAN:** ***This, among others, was the evidence of the coach of the Applewood team, as cross-examined by Paul Smither's lawyer, Arthur Maloney...***

## Scene 5 / In Court

**MALONEY:** ...And who was addressing this kind of language to Smithers?

**COACH:** I heard Barrie say one phrase, but it was also coming from the other players as well.

**MALONEY:** From the other players too?

**COACH:** On our bench, yes.

**MALONEY:** So Barrie Cobby wasn't the only one to call him "fucking coon"?

**COACH:** No.

**MALONEY:** Was the term "coon" used, or was he called a "fucking nigger"?

**COACH:** Oh, I heard the word "nigger" on our bench. I mentioned to the fellows to stick to hockey and forget the name-calling.

**GREENSPAN:** ***Since Barrie's coach was a witness for the Crown, his admission, along with similar testimony from other Crown witnesses, left no doubt that racially abusive language was, in fact, directed at Paul Smithers in the Cawthra Arena. The referee, who would later testify that he had heard no racial insults but simply two boys shouting at each other in foul language, ordered both boys to leave the ice at once. Barrie Cobby and Paul Smithers were thrown out of the game. Both youngsters began walking towards their changing rooms, but, according to the bulk of the evidence, in very different frames of mind...***

## Scene 6 / At the Hockey Arena

**PAUL:** You better watch out, you fuckin' goof...I've had enough of this...I'm not gong to take this anymore...You hear? I'm going to get this straightened out once and for all. You want to fight? Fight! You meet me in the hall in ten minutes and fight.

**BARRIE:** You shake me up, man.

*Barrie enters his dressing-room.*

**PAUL** (*from corridor outside*): In ten minutes, you hear? Come in the hall in ten minutes and fight.

**FRIEND:** Hey, Barrie, whatcha gonna do?

**BARRIE:** What da you mean, what I'm gonna do? What do you expect me to do?

**PAUL:** I'll be here in ten minutes waitin' for you. You hear, goof?

**FRIEND:** You gonna fight him, Barrie?

**BARRIE:** I'm not gonna do anything. I value my life too much, thank you.

## Scene 7 / In Court

**GREENSPAN:** ***Barrie Cobby was in his dressing room, changing into street clothes, evidently disinclined to fight. What happened next was elicited in direct examination from various witnesses by Crown Attorney Leo McGuigan. First, he questioned the manager of Barrie's team...***

**CROWN:** When you saw the accused outside dressing room number 7, what if anything, did you do or say at that time?

**MANAGER:** Well, a fellow by the name of Mike, he came down and asked me if he could be of assistance, and I said, "Yes, would you get a rink attendant or somebody to get Paul Smithers out of there? There's going to be trouble", and this is what he did.

**GREENSPAN:** ***The rink attendant had this to say...***

**ATTENDANT:** Yes, sir, I went down into the dressing-room area to see what the problem was.

**CROWN:** And did you observe anything at that time?

**ATTENDANT:** Yes. There was a negro boy in a white jacket; he was outside the dressing room.

**CROWN:** Now, did you yourself have any conversation at that time, or around that time, with the accused, Mr. Smithers?

**ATTENDANT:** I said to him, there won't be any fighting in the arena; if you want to fight, have it outside.

**CROWN:** And was there any response from him to that?

**ATTENDANT:** Well, not at that exact moment... The coach from the Cooksville team came into the dressing-room area and there was a conversation.

**CROWN:** All right?

**ATTENDANT:** And as the defendant was leaving he says: "Well, I'm going to get him; I'm not going to hurt him, I'm going to kill him."

**CROWN:** "As the defendant was leaving" — who are you referring to?

**ATTENDANT:** Mr. Smithers.

**GREENSPAN:** ***Neither Paul Smithers nor Barrie Cobby left the arena for about another forty-five minutes. Dressed in street clothes, they were both watching the game from the sidelines, Barrie sitting on the bench with his teammates and Paul standing nearby. However, according to the evidence of the referee, Paul was not content with merely watching...***

**REFEREE:** With approximately three minutes to go in the game, I had occasion to go into the corner near the exit where Smithers was standing, and at that time I received foul and abusive language directed at me from Smithers.

**CROWN:** Do you recall what was said to you?

**REFEREE:** I believe I was called a "lousy arsehole"...

**CROWN:** So, what happened then?

**REFEREE:** I stopped the game, I went over and made a note on the game sheet....

**CROWN:** Did you recommend anything?

**REFEREE:** Yes, the disciplinary committee has the grounds to call him in and assess further suspension.

**GREENSPAN:** ***At this point Smithers was clearly, perhaps understandably, distressed — distressed because of the racial insults, no doubt, and distressed at being banished from the game for responding to the insults in similar language. He was standing at the edge of the rink, waiting. As the game was drawing to a close, it became clear to Barrie's coach and manager that they had better get Barrie out of the arena quickly... This was also the impression of Barrie's girlfriend...***

**CROWN:** Whose idea was it to go and get the car?

**MARILYN:** Mine.

**CROWN:** And what... ah, precipitated you to have this idea, if anything?

**MARILYN:** Well, I just wanted to get him out of the arena as quick as he could.
**CROWN:** And why was that?
**MARILYN:** Ah, so he wouldn't get hurt?
**CROWN:** What made you think that he might get hurt?
**MARILYN:** Well, Paul Smithers was waiting... Hm, it was obvious that there was gonna... Well, he was going to try and fight and Barrie didn't want to, so it seemed to be the only way.

**GREENSPAN:** ***Barrie's girlfriend, Marilyn, did leave with some friends to get Barrie's car from the parking lot.***

***Meanwhile, Barrie, surrounded by his coach, his manager, and some of his teammates, walked out the main exit of the arena. According to the Crown's evidence, Paul Smithers was following right behind...***

## Scene 8 / In the Arena Foyer

**PAUL:** Come on... Come on... hey, come on!
**COACH:** Leave him alone, eh, get lost...
**PAUL:** Come on, goof, fight...
**MANAGER:** It was only a game! Don't worry about it, get him next game with a stiff check or something...
**PAUL:** No, I wanna get him right now. Come on...
**MANAGER:** Just... just cool down.

**GREENSPAN:** ***The manager of the Applewood team grabbed Paul and held him, while Barrie ran towards where Marilyn was waiting inside the car. But Paul broke loose and ran after Barrie. When he caught up with him, he threw a punch or two at Barrie's head, which may or may not have found the mark. At any rate, they did little or no damage. Barrie defended himself by crouching and covering up his face; he did not throw any punches at Paul. It was at this point that Barrie's coach and two of his teammates caught up with Paul. They grabbed and held him in a headlock; they pinned back both his arms. Immobilized in every other way, Paul lashed out with his foot, catching Barrie somewhere between the groin and the solar plexus. Barrie turned, took a few steps towards his car, then collapsed and lay on his back, gasping for air...***

## Scene 9 / Outside Arena in Parking Lot

**MANAGER:** Jeez... Is he okay?
**COACH:** I dunno... Get a coat, someone.
**MARILYN:** He can't breathe... Can't you do something?
**MANAGER:** Stand back, stand back, give him some air... Go, get an ambulance, hurry!
**COACH:** Hey, does anybody here know how to do mouth-to-mouth?
**MANAGER** (*to Paul*): You!... Are you happy now?
**PAUL:** I couldn't have hit him that hard.

## Scene 10 / In Court

**CLERK** (*reading*): Members of the jury, look upon the prisoner and hearken to his charge. He stands indicted by the name of Paul Douglas Smithers as follows: The Jurors of Her Majesty the Queen present that Paul Douglas Smithers, on or about the 18th day of February, 1973, in the Town of Mississauga, did unlawfully kill Barrie Ross Cobby by kicking him, and did thereby commit manslaughter, contrary to the provisions of the Criminal Code of Canada. Upon this indictment he hath been arraigned, and he hath pleaded not guilty, and for his trial hath put himself upon his country, which country you are. Your charge, therefore, is to inquire whether he be guilty of the indictable offence charged or not guilty, and to hearken to the evidence.

**GREENSPAN:** ***What were the issues in the case of the Queen*** **versus** ***Paul Smithers? There was no question whatever that Paul never intended to kill Barrie, or to even cause him serious harm. Had there been any evidence of that, instead of manslaughter, the charge could have been murder. Still, as a very conscientious defence lawyer, Arthur Maloney wanted to make sure in the course of his cross-examination of the rink attendant that any possible misunderstandings about Paul's intentions would be removed from the jury's mind...***

**MALONEY:** When you heard Paul Smithers say, quote: "I'm not going to hurt him, I'm going to kill him," end quote, were you... What was your impression as to whether that was a serious threat or not?

**ATTENDANT:** I think it's a threat that's made in anger; it's not a threat that you take actually for his word ——

**MALONEY:** It's not... I don't mean to interrupt, would you finish?

**ATTENDANT:** I don't really know how to put it. It's a threat that just means, I'm going to beat you up, not actually kill a person.

**MALONEY:** You didn't take it very seriously anyway?

**ATTENDANT:** What Mr. Smithers said at the time? No.

**GREENSPAN:** ***But even with any intention to kill out of the way, Paul would still be guilty of manslaughter if the Crown could satisfy a jury beyond a reasonable doubt that: (a) Paul intended, and did, kick Barrie; (b) that the kick was unlawful; and (c) that the kick caused Barrie's death. The fact that Paul could not foresee that his kick would kill Barrie would, in itself, be immaterial...***

**CROWN:** Now, eh, tell us about that kick.

**COACH:** Well, from where I was standing trying to pull Paul's arm off, I could see that the foot came up and Barrie was still kind of hunched over, but the blow landed in the midsection, the lower midsection.

**CROWN:** What makes you think the kick landed?

**COACH:** I could see it, and hear it.

**CROWN:** You heard it?

**COACH:** Yes.

*Later.*

**CROWN:** And what did you observe, if anything?

**MANAGER:** Well...ah, there was some people pulling Paul Smithers off; they had him by the arms, and I saw a boot, or a foot lash out and Barrie double over.

**CROWN:** Did you see whether that foot made contact with Mr. Cobby?

**MANAGER:** Yes, I believe... Yes, yes, I did.

**GREENSPAN:** ***So, there was a kick and it landed, according to the coach, the manager, and other eye-witnesses. But was the kick unlawful? Although, on the Crown's evidence, Paul had been the initial aggressor, still, by the time he lashed out with his foot, he was being pinned down by three people. Had Barrie attacked him then, Paul could have kicked him in lawful self-defence...***

**CROWN:** What was Barrie Cobby doing at this time?

**MANAGER:** Well, just defending himself.

**CROWN:** Oh, when you say he was defending himself...ah, what was he doing?

**MANAGER:** Well, just covering himself up, like so.

**CROWN:** From your observations, did you observe any active defence, if I might use that phrase?

**MANAGER:** No, no active defence, no...

*Later.*

**CROWN:** What did Barrie Cobby do at this time?

**BOY:** He just stood back while we grabbed Paul Smithers.

**CROWN:** Did he take any active steps to defend himself at that time?

**BOY:** No, he just ducked down and hid his face.

**CROWN:** How did he hide his face?

**BOY:** Well, should I demonstrate?

**CROWN:** Yes, if you would.

**BOY:** He bent over like this.

**CROWN:** You are indicating bending forward and the hands covering the facial area... Would that be a fair description, Mr. Maloney?

**MALONEY** (*dryly*): I think that accurately describes what this witness did.

**GREENSPAN:** ***But assuming that the kick did land and it was unlawful, did it in fact cause the death of the victim? This was a much more difficult question, and a much more difficult point for the Crown to prove...***

**CROWN:** Now, Dr. Brunsdon, I understand, sir, that on February 19 last year you performed an autopsy on the body of Barrie Cobby, is that correct?

**BRUNSDON:** Yes.

**CROWN:** As a result, were you able to come to an opinion as to the cause of death?

**BRUNSDON:** Yes, sir. I considered that the death was due to asphyxiation, due to the aspiration, the breathing in, of foreign material into the lungs.

**CROWN:** How does that bring about death?

**BRUNSDON:** There would be regurgitation, that is, upward passage of material from the stomach, which sometimes goes into the mouth, and then somehow or other would pass backwards down through an opening, the epiglottis, which at the time cannot have been properly protected by the normal reflexes.

**CROWN:** Now, Doctor, I would ask you to express an opinion as to what possible effect on this reflex action you have indicated would be caused by a sudden kick in the abdomen or the groin area?

**BRUNSDON:** A sudden kick or blow on the abdomen or groin area, would, I think — I couldn't say always — but it certainly would predispose to regurgitation.

**GREENSPAN:** ***The doctor explained, with proper scientific caution, that Barrie seemed in perfectly good health before he suddenly started vomiting and then choking on his own vomit. In the absence of any other medical reason for this, the doctor seemed to agree that Paul's kick could have induced the vomiting and perhaps even the absence of a normal reflex, the closing of the so-called epiglottis that ordinarily prevents food or other foreign matter from being breathed into the lungs. Another medical expert, Dr. Hillsdon Smith, agreed — but even more cautiously...***

**CROWN:** Now, Doctor, assume if you will the following facts. That a young man, previously in good health, with no propensity for vomiting, no evidence of drugs or alcohol, had participated for about ten minutes in a rough hockey game; had been in a verbal confrontation with the accused; and for about forty-five minutes after that was in a state of anger and was quite nervous and frightened due to a challenge for physical combat by the accused. Assume that he was then kicked in the abdominal area, gasped, and died of aspiration due to inhalation. Assuming those facts, can you express an opinion as to whether or not there was any probable connection between the kick and the vomiting of the deceased?

**SMITH:** I can say that there *probably* is a connection between the kick and the vomiting, or there could be. I can't say there *is*.

**CROWN:** And the reason for that, Doctor?

**SMITH:** Because this boy was in this mental state, he was apprehensive; those are conditions which can induce vomiting without any kick.

**CROWN:** Take a person who is in an apprehensive state, add to that the element of the kick, would that increase or decrease the probability of someone vomiting?

**SMITH:** Oh, I think it would increase it.

**CROWN:** Assuming all those facts again, can you express an opinion as to whether the kick would have any connection with the aspirating, the breathing in, of those materials?

**SMITH:** Whether the food material was ejected through the mouth, or whether it found itself in the air passages, is in my opinion, purely a matter of chance. Once the vomit reaches the back of the throat, whether it goes by what appears to be a not very well functioning epiglottis or not, is accident.

**CROWN:** The kick to the abdominal area, would that alter your opinion on that particular aspect?

**SMITH:** No, no.

**GREENSPAN:** ***So, the Crown's own expert believed that the breathing in of the stomach contents, the immediate cause of Barrie's death, was merely an accident, due to the rare chance of a poorly functioning epiglottis. It had nothing to do with the kick. But incalculable as this might be in its effect on the jury, from a legal point of view it was less than crucial. It is a well-established principle in law that an assailant must take his victim as he finds him. This is often referred to as the principle of the thin-skulled man: if a light tap on the head kills the victim, the accused can't escape a manslaughter conviction merely by pointing out that his victim had an unusually thin skull.***

***But the experts could not even say for certain that Paul's kick caused Barrie to vomit; it may have been due to other causes — anger, nervousness, or fear. It is, of course, not manslaughter merely to incense or frighten a healthy adult so that he vomits and chokes. The defence wasted no time in challenging the Crown's evidence on this point...***

**MALONEY:** As I understand it, Doctor, you are saying it'd be quite impossible to say the kick and the aspiration had *any* relationship?

**SMITH:** Yes.

**MALONEY:** And that you could say there is *probably* a connection between the kick and the vomiting; there could be, but you can't say there *is*?

**SMITH:** That's right.

**MALONEY:** And that is the extent of your opinion, as far as you are prepared to go?

**SMITH:** Yes.

**MALONEY:** And you have, as you told my friend, a very long background of experience in the field... Thank you.

**GREENSPAN:** ***During cross-examination, the defence, of course, also tried laying some groundwork for countering the Crown's suggestion that the kick was unlawful, by raising the question of self-defence. First, in questioning Barrie's coach...***

**MALONEY:** So, even before you got to Smithers, he was being held by the neck and by the right arm? And all that was left to get hold of was his left arm, and that's what you did?

**COACH:** I was trying to free his arm so that Barrie could run.

**MALONEY:** Well, suppose Mr. Smithers had to defend himself at that stage, just suppose that he did, the only part of him that was free for defence was his foot?

**COACH:** Yes.

**GREENSPAN:** ***And then, in questioning Barrie's manager...***

**MALONEY:** Assuming the jury should come to the conclusion that Smithers had to defend himself, his arm was being held, his right arm was being held and his left arm was being held, is that right?

**MANAGER:** Yeah, that would be right, yes.

**MALONEY:** And that the only part of him free for defence would be what?

**MANAGER:** His lower half, I guess.

**MALONEY:** His what?

**MANAGER:** His leg.

**GREENSPAN:** ***The defence also spent considerable time in establishing the insults Paul Smithers had to endure that Sunday in the Cawthra Arena. Though this would be of limited legal significance — provocation not being a defence in law against a charge of manslaughter — it was a very legitimate bid for the sympathy of the jury...***

**MALONEY:** Sir, one of the last questions put to you by my friend, the counsel for the prosecution, was that from the time Smithers and Cobby were banished from the hockey game until the time of the kick outside the arena, you never saw Cobby strike out at Smithers?

**MANAGER:** That's right.

**MALONEY:** I suppose calling another player a "fucking nigger" is a form of striking out, isn't it?

**MANAGER:** Hm, well, as it was implied, I thought it meant physical...ah, if you want to go to the term, yes.

**MALONEY:** Did it occur to you that it might be a more cruel form of striking out than a blow from the fist?

**MANAGER:** Possibly, sir.

**MALONEY:** Did you hear Cobby call Smithers a "fucking nigger"?

**MANAGER:** Yes, sir.

**MALONEY:** How many times?

**MANAGER:** Why, I can't...I can't recall, sir.

**MALONEY:** So many you don't remember?

**MANAGER:** No, no, no, sir. Possibly two or three times...

**MALONEY:** Do you feel that he had a real grievance if somebody had called him that?

**MANAGER:** Hm. I...I don't know how he would feel, sir. I don't know. I'm...I'm not in that position.

*Later.*

**MALONEY:** Smithers was the best player on his team?

**COACH:** I would say he probably was.

**MALONEY:** Is it regarded as good tactics to try and get the best player on the opposite team mad, so he will lose his judgement?

**COACH:** No, stick on him, check him, that's the name of the game.

**MALONEY:** But you didn't think the use of the terms "fucking coon" and "fucking nigger" was designed to bait him in any way?

**COACH:** No way.

**MALONEY:** Just a spontaneous outburst from some healthy young Canadian boys?

**GREENSPAN:** ***In one sense, it was the plain duty of defence counsel to emphasize the element of provocation. While it was in no way a defence to the charge of manslaughter, it could become very important if Paul Smithers was convicted because evidence of provocation could significantly affect an eventual sentence, and rightly so. However, in the daily press this aspect of the defence acquired a totally unwarranted magnitude. First, it created the impression that the victim and his entire environment in a normal Canadian suburb had been monstrously racist — a conclusion unsupported by any evidence.***

***Second, it mistakenly suggested that Paul Smithers' defence was, or ought to be, relying on some kind of licence to respond to racial insults by an act of assault. But this, of course, was not the defence's point when, at the end of the Crown's case, it made a submission to His Honour, County Court Judge Shapiro...***

**JUDGE:** Mr. Maloney, you propose to present a motion at this time?

**MALONEY:** Your Honour, my respectful submission to Your Honour, at this stage, is that the jury should be directed to return a verdict of not guilty. Now I am quite mindful that you are not entitled to take away from the jury a case of this nature if there is *some* evidence on which it would be open to them to find that the death was caused by the kick. But there is no evidence at all as to what caused the death in this case. None of the medical witnesses go beyond a probable connection between the death and the kick.

**JUDGE:** Probable connection.

**MALONEY:** If this were a civil proceeding it would have to go to the jury to determine on the balance of probabilities whether or not the kick had caused death. But this is a criminal proceeding which requires a standard of proof beyond a reasonable doubt.

**JUDGE:** Mr. McGuigan?

**CROWN:** Your Honour, we have heard evidence that medicine is not a definite science; it deals in the area of probabilities. The jury must consider all of the evidence, not just the doctors' — the evidence of each and every person who testified what he observed after the kick. The gasp, the turning around...

**MALONEY:** Your Honour, that's the very danger that I want to avoid, that a jury of laymen will say to themselves, well, the coincidence of the kick, and the falling down, and the gasping, we don't care what the doctors say. We figure that's what must have caused the death.

**JUDGE:** Yes. Well, gentlemen, I appreciate the argument that you have each advanced. However, I am going to allow this to go before the jury.

**GREENSPAN:** ***The judge's ruling made sense in law. If juries were forced to accept expert evidence only and not allowed to draw their own conclusions, our system could change from trial by jury to a system of trial by experts, which would be very, very dangerous. Eventually the Supreme Court of Canada would unanimously support the trial judge on this point. But assuming the jury did find that Paul's kick caused***

***Barrie's death, what could be Paul Smithers' defence? The Crown's own evidence supported one excellent possibility. Having thrown a couple of punches, Paul might have finished his assault. When three men grabbed him by the upper body in the icy parking lot, Paul could have lost his footing. His leg could have moved up in a totally unconscious effort to regain his balance, making contact with Barrie, who was still crouching in front of him. That would have been a real accident. If that had been Paul's evidence, the Crown might have found it very difficult to prove the contrary beyond a reasonable doubt. But, in all honesty, Paul made no such claim on the witness stand. Instead he raised the issue of self-defence...***

MALONEY: When you went down the steps to Barrie Cobby, what was in your mind?

PAUL: Well, I sort of... I didn't want to leave without getting something or other straightened out. Because I didn't feel, like, I came out to play, you know, I guess hockey, I didn't come there to be called nigger, whatever... because I get enough of that where I live and things like that — so... so I w... I was prepared to fight.

GREENSPAN: ***Paul did claim that he had given Barrie a chance to apologize just moments earlier... in the presence of witnesses...***

PAUL: ... at that point I said "Apologize and we'll forget the whole thing", like that, I... I wasn't yelling or I wasn't whispering, and at that point Barrie turned around and his coach, they turned around, and it looked like in amazement, and, and Barrie goes, "Ha, me apologize to you?" And it was loud enough that anybody who was around there would have heard it, but evidently I guess they didn't.

GREENSPAN: ***As for the fatal kick, Paul described it in this fashion...***

PAUL: They were sort of pulling my neck back, and two people had one arm and one person had the other arm, and at that time Barrie was facing me and it looked like he was ready to hit or kick me, whatever, and at that point... at that point I kicked him...

MALONEY: Your head was tilted back?

PAUL: Yes, sir.

**MALONEY:** And what was it...from that position that you could see, what was Barrie Cobby doing?
**PAUL:** To me he had appeared, like, I couldn't say if he was going to hit me or not, but it sort of looked like "Here's a chance". This is my assumption anyway, that it appeared like "Here's a chance to get this guy"...That sort of thing, you know...
**MALONEY:** So, what happened next?
**PAUL:** At that point, I guess I just kicked him.

**GREENSPAN:** ***So, on Paul's own evidence, he intended to kick Barrie. It was something he meant to do and did do, though under the impression that it was necessary for self-defence. True as this may have been from Paul's subjective point of view, it may not have been enough for a jury that heard not one iota of independent evidence but that Barrie was running away and never lifted a hand, except to cover his face...***

## Scene 11 / In Arena Parking Lot

*A crowd is milling about as the ambulance arrives.*

**BYSTANDER:** Now, take it easy, eh, Paul...Just relax.
**PAUL** (*breathing hard*): Yeah, okay.
**MAN:** I hope you're satisfied, you black bastard. He's hurt bad!
**BYSTANDER:** Easy...
**PAUL:** I couldn't have hit him that hard...If he's hurt badly I'm going to kill myself...
**BYSTANDER:** Come on, Paul, I...I'd better take you home.
**PAUL:** No...If the police are coming I'll stay here.

**GREENSPAN:** ***This was the defence evidence. There was nothing left but for the defence, and then for the Crown, to address the jury, before the trial judge would deliver his final charge. In his eloquent address, Arthur Maloney made two main points...***

## Scene 12 / In Court

**MALONEY:** ...You may think, in the light of the evidence you have heard, that the kick might have caused the death. You may even think it is likely to have caused the death. You may even think that it is probable. But in my submission all those states of mind are insufficient on your part, because of the standard of proof required in a criminal case, that standard being proof beyond a reasonable doubt to the point of moral certainty...

**GREENSPAN:** ***This was Maloney's first point. The second was...***

**MALONEY:**...You may feel in the light of the evidence you have heard, that Barrie Cobby wanted to avoid a fight. Quite reasonably, you may feel that Paul Smithers' belief that Barrie Cobby was going to fight him was mistaken. But if you accept Smithers' evidence about the beliefs he entertained, or if you have any reasonable doubt about whether or not this is what he believed, then as far as the law is concerned he is to be judged as though the facts were as he mistakenly believed them to be and not as you or I may now feel they were...There is no burden on Paul Smithers to prove he was acting in self-defence. The burden is on the Crown to satisfy you beyond a reasonable doubt, to the point of moral certainty, that he was not.

**GREENSPAN:** ***The key point in the Crown's address, delivered by Leo McGuigan, was perhaps this:***

**CROWN:** ...Members of the jury, you have had an opportunity to observe the accused as he testified in the witness box. As I recall his evidence, he testified that even today, looking back on the incident, it was his opinion that Barrie Cobby was going to attack him that night of February 18, 1973. That is his opinion at this time, after hearing all the evidence. If that is the case, what would Barrie Cobby have to do on that particular evening to have convinced the accused that he didn't intend to attack...

**GREENSPAN:** ***Then it was the turn of the trial judge...***

**JUDGE:** Ladies and gentlemen of the jury, at one time in sport, the losing team used to call for three cheers for the winners, and the winning team reciprocated with three cheers for the losing team.

How far have we travelled away from this concept when on the 18th of February, 1973, one boy had to be taunted and insulted for the accident of birth which gave him a darker skin, and another boy, at least according to many Crown witnesses, was in such fear that when he left his dressing room, he was accompanied by an escort.

I say these things because I am sure that you have been appalled, as I have been, to hear how sportsmanship has been so lost...

But no matter how you or I may disapprove, our duty is not to sit in judgement on present Midget Hockey, but to try the case on the indictment before us, namely, did Paul Douglas Smithers unlawfully kill Barrie Ross Cobby by kicking him and thereby commit manslaughter, or not. In this we have a solemn oath to honour, the one I took when I was sworn in as a judge, and the one you...

**GREENSPAN:** ***In a long, meticulous charge His Honour dealt with the law and with the evidence, but it was the following remarks that may have especially impressed themselves on the jury's mind...***

**JUDGE:** ... You should not be prejudiced against the accused because of his colour — nor should you, on the other hand, lean over backwards in his favour solely out of any feeling of compassion or sympathy that you may have, resulting from his having been wronged by the racial slurs... This case must be decided in a cold, analytical, impartial, and fair way... I'm sure that you've seen pictures of the female form of justice holding the scales of justice, and across her eyes is a blindfold — so those scales of justice shall be equal for all...

**GREENSPAN:** ***Following the judge's charge, at 3:27 p.m., the jury retired. After a relatively short deliberation, about two and a half hours later, they returned to the courtroom...***

**JUDGE:** Mr. Foreman, I see you have an envelope in your hand.
**CLERK:** Have you agreed upon your verdict?
**FOREMAN:** Yes, we have, Your Honour. We, the jury, find the accused guilty as charged. However, due to his age we recommend a light sentence.

**GREENSPAN:** ***The jury's verdict was returned on Monday, April 22, 1974. But more than two months would pass before Judge Shapiro***

***would pronounce his sentence. And the sentencing was clearly going to be one of the most difficult aspects of a difficult case. And it was complicated by outside forces...***

## Scene 13 / At the Unitarian Church

**SPEAKER 1:** Okay, brother... Freedom for Paul Smithers. Framed-up and convicted for manslaughter for challenging some racist insults... Freedom for Paul Smithers...

**WOMAN 1:** Freedom for Paul Smithers... Convicted for manslaughter for challenging some racist insults... Freedom for Paul Smithers...

**GREENSPAN:** ***Throughout the trial, the press had played up the racial issues behind the case in a sensational fashion. Any evidence of racial slurs or prejudice would be turned into headlines. Most readers, of course, would never attend the trial or hear the whole of the evidence, and could therefore easily gain the false impression that the entire game, or indeed the suburbs of Toronto and all of house-league hockey were permeated by an atmosphere of racial hatred. Or so the papers made it seem...***

**WOMAN 2:** It's all imperialist, legal shit... They should never have charged him. In a decent, non-racist society they'd charge the people who were calling him names...

**GREENSPAN:** ***In fact, it was the reporting that was inaccurate as the press itself was moved to admit a year later. In the words of a senior editor of the*** **Toronto Star*****:***

**EDITOR:** The reporting, in the press and on the air, left much to be desired. Cobby and Smithers were the outstanding players on their two teams; they had roughed each other up before and there was evidence that their animosity was personal, not racial. This evidence was not reported.

**GREENSPAN:** ***Barrie's parents had reason to be bitter.***

**MR. COBBY:** Sickening, that's what the reporting was. It was as though our boy was the villain and Smithers lily-white... I mean, we're all called names at times, aren't we? I've been called a limey what's-it many a time.

**MRS. COBBY:** You see, it doesn't matter to us what colour Smithers is, he killed our boy. The papers, oh, they make me ill the way they turn things around...

**GREENSPAN:** ***Beyond the tragedy of losing their son, Mr. and Mrs. Cobby had to endure a highly inaccurate portrayal of Barrie, and, by extension, themselves, as bigoted. It wasn't until much later that the papers got around to looking for people to talk about the other side of the story...***

**TEACHER:** In the time I knew Barrie I found him to be warm and sensitive, possessed of a sense of friendship and loyalty, and above all endowed with a quiet sense of humour...

**BARRIE:** *The Adventures of Huckleberry Finn* probably taught me more than any other book we've read in high school... I learn about friendship between two races and I hope that some day we'll all be able to get along together...

**GREENSPAN:** ***Such balanced reporting — quotes from Barrie's teachers or his high-school essays — was in the future, however. During the year following Barrie's death, the victim's parents could hear no public voices raised in sympathy. Not surprisingly, positions hardened. It was during this time that the mail delivered a Christmas card to the Smithers house...***

**MRS. COBBY:** "... His future crushed e'er it came to bloom
By a hand that he doth know
That they are marked for eternal doom
He waits for the death that you owe."

**GREENSPAN:** ***The card was signed "Barrie's mother". But if positions had hardened on one side, on the other side they had attracted the most irresponsible and disruptive forces, trying to exploit the tragedy for their own political purposes. These forces, genuine as their concern for Paul Smithers and for social justice may have been according to their lights, were striking at the very roots of the rule of law that forms***

***the basis of our society. It was the National Black Coalition and a New Left group calling itself "Students for a Democratic Society", along with some radical activists from the United States, that urged protesters to gather in the court where Paul Smithers was going to be sentenced...***

**SPEAKER 2:** ...Say we will not tolerate this kind of racism, this kind of legalized lynching...

**PAUL:** Thanks...I...I'd like you all to come to court next Tuesday, to...ah, to fill the court when they sentence me...

**GREENSPAN:** ***Paul, still only seventeen, became caught up in the atmosphere created by the group calling itself "Friends of Paul Smithers". His father, however, expressed himself with much more wisdom...***

**MR. SMITHERS** (*to interviewer*): Well, I...I'm against this kind of protest..This should be a legal issue rather than a political one...I only hope these people are interested in Paul as a human being, not as an instrument...

**GREENSPAN:** ***Mr. Smithers' instincts were right. When the court convened for sentencing on June 24, 1974, it became clear that the "Friends of Paul Smithers" were potentially his worst enemies...***

## Scene 14/In Court

**JUDGE:** Paul Smithers, you may be seated during the pronouncement of sentence. For what I have to say may take a little while.

I think it's unfortunate that the racial issue had to enter this case at all, for I've the opinion that had it not been you and Barrie Cobby, before long it would have been two other boys, probably of the same colour and race. Maybe this most unfortunate case will act as a stern warning to excessive player and excessive fan alike, and our hockey arenas might then remain places where decent people are not ashamed to bring their children.

You gave evidence, and it was your evidence alone, that you thought Barrie was going to attack you. This theory was properly presented on your behalf and rejected by the jury. I am satisfied that their rejection was on the weight of the evidence and not because you are black and the other boy, white.

The record will reveal amply that there was evidence to support the jury's finding. How, then, can people who were not present during the trial, some who do not live in this country, how can they denounce the trial as a frame-up, or as legalized lynching? One has to be suspect of such people...

Whether you are being used by people who have other motives for their actions and advice I don't know, but I strongly suspect this... To request a demonstration to be made at the Court House prior to your sentence, leads to the conclusion that it was intended to deter me, or intimidate me from carrying out those duties which I have been sworn to uphold. To attempt to coerce in this way is reprehensible, and an attempt to interfere with the administration of justice. I assure you it will not work with this Court, or any other in Canada.

The greater danger is that I, or others, might react to these demonstrations and punish you more severely... I mention this by way of assuring you that I will not fall into this error either. Taking all matters into consideration, I consider that an appropriate period of custody in your case will be six months. Now, had you not been provoked by racial slurs, and had the jury not made their recommendation for a light sentence, I assure you that my sentence would have been much more severe.

**MR. COBBY:** I think it's a pretty poor effort when Smithers gets six months for taking fifty years from my boy...

**PAUL:** I'm terribly, terribly sorry about this tragedy. I'd do anything to change it... But I don't think I should be called "nigger". I don't really think I have the right answer even now. I don't know if I should just stand there and take it, or fight back... I didn't get a fair deal. I was judged not by my peers... I wasn't judged by one black person. I wasn't judged by anyone but twelve white people...

**GREENSPAN:** ***After his conviction Paul Smithers remained free on bail for nearly three more years while his case was being appealed through***

*the courts, to the Supreme Court of Canada. In May 1977, the highest court ruled unanimously that Paul Smithers did get a fair deal. It would be hard to disagree. Sad as Barrie's death and some of the underlying issues were, and unresolved as the human conflict might remain, the case was marked by a spirited defence, a restrained prosecution, a balanced interpretation of the law, and a moderate sentence. It has come as close as any case can in balancing the scales of justice.*

# Producer's Notes

I have always been interested in the 1973 case of Paul Smithers, an Ontario teenager of racially mixed ancestry. His conviction for manslaughter, arising out of an incident during a high-school hockey game, was seen by some people as evidence for the inherent racism of Canadian society.

The facts were straightforward. Angered by some racial slurs hurled at him during an altercation on the ice, Smithers decided to have it out with another teenager named Barrie Cobby after the game. Smithers only wanted to fight; he clearly had no intention of killing the other boy. Nevertheless, at the end of a very brief fight outside the hockey arena, as a result of an unfortunate physical reaction to a kick, Barrie Cobby was dead.

The case raised some hard medical and legal questions relating to accidental death, culpable homicide, and homicide justifiable by self-defence. These were resolved by the jury's finding that Smithers' kick killed Cobby and that his kick was unlawful. An unlawful act resulting in death, however unintended, is one of the classic definitions of manslaughter. The law's view is that a killer must always take his victim as he finds him, physical infirmities and all.

On a human level it was easy to sympathize both with Smithers, understandably hurt and angered by thoughtless racial abuse, and with the parents of Barrie Cobby, whose son seemed to have tried to avoid the fight and in any case did not deserve to die at age sixteen for whatever he may have said in the heat of a hockey game. It was much more difficult to sympathize with those who, under the guise of opposing racism and supporting Paul Smithers, tried improperly to influence and interfere with the orderly conduct of a Canadian court. The issues were put in context by Judge Shapiro, whose eventual sentence (and remarks before sentencing) stood as a model for the fairness, compassion, and incorruptibility of the judicial process at its best. Unlikely as Judge Shapiro's remarks were to alter the views of those whose positions had hardened on either side of the case, they underlined the attitude of a civilized society under the rule of law, and the empty demagoguery of those who called Smithers' trial and sentencing "legalized lynching".

In the program the role of Paul Smithers was recreated by the very talented black actor Phil Akin. Barrie Cobby was played by Angelo Rizacos with his customary excellence. Henry Ramer rendered the tolerance and firmness of the trial judge with quiet, controlled power. Other outstanding performances were by Michael Tait as Smithers' defence lawyer, the late Ontario Ombudsman Arthur Maloney; and by Frank Perry as Crown Attorney Leo McGuigan. Tom Hauff played perfectly the brief role of the referee. Also first-rate in their supporting roles were veteran actors Jon Granik, Leslie Yeo, Mia Anderson, Bill Lynn, Jack Scott, and the late Sean Sullivan.

"Game Misconduct" marked the debut of Guy Gavriel Kay as a director. It was his view at the time that, given a choice between directing one of his own scripts or one of mine as his first effort in studio, he'd rather make a mess of my script. As it turned out, he could have safely chosen his own. Even Greenspan, a stern critic of all his former articling students, could find no fault with Kay's work.

G.J.

# Second Time Around

*Guy Gavriel Kay*

**The Cast**

Commentary by Edward L. Greenspan, Q.C.

| | |
|---|---|
| **GARY STAPLES** | Chuck Shamata |
| **MARY CONKLIN** | Jayne Eastwood |
| **MR. MALONEY** for the defence | Michael Tait |
| **MR. FRESHMAN** for the Crown | Lawrence Dane |
| **MRS. EMMA STAPLES** | Nonnie Griffin |

With the support of (in alphabetical order): Grant Buchanan, Rex Hagon, Terri Hawkes, Shawn Lawrence, Sean McCann, James Morris, Frank Perry, Wayne Robson, Dixie Seatle, Nicky Guadagni, and Murray Westgate

## Scene 1 / In Court

**CROWN:** Now, Mrs. Conklin, you have told the Court that you commenced a sexual relationship with the accused person in the summer of 1969. Would you now relate to the jury, in your own words, what transpired when the accused man, Gary Staples, arrived at your farmhouse on the night of December 5, 1969?

**MARY CONKLIN:** Ummm. Gary got to my place about 10:30 or 11:00 that night. I was watching TV; my cousin Ken Shellerd was lying on the couch. Ah, Gary came in and sat down on the floor, and he took a pistol out of his pocket and a plastic bag and some black tape, and he started wrapping the gun up in the bag with the tape. Then he pointed at me and said "Let's go in the kitchen".

**CROWN:** Why was this?

**MARY:** Well, I don't think he wanted to say anything in front of Ken.

**CROWN:** And what was said in the kitchen?

**MARY:** Well, I asked him what he was doing and he said, "Well, I've got to get rid of it." And I asked him why and he said, "Well, I have just used it on somebody" and then I asked who, and he said a taxi driver in Hamilton.

**CLERK 1:** Members of the jury, have you agreed upon your verdict?

**FOREMAN 1:** We have.

**CLERK 1:** And what is your verdict?

**FOREMAN 1:** We find the accused guilty as charged of non-capital murder.

**GREENSPAN:** ***And that is undoubtedly the quickest conviction we've ever had on "The Scales of Justice". A Hamilton cab driver named Gerald Burke had indeed been murdered on the cold winter night of December 5, 1969. He had been robbed of the money he had that night***

*— not much more than forty dollars. The jury evidently believed the story told them by Mary Conklin, a woman in her thirties, separated from her husband, who lived on a farm about thirty-two miles from Hamilton. Conklin's story was virtually the whole Crown case against twenty-five-year-old Gary Staples of Dunnville, a town also about thirty miles from Hamilton...* That *jury believed her story, at any rate, because in fact, the conviction of Gary Staples was in many ways only the beginning of an extraordinary case that conjured forth from the sordid facts of that murder for cash remarkable extremes of love and hate... My name is Edward Greenspan and the story you are about to hear is reconstructed from the trial transcripts and the documents filed in the Ontario Court of Appeal.*

*Gerald Burke was found dead in his taxi at about 2:45 a.m. by a police constable on a routine check of a quiet laneway behind the busy Hamilton Place shopping centre. Burke had been shot twice in the head and his wallet had been taken. There were no recognizable fingerprints in the taxi and no other clues at all to the identity of the killer. This sort of robbery-murder is often the very hardest crime for police to solve, and, in fact, despite diligent attempts, the Hamilton police got absolutely nowhere. It wasn't until almost four and a half months later, when the file was virtually closed, that the police, investigating a completely different matter, got more than they had bargained for...*

## Scene 2 / Mary Conklin's Home

**HANES:** Mrs. Conklin, my name is Sergeant Hanes, of the Cayuga OPP. This is Constable White. We'd like to ask you a few questions about a break-in in Selkirk, Ontario.

**MARY:** I don't know anything about anything like that.

**HANES:** Well, I'm afraid your daughter, Donna, has given us some information to the contrary.

**MARY:** Little bitch!

**HANES:** She alleges that you are in possession here of some goods that...ah, don't belong to you.

**MARY:** That little bitch! Listen...ah, listen, why're you guys bothering with me? You go to Gary's house...Gary Staples. You just go and see what you can find in *his* house. It was his idea anyhow.

**HANES:** Your daughter mentioned Mr. Staples as well. We've been to see him. There's nothing there at all, Mrs. Conklin, but I'd like some answers from you, please.

**MARY:** Ah...look, I mean, this is nothing stuff. You guys forget about me. I mean, if you think a B & E is important I can tell you about something far more important.

**HANES** (*carefully*): And what would that be, Mrs. Conklin?

**MARY:** I can tell you something about Staples that in the old days they used to hang a man for.

**GREENSPAN:** ***And Mary Conklin did just that. She told the police that Gary Staples had confessed to her that he had murdered Gerald Burke. In a little while we'll take a closer look at the controversy surrounding that alleged confession, but for the moment we'll just note that it was that statement by Mary Conklin and nothing else that led a large number of police officers to knock on the door of the Staples home in Dunnville at 2:40 a.m. on April 26, 1970. Why that hour? Frankly, I can think of no good reason...***

## Scene 3/Gary Staples' House

**STAPLES** (*sleepily, answering the door*): Yes? Uh...oh!

**THOMPSON:** Are you Gary Staples?

**STAPLES:** Uh-huh.

**THOMPSON:** I'm Sergeant Thompson of the Hamilton police. This is Lieutenant Campbell, Sergeant Williams. May we come in?

**STAPLES:** Uh, yeah. I guess so.

**ALICE** (*from another room*): Gary, what's happening?

**THOMPSON:** Go ahead.

**WILLIAMS:** This is a copy of a warrant we have to search this house. (*Hands paper to Staples.*) Gary Staples, you are charged with the non-capital murder of Gerald Burke on December 5, 1969.

**STAPLES:** What?

**WILLIAMS:** Do you wish to say anything in answer to the charge? You are not obliged to say anything unless you wish to do so, but whatever you say may be given in evidence.

**STAPLES** (*in shock*): Murder, me murder? You must be joking.

**GREENSPAN:** ***It was, of course, no joke at all. As we heard at the outset, Staples was convicted, after a nine-day trial in Hamilton, of the murder of Gerald Burke. We'll examine the evidence against him when we come to consider the second trial of Gary Staples. The second trial? Yes, indeed, for after his conviction Staples hired a new lawyer to appeal that conviction and the lawyer he hired was one of the great barristers of our day: Arthur Maloney, Q.C.***

## Scene 4 / In the Law Office

**MALONEY** (*calls out*): Niels, come into my office a minute. I want to talk about Gary Staples.

**NIELS ORTVED:** Yes, sir. I'll get the file.

**MALONEY:** I've *got* the file. Come on in. (*A little wryly*) Ah, it says somewhere in your articles of clerkship that I'm supposed to spend part of the year teaching you, doesn't it?

**NIELS:** Ah, yes, sir...

**MALONEY:** All right, let's see what you've learned. How do we get the Court of Appeal to order a new trial for Staples?

**NIELS:** Ummm, you can argue that the judge didn't instruct the jury that there was no corroboration for Mary Conklin's evidence?

**MALONEY:** True enough, he didn't tell them that. Problem is, I don't think he had to. He *did* warn them that because of her character and all the circumstances it would be dangerous to convict on her evidence alone. I don't think the Court of Appeal is going to say he should have done more. Now, we'll argue for it, but we won't win. What else?

**NIELS:** The Crown attorney? His address to the jury was pretty inflammatory. Close to prejudicial.

**MALONEY:** Mmm-hmm. Mr. Freshman *is* a rather aggressive Crown. But "pretty inflammatory" isn't enough, and I've seen and heard addresses that were a lot worse. Dig up the Wilbert Coffin file some time and see what the two Crowns said then — got away with saying.

**NIELS** (*scribbling a note*): Coffin file... Yeah, I'll do that, sir.

**MALONEY** (*into intercom*): Yes?

**SECRETARY:** Mrs. Staples is here, Mr. Maloney.

**MALONEY:** Show her in please. (*To Niels*) Isn't much else in the trial record, is there, Niels? Which means we have to come up with something new. And the woman who did that for us has just arrived.

**NIELS:** Alice? His wife?

**MALONEY** (*dryly*): Nooo, I don't think we could expect his wife to have done this. Gary was running around with another woman... I don't imagine Alice is all that happy with her husband.

*Mrs. Staples is shown into the office.*

**MALONEY:** Mrs. Staples, come in please.

**EMMA** (*shyly*): Thank you, sir.

**MALONEY:** Niels, meet Gary's mother, Mrs. Emma Staples. This is my articling student, Niels Ortved. Now, why don't we all sit down, and Mrs. Staples, you tell Niels about what you've come up with.

**EMMA:** Well, it's as I said before, Mr. Maloney. There's four people — the two children, Ronald Stire and Marilyn Burdiak, and the Longley couple — and they've all told me, ummm, evidence, that backs up what Gary's been saying all along.

**MALONEY:** All right, now, before we get into the details, Niels, you tell us what the problem with new evidence is.

**NIELS:** Well, the Court of Appeal won't even hear it or read it unless you can prove that you couldn't have known about it at the time of the original trial.

**MALONEY:** Hmmm. Good... Good. Mrs. Staples, what do you say to that?

**EMMA:** Well, that's just it! We couldn't have known back then because the mothers of both children have told me they ordered their kids to say nothing.

**MALONEY:** Ah, ha. Which reminds me... Niels, we'll need affidavits from the mothers to that effect.

**NIELS:** Yes, sir.

**MALONEY:** Yes, what about the Longleys, Mrs. Staples?

**EMMA:** The Longleys saw Gary in their house on December 5, in Dunnville, around 8:30 — right at the time that poor man was killed thirty miles away in Hamilton... but they didn't realize that it was December 5... They didn't know what night it was until after the trial when they were... well, they were doing their tax returns and they found out that Dennis — Mr. Longley — went back to work on that Friday after being laid off. And they always knew they'd seen Gary the day Dennis went back to work, but they didn't know it was December 5 until they did their taxes.

**MALONEY:** Four new witnesses. Heh, Niels? And pretty good reasons why they weren't called at trial. Mrs. Staples, if we do get your son a new trial, it'll be because of the work you've done.

**EMMA** (*with dignity*): I'm his mother, sir.

**MALONEY:** I know that, ma'am. I hope he appreciates it.

## Scene 5 / In Court of Appeal

**GALE:** An application to receive fresh evidence was made to this court in the form of seven affidavits. These affidavits appear to be relevant to the alibi defence and to the vital issue as to whether the appellant confessed to the principal Crown witness that he had committed the crime. We granted leave to the filing of these affidavits, being satisfied that the evidence set forth in them could not have been discovered by reasonable diligence by the time of the trial. We've come to the conclusion that the evidence now submitted is of such strength that it might reasonably affect the verdict of a jury. That being so, there simply must be another trial...

## Scene 6 / In Court

**CLERK 2:** The accused stand please... Gary Staples, you stand charged that, at the City of Hamilton, in the County of Wentworth, on or about December 5, 1969, you did murder Gerald Burke, and thereby did commit non-capital murder, contrary to the...

**GREENSPAN:** ***And so, on January 11, 1972, the second trial began, and this time Arthur Maloney was defending Gary Staples who had been in jail since his arrest in April 1970. A second trial should be a sharper one than the first. In this case it was — bitterly sharp. The evidence at the first trial had taken nine days to present. This time around, although the witnesses were virtually the same, the trial took four weeks... Arthur Maloney knew that for Staples to be acquitted, Mary***

*Conklin had to be discredited as a witness. Although he expected to be able to cast a lot of doubt on her character and motivation for turning Staples in, the lawyer at the first trial had done that very well — and still lost. The problem was that Mary Conklin knew an awful lot about how Gerald Burke had died. She had to have learned that* somehow *and, very early in the game, Maloney began to steer his cross-examination of routine police witnesses towards planting some possibilities in the minds of the jurors...*

**MALONEY:** Sergeant Williams, have you ever met a man named Freeman on Mary Conklin's property?
**WILLIAMS:** Yes, I have.
**MALONEY:** Now, was it your understanding that he was living there?
**WILLIAMS:** I don't know. I didn't ask.
**MALONEY:** You don't know whether he has a criminal record, or anything? You know nothing about him?
**WILLIAMS:** No, sir.
**MALONEY:** Well, what about a chap named Roland Savard? Did you hear of a connection between him and Mary Conklin?
**WILLIAMS:** Only through the proceedings in court.
**MALONEY:** So, what do you know about him?
**WILLIAMS:** Not a thing, sir.
**MALONEY:** Do you know whether he has a criminal record?
**WILLIAMS:** No, sir, I do not.
**MALONEY:** Well, what about his brother, Dennis Savard?
**WILLIAMS:** I don't know anything about him.
**MALONEY:** Nothing about his relationship with Mary Conklin?
**WILLIAMS:** No, sir.
**MALONEY:** What about a man named Guy Hall? What do you know about him?
**WILLIAMS:** Not a thing.
**MALONEY:** How old he is, his relationship with Mary Conklin, whether he has a record — you know none of these things?
**WILLIAMS:** No, sir, I do not.
**MALONEY:** What about a chap named Ray Stirling? His name was dropped at the preliminary hearing.
**WILLIAMS:** I believe it was.
**MALONEY:** What do you know about him?
**WILLIAMS:** Not a thing.
**MALONEY:** What about a man named William Willemanka?

**WILLIAMS:** I believe the name used at the previous hearing was Hans.
**MALONEY:** I stand corrected. What do you know about him?
**WILLIAMS:** Nothing, sir.
**MALONEY:** You don't know anything about his relationship with Mary Conklin?
**WILLIAMS:** No, sir.
**MALONEY:** What about Ken Shellerd?
**WILLIAMS:** Yes, sir.
**MALONEY:** He is related to Mary Conklin, isn't he?
**WILLIAMS:** To the best of my knowledge.
**MALONEY:** Well, what about him? Did you check him out to see if he has a record?
**WILLIAMS:** Yes.
**MALONEY:** A short one or a long one?
**WILLIAMS:** It's long, and growing longer.

**GREENSPAN:** ***There was a carefully thought-out purpose behind this early exchange. Maloney was letting the jury know that there were plenty of other men around who could have been Mary Conklin's source of information. How* had *Gerald Burke died on that cold night of December 5? Well, as it happens, there was a young man who gave evidence at both trials, a young man who was very nearly an eyewitness to the killing…***

**CROWN:** Mr. Johnstone, you are sixteen years of age at this time?
**JOHNSTONE:** Yes, sir.
**CROWN:** And you would have been fourteen on the evening of December 5, 1969?
**JOHNSTONE:** Yes, sir.
**CROWN:** Now, on that evening of December 5, what were you doing, if anything, that would be of interest to this court?
**JOHNSTONE:** I was at home by myself. At 8:30 I started watching a TV show, "Bracken's World". I'd only watched a few minutes —
**JUDGE:** Slowly, please
**JOHNSTONE:** Sorry. I'd only watched for a…small while. Then I went out. I went down the street towards the tracks… I went along the small road behind the Hammant Engineering Building. And in about five minutes or less a car pulled into the same laneway that runs beside the tracks and when I saw the car I crawled in behind a green scrap box because I thought it was

the police or a CNR cop and they might think I was doing something wrong or breaking in...So, I was hiding there, and then the car pulled up and stopped and it wasn't long after that I heard two small muffled bangs. Then I heard a door open and close and, like, as if someone were walking in front of the car, the lights flickered off and on. Then I heard a door open again, and then the headlights went out. Then the door shut again and I heard someone walking towards me. The person walked in front of me, but I never saw his face. He had a light build, five seven or five eight, and he had a heavy jacket with a white collar...Well, after he left I walked out again and I saw that the car was a taxi...

**CROWN:** Yes, go on.

**JOHNSTONE:** Then I went back home, and after, when I read about the murders in the papers, I realized that it must have been while I was there so I called one of my teachers and then I ended up phoning the police.

**GREENSPAN:** ***Almost an eyewitness, but not quite. Gary Staples was about five foot six inches tall, and he did own a jacket with a white fur collar, which the police seized at the time of his arrest, but beyond these two tenuous pieces of circumstantial evidence, the testimony of young James Johnstone, although it revealed a good deal about how Gerald Burke died,*** **didn't** ***do a great deal to connect Gary Staples to Burke's death. The person who did that, the only person to do that, was the next witness, the woman who was the key to the whole trial...***

**CROWN:** Mrs. Conklin, in the month of December 1969, where were you living?

**MARY:** I lived at R.R. 4, Dunnville, on a farm.

**CROWN:** Were you living with your husband?

**MARY:** No, I was not.

**CROWN:** Do you have any children?

**MARY:** Yes, I do. I have eleven children and nine of them was living at home with me.

**CROWN:** Now, Mrs. Conklin, would you be good enough to look at the accused and tell me if you know him?

**MARY:** Yes, I do.

**CROWN:** And would you be good enough to tell us for how long you have known him?

**MARY:** I met Gary the month of June, in 1969.

**CROWN:** Under what circumstances did you meet him?
**MARY:** I met him on my farm when he drove in on a motorcycle to see Roland Savard who was there at the time.
**CROWN:** Now whose friend was this Roland Savard?
**MARY:** He was both our friends, a mutual friend, like.
**CROWN:** Now, when did you next see the accused?
**MARY:** I think it was a couple of days later he came back to the farm...

## Scene 7/Outdoors at the Farm

*A man on a motorcycle pulls into the yard.*

**STAPLES:** Hi.
**MARY:** Hi.
**STAPLES:** You remember me? I'm Gary Staples.
**MARY:** I remember.
**STAPLES:** I was here couple days back to help Roland with his car.
**MARY:** I remember. He's not here now.
**STAPLES:** Oh. Ah... Mary, ah, do you have any friends, ah, I mean boyfriends, any steady boyfriends, just now?
**MARY** (*pausing and sizing him up*): No. Not just now.
**STAPLES:** Well would you... object if I came up now and again to see you?
**MARY:** No... no, I wouldn't object.

## Scene 8/In Court

**CROWN:** At that time did you know if he was married or not?
**MARY:** No, I didn't know at the time. It was about a month later I found out he was married and had a boy.
**CROWN:** I see. Well, after he asked you the question you say he asked you, was that the last time you saw him?
**MARY:** No, about two or three times a week he'd come and visit me.
**CROWN:** And what was your relationship with him?
**MARY:** Well, it was quite close.
**CROWN:** How do you mean?

**MARY:** Well, we did have sex together. I think that's close.
**CROWN:** And how long did this association last?
**MARY:** I believe until about April 1970. Right up to the night before they arrested him, you know, but not as often.

**GREENSPAN:** ***The Crown now moved into some very controversial issues. It had been established that Gerald Burke had been shot with a .32-calibre handgun, and the police had found shells for a type of gun that was known as a .32 rim-fire on the Staples premises at the time of the arrest...***

**CROWN:** Mrs. Conklin, did you ever see Gary Staples with a pistol?
**MARY:** Yes, a little gun, a little pistol.
**CROWN:** What sort of pistol was it?
**MARY:** It was eight inches, maybe six inches long. It had a chrome barrel and a little white ivory handle.
**CROWN:** Yes?
**MARY:** Well, that's what kind it was. What calibre it was, I couldn't have told you.
**CROWN:** Could you tell the jury...this gun you have described, was this *your* gun?
**MARY:** It was never my gun.

**GREENSPAN:** ***As we shall soon see, Gary Staples would dispute this. In the meantime, Crown Attorney Freshman now took his key witness to the heart of the case...***

**CROWN:** I wonder if you can help us as to whether you saw Gary at any time at or around December 5, 1969?
**MARY:** Well, I seen Gary on December 5, at night between ten and eleven ——
**JUDGE:** Slowly, please
**MARY:** Sorry. He came in the house, took off his shoes, and walked into the living room where the television was. I was sitting on the chesterfield. My cousin Kenneth Shellerd was lying on the other chesterfield, face down. Gary sat down in the middle of the floor, took the gun out of one pocket and a plastic bag out of the other, and he proceeded putting the pistol into the plastic bag. Then he took black electrical tape, I call it, and he wrapped it all around the plastic.

## Scene 9/Conklin Living Room

**MARY:** What are you doing that for?
**STAPLES** (*tense, but in control*): I have to get rid of it for awhile.
**MARY:** What for?
**STAPLES:** 'Cause I just used it on somebody.
**MARY:** For heaven sakes, who?
**STAPLES:** A taxi driver.
**MARY:** Where?
**STAPLES:** Hamilton... Now, let's go in the kitchen...

## Scene 10/In Court

**CROWN:** Why did he say this?
**MARY:** Well, he kind of motioned over to my cousin, as if he didn't want him to hear any more.
**CROWN:** All right. Did anything occur in the kitchen?
**MARY:** Yes. I was kind of curious as to whether he was telling me the truth or not, because, honestly, I didn't believe him at the time, and I questioned him about where it was and how he did it...

## Scene 11/Conklin Kitchen

**STAPLES:** Make me some coffee, will ya?
**MARY:** What did you do, Gary? How did you do it?
**STAPLES:** I parked my car downtown in Hamilton, and I phoned for a taxi from a phone booth near a Laura Secord store. And when he came I got in the front seat and I told him I didn't know the name of the street but I'd show him where to go and then, when we got there, I pulled the gun out and told him to give me his money.
**MARY:** What did he do?
**STAPLES:** He emptied his pockets on the front seat of the cab, all the change and his wallet.
**MARY:** Yeah?
**STAPLES:** Then I put a bullet in the side of his neck and took the money. I wasn't sure if he was dead so I put another bullet in him, but I didn't see where that one went.

**MARY:** Jesus. Then what?

**STAPLES:** I got out. Walked around the front, and I seen that the lights were still on, so I opened the driver's side door and I turned them off, and then I wiped any fingerprints off, and then I walked back to my car.

**MARY:** Do you expect me to believe all that?

**STAPLES:** Mary, I'm not joking. All I got out of it was forty lousy dollars.

**GREENSPAN:** ***And that, essentially, was Mary Conklin's evidence, and it was also the essence of the Crown's case against Gary Staples. It was quite clear that Mary Conklin had — somehow — come to know a great deal about how Gerald Burke had been killed and the defence was going to have to face up to that. In the meantime, Arthur Maloney had been waiting a long while for his chance to cross-examine Mary Conklin...***

## Scene 12 / In Court

**MALONEY:** Mrs. Conklin, would you ever tell a lie under oath?

**MARY:** No.

**MALONEY:** Sure of that?

**MARY:** Yes.

**MALONEY:** Do you know the Burdiak family?

**MARY:** Yes, I know them. They lived a quarter of a mile up the road from me.

**MALONEY:** Did they have a daughter, Marilyn?

**MARY:** Yes, they did.

**MALONEY:** And did Marilyn sometimes come over to your house?

**MARY:** Yes, she did.

**MALONEY:** I put it to you that, in the presence or the hearing of Marilyn Burdiak, when Gary Staples came to your house on Saturday, December *6th*, that you shouted at him, you swore at him, because he had *not* come to your house the night before and you'd waited for him.

**MARY:** No, I did not.

**MALONEY:** Yeah, but when Marilyn Burdiak goes into the witness box and swears that that is what she heard you say, will that be true or false?

**MARY:** That's false.

**MALONEY:** You say that a young child will be telling a lie to His Lordship and the jury if she comes into the court and says that?
**MARY:** I am.
**MALONEY:** Well, she has nothing against you?
**MARY:** Not as far as I know.
**MALONEY:** No reason to lie against you?
**MARY:** No.
**MALONEY:** And yet you say if she comes into the witness box and says that, she is telling a lie under oath?
**MARY:** Yes, she is.

**GREENSPAN:** ***Marilyn Burdiak, of course, was one of the four new witnesses whose affidavit evidence had led to the new trial. What Maloney had just done was set up a credibility contest between Mary Conklin and this young girl. Now he shifted ground…***

**MALONEY:** When did you first tell the police that Gary Staples said anything to you about the murder of Gerald Burke?
**MARY:** April 1970.
**MALONEY:** And the police had come to see you because of your involvement in some break-ins in Selkirk, Ontario?
**MARY:** Yes.
**MALONEY:** They had heard that you were in possession of items that didn't belong to you?
**MARY:** Yes.
**MALONEY:** And you told them to go to Gary Staples' house and they said they'd already been there and couldn't find anything there?
**MARY:** Yes.
**MALONEY:** So this made you pretty mad, didn't it?
**MARY:** Well, you might say mad. I was more hurt than angry.
**MALONEY:** That's why you told the story on Gary, isn't it?
**MARY:** No, not really. I wasn't really that mad. I could never get mad at him.
**MALONEY:** Well, do you remember giving evidence at the preliminary hearing in this matter?
**MARY:** Oh, yes.
**MALONEY:** Do you remember being asked this question and giving this answer? "*Question*: Could you tell the Court why you eventually did inform the police? *Answer*: Well, I was getting involved with these B & E's and being charged with possession and stuff like that and then he didn't bother coming around so

often, as much as to say, 'Well you're in it, I'm staying out of it' so I thought 'if that's the way you want to be and let me take it all, why should I?'" Remember that question and answer?

**MARY:** Yes, I do.

**MALONEY:** Was it a true answer?

**MARY:** Yeah.

**GREENSPAN:** ***And so, having made the jury forcefully aware of the highly dubious circumstances of how Mary Conklin had accused Staples of the murder of Gerald Burke, Maloney moved into territory he had so carefully prepared with the police witnesses...***

**MALONEY:** Now, let's consider a man named Hans Willemanka. When did you first meet him?

**MARY:** I think a year before I left my husband. In 1967.

**MALONEY:** Did you have any sort of an affair with him?

**MARY:** No, I wouldn't have an affair, no.

**MALONEY:** Well, were you going out with him, keeping company with him?

**MARY:** Yes, I was.

**MALONEY:** I was under the impression — I have never met you before — I was under the impression from the material I read that in previous hearings in this matter you made it very plain that you never went out with anyone before you and your husband separated.

**MARY:** I did at that time, yes. I tried to make that plain.

**MALONEY:** Why did you say that, under oath, when you knew it wasn't true?

**MARY:** I don't know. I just didn't want to. I... I don't know ——

**MALONEY:** You knew it wasn't true.

**MARY:** That's right.

**MALONEY:** Now, at the preliminary enquiry, do you remember this question and answer: "*Question*: What is Hans' last name? *Answer*: I don't know." Do you remember that question and answer?

**MARY:** Yes.

**MALONEY:** Again, that wasn't true, was it? You knew his last name, didn't you?

**MARY:** Yes, I knew his last name.

**MALONEY:** That was a lie?

**MARY:** Yes.

**MALONEY:** And you were under oath?

**MARY:** Yes. I didn't think it was anybody's business.
**MALONEY:** May we assume you hold back anything you don't think is our business?
**MARY** (*defiantly*): My personal business, yes.
**MALONEY:** Even if you are under oath?
**MARY:** Look...if I feel you should know, I'll tell you.
**MALONEY:** *You* will determine what I should know?
**MARY:** Well, as far as my life is concerned, yes.
**MALONEY:** Mrs. Conklin, have you ever discussed the matter of Gerald Burke with any one of the men whose names we have mentioned here?
**MARY:** No, never.
**MALONEY:** With Freeman?
**MARY:** No.
**MALONEY:** With Willemanka?
**MARY:** No.
**MALONEY:** With Stirling?
**MARY:** No.
**MALONEY:** With Hall?
**MARY:** No.
**MALONEY:** Goodfallaw?
**MARY:** No.
**MALONEY:** Shellerd?
**MARY:** No.
**MALONEY:** Mrs. Conklin, I put it to you that the evidence you have given in this court that Gary Staples made any confession to you on the night of Friday, December 5th, 1969, or any other day or night, is a total falsity and that you lied when you said it.
**MARY:** That's not true.
**MALONEY:** I put it to you that he wasn't even in your house on Friday night, December 5, and you know it.
**MARY:** Yes, he was.
**MALONEY:** And that you got all this information about this murder from someone else and I don't know who.
**MARY:** I did not.
**MALONEY:** Thank you, madam.

**GREENSPAN:** ***Before the Crown case closed and the defence began, a furious, hot-tempered legal argument occurred over an issue of some importance...***

**CROWN:** Ah, My Lord, there is a name that appears on the indictment, a Ken Shellerd. With a great deal of difficulty we have located him. He was literally picked up and subpoenaed in Toronto yesterday. He is present in this courtroom, but his evidence is, in my submission, not material in any regard; I don't propose to call him.

**MALONEY** (*becoming angry*): Well, it seems to me my friend has a real duty to call this witness. If Mary Conklin's story is right, well then, this mean Shellerd was present when everything was said and done by Staples in the room where Mary Conklin and Shellerd were watching television. My friend knows the background to this very well. This chap gave the police a statement while he was an inmate at Burwash that confirmed Mary Conklin's story. Now, he was called at the preliminary hearing and he said the statement was untrue. He said he made it because the police told him if he didn't give them a statement implicating Staples they would press certain charges against him, but if he did they would see that these charges were withdrawn. Now that is the case with respect to Ken Shellerd, and if my friend doesn't call him as a witness I... I certainly assure the Court I intend to make the most of it, because I think I should. It is a very serious matter.

**GREENSPAN:** ***This issue of Ken Shellerd was indeed very serious, and it rested squarely on the shadowy borderline of what the duties of a Crown attorney are in Canadian law. Maloney and the trial judge agreed that there was no power in the Court to compel the Crown to call a witness under the law as it existed then. But, at the same time, given that Shellerd was alleged by Mary Conklin to have been in the room when Staples confessed to a murder, Maloney had a very strong argument that the Crown had a duty in the interests of justice to call him as a witness. Why couldn't the defence call him? That would be totally unfair. He was Mary Conklin's cousin, he had been a Crown witness at the preliminary, and he was a man of such character that to force the defence to make him their witness, and then let the Crown cross-examine, would be a travesty.***

***Shellerd was never called, and Crown Attorney Freshman closed his case. It was now the turn of the defence to lead evidence, and Maloney's first witness was his most important...***

**MALONEY:** You are Gary Francis Staples?

**STAPLES:** Yes, sir.

**MALONEY:** You are now twenty-six years old, you are married, have one child, and you live in Dunnville, Ontario. Is that correct?

**STAPLES:** Yes, it is, sir.

**MALONEY:** Now, evidence has been given about the tragic events that occurred on Friday, December 5, in Hamilton when one Gerald Burke was brutally murdered. Did you kill Gerald Burke?

**STAPLES:** No, I did not.

**MALONEY:** Where were you on that night.

**STAPLES:** I spent that night in Dunnville, Ontario.

**MALONEY:** Now, I want you to tell me in your own words how it was that you first met Mary Conklin.

**STAPLES:** I first met Mary Conklin in June 1969...

**GREENSPAN:** ***Maloney took Staples through his first meetings with Conklin and the beginnings of their relationship, then he reached a critical area...***

**MALONEY:** Now, let's get to November 1969. Do you remember any discussion with respect to guns?

**STAPLES:** Ah, yes. One night when I went to Mary Conklin's farm in November ——

**JUDGE:** Slowly, please.

**STAPLES:** On entering the farm Mary Conklin came running to me. She was excited. She said she had something in the bedroom she wanted to show me.

**MALONEY:** What happened?

**STAPLES:** Well, on entering the bedroom she lifted up the mattress and there was two guns. A .22 rifle and a handgun. I picked up both guns. Ah...she asked me if I knew what calibre the handgun was.

**MALONEY:** Yes.

**STAPLES:** I said no, but I could find out. I offered to clean the gun for her plus find out what calibre it was.

**MALONEY:** Was there any discussion with respect to where she got the gun?

**STAPLES:** Yes, sir. That was the first question I asked her. She said a friend of hers in Hamilton had given them to her and she wanted the guns for protection. She said she didn't want me showing the gun to anyone, and I asked her why, was the gun hot? And she said yes, it was.

**GREENSPAN:** ***And so the lines of conflict were clearly drawn on this issue too. Maloney then went to even more important terrain…***

**MALONEY:** All right, I want to get to Friday, December 5. What shift were you working at the Exomet plant?

**STAPLES:** Day shift.

**MALONEY:** What time did you get home?

**STAPLES:** Approximately five o'clock.

**MALONEY:** What happened from then on?

**STAPLES:** I watched television. I always watch "Star Trek" at five o'clock and then "Twilight Zone" at six. And then when the shows were over I got up and I asked my wife…

## Scene 13 / Staples' House

**STAPLES:** Alice, I need some cash. I'm short. I gotta go buy a part for my car.

**ALICE:** No.

**STAPLES:** What d'ya mean, no? I gotta buy a part.

**ALICE:** Do you think I'm stupid? You think I don't know what you want money for?

**STAPLES:** Ah, Alice. Come on, let's not start it again.

**ALICE:** We won't start anything at all. I'm just not giving you money so you can go out chasing and running around. You think I don't know what you're doing?

**STAPLES:** You're wrong. You're dead wrong. I'm just getting the car fixed.

**ALICE:** Gary, I don't want another of your stories. I —

**STAPLES** (*putting on the charm*): Alice, listen to me, will ya? There's no story. I need a part for the car. I gotta go to Canadian Tire and get a part. Then I gotta go and get the car fixed. That's all I'm doing, so just take it easy, okay…

## Scene 14 / In Court

**STAPLES:** In the end, she gave me the money and I went out —

**MALONEY:** Let me just interrupt you. When you were arrested on April 26 were you able to recall where you had been on December 5, five months before?

**STAPLES:** No, sir.
**MALONEY:** How long did it take you to piece together your activities on that Friday night?
**STAPLES:** Quite a few weeks. I had remembered that it was my sister Susan's birthday on December 6 and that's what led me to remember other things that occurred at that time...

**GREENSPAN:** ***The birth certificate of Susan McIntee, Staples' sister, was later filed, and it turned out that her sixteenth birthday was indeed December 6. A very important coincidence for the Staples family in helping them to recall the events of the night before. According to Staples, on that Friday night he visited his parents, wished his sister a happy birthday, then went to Canadian Tire to buy a universal joint for his car. He said he was there between 8:00 and 8:30 and then went to Stollar's Sunoco Station in Dunnville to have the universal joint installed. He was there until about 10:30. He left, stopped in at his father's briefly, and then went home at about 11:00. His wife made him a snack and they watched the late show together and went to bed. Not until December 6, at about 3:00 p.m., according to Staples, did he go out to Mary Conklin's farm...***

## Scene 15/Conklin Farm House

**STAPLES** (*a little nervously*): Hi. How ya doin'?
**MARY** (*furious*): Don't give me that little boy look, you asshole!
**STAPLES:** Ah, look, Mary ——
**MARY** (*mimicking*): Ah, look, Mary... You're full of it, Gary! You're just full of it! Where the *hell* were you last night?
**STAPLES:** I had to get my *car* fixed. I was freezin' my butt off at a garage and ——
**MARY:** Oh, Christ! So now it's your car. That goddamn car means more to you than I do!
**STAPLES** (*starting to get angry*): Well, yeah, it does. I need that car to get to work.
**MARY:** Oh, hah!
**STAPLES:** Ah, stuff it, Mary. If I don't get to work you sure as hell aren't gonna pay my wages.
**MARY:** Oh, stuff it yourself! You promised me you'd be here last night and you didn't make it.

**STAPLES:** I *couldn't* get here last night. I was getting my goddamn *car* fixed!
**MARY:** That's a lousy goddamned excuse on a Friday night, you son of a bitch, and I want you to know…

**GREENSPAN:** ***And so Gary Staples denied the murder, he denied the confession, he denied owning the handgun everyone was talking about, and he even denied being at Mary Conklin's on the night of December 5. There were a number of witnesses to support various aspects of this story, but first Staples had to weather a cross-examination from a very determined Crown Attorney Freshman who had convicted him of murder once already…***

## Scene 16/In Court

**CROWN:** Were you out west, at any time, sir?
**STAPLES:** Yes, sir. I was stationed at Curry Barracks.
**CROWN:** What were you doing there?
**STAPLES:** I was a soldier. I was in the army.
**CROWN:** After many years ——
**MALONEY** (*interrupting*): My friend is on dangerous ground here. He knows my position with respect to this line of questioning. I would have expected him to have raised this in the absence of the jury.

**GREENSPAN:** ***Gary Staples may have been facing a determined Crown, but this time he had on his side an extraordinary lawyer who would leap to his defence at the slightest hint of irregularity. The issue now was that the Crown wanted to lead evidence of Staples' theft of guns from the army supply barracks and his subsequent dishonourable discharge. There was no question that the criminal record itself was admissible, but Maloney argued successfully that a dishonourable discharge was not a criminal record and so was inadmissible, and he also kept out the fact that it was guns that were stolen on the grounds that this was prejudicial and irrelevant. Both those details had gone to the jury in the first trial.***

***The Crown shifted, with more success, to a different line of attack…***

**CROWN:** Mr. Staples, I understand you are trying to tell us that Mrs. Conklin was the one whose gun this was?

**STAPLES:** Yes.

**CROWN:** The only purpose for which you had it was to clean it?

**STAPLES:** Yes, sir.

**CROWN:** Then, would you be good enough to explain what you were doing with Exhibit 26 — the partially filled box of shells the police found at your place.

**STAPLES:** Yes, sir.

**CROWN:** Explain that, would you please?

**STAPLES:** When I gave the gun back to Mrs. Conklin I did not give her back the shells I had bought. I only gave her the gun.

**CROWN:** Why would you buy the shells?

**STAPLES:** I bought them for the gun.

**CROWN:** But why?

**STAPLES:** Mrs. Conklin wanted them.

**CROWN:** Well, if she wanted them and if you bought them for her, why did you not give them to her?

**STAPLES:** I don't really know. Ah, she didn't give me any money for them, and I couldn't see any sense in buying shells and just giving them to her.

**GREENSPAN:** ***Maloney couldn't help his client on that issue, but on another one he very definitely did...***

**CROWN:** Mr. Staples, I am reading from a previous time when you gave evidence under oath in this matter. You were asked: "*Question:* You were a confidant of Mary Conklin's, weren't you? *Answer:* Yes. *Question:* You exchanged secrets? *Answer:* Yes. *Question:* On a great many occasions? *Answer:* Yes." Do you recall these questions and answers?

**STAPLES:** Yes, sir.

**MALONEY** (*irritated*): Just read the next question too, Mr. Freshman. Read the next *two* questions and answers.

**CROWN:** Well, I think His Lordship should decide ——

**JUDGE:** I think you ought to, Mr. Freshman. It is on the same issue, after all.

**CROWN:** Yes, My Lord. Ahh..."*Question:* Mrs. Conklin — you trusted her did you not? *Answer:* No more than any other woman. *Question:* Well, isn't it fair to say you trusted her with secrets you would not share with anyone else? *Answer:* No."

**MALONEY:** "No, I didn't," is the answer.
**CROWN** (*sullenly*): I beg your pardon. "*Answer:* No, I didn't."

**GREENSPAN:** ***The art of defence advocacy is far more than a matter of flashy cross-examination or passionate jury addresses. It involves a constant, careful monitoring of all the evidence and legal issues relating to the case, with a view, among other things, to protecting one's witnesses. And on this score, among others, Arthur Maloney's defence of Gary Staples was masterful...***

**CROWN:** Now, Mr. Staples, I suggest to you that on the Saturday afternoon you were very interested in getting back out to Mary Conklin's and you drove there immediately.
**STAPLES:** I went to her farm that afternoon, but I wasn't in a big hurry. I remember I also drove around in Dunnville that afternoon looking at cars.
**CROWN:** Isn't this the first time you have ever mentioned looking at car lots that afternoon?
**STAPLES:** Ah, no sir, I don't believe so. I believe I mentioned it a year ago at the last proceeding.
**MALONEY** (*interrupting*): Excuse me, My Lord. My friend says there is nothing in the record. On page 875 of the earlier proceedings Mr. Staples says, quote: "I was looking at cars in the car lot that day, and I went to Mary Conklin's farm," end quote.
**CROWN** (*deflated*): I stand corrected.

**GREENSPAN:** ***Of the four new witnesses Mrs. Staples had tracked down for her son, the most important was undoubtedly Marilyn Burdiak. This young girl, who was thirteen in December 1969, lived down the road from the Conklin farm. She said she was there playing with Mary Conklin's daughters almost every day and she corroborated Gary Staples' account in two important ways...***

**MALONEY:** Now, during the summer of 1969 did you make any observations at the Conklin residence with respect to guns?
**MARILYN:** Yes. I saw a rifle in the basement under some sacks and I saw one in her top dresser drawer. It was a small handgun with a whitish handle.

**GREENSPAN:** ***Marilyn's other key evidence was even more important...***

**MALONEY:** Were you at the Conklin House on Saturday, December 6?
**MARILYN:** Yes.
**MALONEY:** What is your best recollection as to when Gary Staples got there?
**MARILYN:** Between 5:00 and 5:30.
**MALONEY:** Where were you when he came into the house?
**MARILYN:** Berta and I were sitting on the porch.
**MALONEY:** Did you hear anything from where you were?
**MARILYN:** Well, Berta and I were going to go saddle up the horses and I was going to go in to ask Kenny Shellerd if he wanted to come and ride with us. I went to open the door and Gary and Mary were having a fight.
**MALONEY:** What did you hear?
**MARILYN:** Mary was yelling at him, cursing at him and yelling at him because he wasn't there the night before and she was waiting for him. He said he couldn't because he had to get his car fixed.

**GREENSPAN:** ***The next witnesses for the defence were the ones who raised and supported Gary Staples' alibi... Perhaps because of television crime shows, the word "alibi" has come to have a negative connotation in the public mind. In reality it is simply one of the most basic defences to a criminal charge: all an alibi is, is a statement by an accused that he didn't commit the crime with which he is charged because he wasn't there. Staples' father and his sister Susan corroborated his account of visiting their house in the early evening of December 5, and Mr. Staples remembered Gary coming back to see him at eleven. The key support for Staples' alibi, though, came from people with no real connection to him at all...***

**MALONEY:** Mrs. Marshall, I understand you worked for the Canadian Tire store in Dunnville in December 1969.
**MRS. MARSHALL:** Yes, I did.
**MALONEY:** What was your position in that store?
**MRS. MARSHALL:** I was a cashier. I had just been promoted to assistant manager.
**MALONEY:** I am showing you a card; can you recognize it?
**MRS. MARSHALL:** That is our stock-control card. This one is in respect to a universal-joint kit for a Buick.
**MALONEY:** Can you assist the jury as to whether anything took place on this card on December 5, 1969?

**MRS. MARSHALL:** On December 5 there was one universal joint in stock, and it was sold and re-ordered on that day.
**MALONEY:** Did you make any further checks for related invoices?
**MRS. MARSHALL:** Yes, I checked all our whiz bills — ah, the invoices we make the sales out on — and I found the whiz bill for that universal joint. I also checked the cash-register tape and that sale was the fifth-to-last one before the end of the day on December 5.
**MALONEY:** What were your business hours on that day?
**MRS. MARSHALL:** From 8:30 in the morning until 9:00 at night.
**MALONEY:** Now, based on your experience as a cashier and as assistant manager, can you tell the court the approximate time this fifth-last purchase might have been made?
**MRS. MARSHALL:** Yes. It would have been made between 8:00 and 8:30 on Friday.

**MALONEY:** Peter Stollar, would you be good enough to tell His Lordship and the jury what your present business is?
**STOLLAR:** I operate a Sunoco service station in Dunnville.
**MALONEY:** Do you recall a night in December 1969 when Gary Staples was in your garage?
**STOLLAR:** There were several nights that he was in. He had an old car with a noisy motor and he had trouble with it.
**MALONEY:** All right. Do you know a young man named Roy Graham?
**STOLLAR:** Yes, sir.
**MALONEY:** Now, was there ever a time when he and Gary Staples were in your station at the same time?
**STOLLAR:** Yes, sir, only once that I recall.

**GREENSPAN:** ***Maloney then took Stollar concisely through an explanation of how he could date his story. It appeared that he used to do carwash jobs for a dealer nearby. One night the dealer asked him to store a car overnight for him after washing it. This was the only time that happened. And that night was the only night that Gary Staples and Roy Graham were in the station together...***

**MALONEY:** Now, I am showing you an invoice. Do you recognize it?
**STOLLAR:** Ah, that's my invoice. It's in my writing. It's addressed to Jack Hay Motors; it's an invoice for $2.50 for washing a 1970 Marquis on December 5, 1969.
**MALONEY:** Bring your mind back to Staples arriving at your garage. Do you recollect the time?

**STOLLAR:** Approximately is the only answer I can give you and I'd say between 8:00 and 9:00.

**MALONEY:** What did he want you to do?

**STOLLAR:** Well, he arrived with a universal joint in his hand and he wanted me to put it in for him.

**MALONEY:** And did you?

**STOLLAR:** Yes, I did. It took me an hour and a half, two hours, because I was busy. As I was doing that, Roy Graham came in.

**MALONEY:** What did he want?

**STOLLAR:** Well, he wanted to wash his car inside because it was cold out. So I had him move the Jack Hay Marquis outside and bring his own car inside to wash it.

**GREENSPAN:** ***Roy Graham was called as well, and he confirmed the details of this story. The interesting question was, how had Staples and his lawyers managed to track down these vital witnesses? The answer to that came in the evidence of the last key witness for the defence...***

**MALONEY:** You are Mrs. Emma Staples?

**EMMA:** Yes, sir.

**MALONEY:** You are the mother of the accused man?

**EMMA:** Yes, sir.

**MALONEY:** Do you recall the time of your son's arrest?

**EMMA:** Yes, I do.

**MALONEY:** Who first told you about it?

**EMMA:** His wife, Alice.

**MALONEY:** And what was your condition emotionally that day?

**EMMA:** I was hysterical.

**MALONEY:** Did you have a discussion that evening about what could have been Gary's whereabouts on December 5?

**EMMA:** My husband and I did. I went hysterical in the house, and he had to shake me to calm me down. And he says: "You have got to think hard. Remember back to December." Then we remembered that it'd been the evening before Susan's birthday, and I remembered she and I went to bingo, and Gary had come by before, and Susan was so dressed up, so pretty. That's why I remembered.

**MALONEY:** Did you discuss this with your son?

**EMMA:** Yes, about two weeks later, in the jail.

**MALONEY:** Now, you can't tell us what you said, but as a result of this conversation, what did you do?

**EMMA:** I went to see the detectives.
**MALONEY:** Yes, anyone else?
**EMMA:** Pete's Sunoco. I spoke to Mr. Stollar.
**MALONEY:** Did he give you some information?
**EMMA:** Yes, he sent me to see a man a few doors down.
**MALONEY:** Again, don't tell us the conversation, but what did you find out?
**EMMA:** The name of a man and his phone number.
**MALONEY:** Yes, and whom had you been looking for?
**EMMA** (*not wanting to do the wrong thing*): Mr.... Can I tell you his name?
**MALONEY:** Yes, you can, Mrs. Staples.
**EMMA:** Mr. Roy Graham.
**MALONEY:** Good. Now, did you ever go to the Canadian Tire store?
**EMMA:** Yes, I did that too. I went to see the manager, but he referred me to Mrs. Marshall, and she found the bill of sale for me.
**MALONEY:** Did you ever go and see Mr. Jack Hay, of Jack Hay Motors?
**EMMA:** Yes, after I finally found Mr. Roy Graham, and from what he told me I went to find Mr. Hay...

**GREENSPAN:** ***All of this investigating had been done* before *the first trial. Then, after her son had been convicted, Mrs. Staples kept working for him. She was the person who had tracked down the evidence of Marilyn Burdiak, of Ronald Stire — a boy who gave further evidence corroborating the events that were said to have taken place in Stollar's garage — and of the Longley couple, who also said they'd seen Gary in Dunnville on the night of December 5. Mrs. Staples had done a great deal indeed for her son, and she had a last piece of evidence to offer in his defence...***

**MALONEY:** One final matter then, after your son's arrest did you have any occasion to meet Mary Conklin?
**EMMA:** Yes, I did, sir.
**MALONEY:** When was that?
**EMMA:** A few weeks after his arrest. In May 1970.
**MALONEY:** And where was this?
**EMMA:** At Ray Stirling's farm. She...she wasn't there, but I waited for her, and she came with Ray Stirling in a truck.
**MALONEY:** Yes, what was it you said to her? And what was it she said to you, as best you can recall?

**EMMA:** I asked her why she did this thing, this terrible thing, to my son, Gary, and she said that if she couldn't have him nobody else was going to have him, and she loved my son. She kept saying she loved him. I told her that she was too old for my son and the only person that would ever love my son was his wife and his little boy.

**MALONEY:** That concludes my examination in chief, My Lord.

**GREENSPAN:** ***Second time around has its advantages. In the first trial, Emma Staples had not been allowed to recount that exchange with Mary Conklin. It was hearsay. This time, though, Maloney had deliberately asked Mary Conklin during his cross-examination of her if she had had this exchange with Gary's mother. She had denied it flatly. As a result, the law of evidence allowed Emma to contradict Mary's sworn testimony and Maloney managed to get some vital evidence before the jury. Both lawyers made their closing addresses and the judge charged the jury as to the evidence and the law. Only, a few minutes after retiring, the jury were back, not with a verdict, but a request...***

**FOREMAN 2:** My Lord, could the members of the jury have the evidence of Mrs. Marshall of Canadian Tire read back to them, please? Would...would this be possible at this time?

**GREENSPAN:** ***Elizabeth Marshall had just gone through a difficult childbirth. There had been some real doubt as to whether she was well enough to come to court — there had been a defence motion to have the trial adjourned to her bedside so she could testify there. The judge had refused. But Arthur Maloney knew*** **something**. ***He juggled the order of his witnesses, he made accommodations to allow Mrs. Marshall time to recover and testify later in the trial, and it was Elizabeth Marshall's evidence that the jury wanted to hear again...***

**MARSHALL:** The sale of the universal joint was the fifth-to-last before the end of the day on December 5.

**MALONEY:** Based on your experience, can you tell the Court the approximate time this purchase might have been made?

**MARSHALL:** Yes. It would have been made between 8:00 and 8:30 on Friday...

**CLERK:** Members of the jury, have you agreed upon a verdict?

**FOREMAN:** We have, My Lord.
**CLERK:** Do you find the prisoner at the bar guilty or not guilty as charged?
**FOREMAN:** Based on the evidence presented, not guilty.

**GREENSPAN:** ***There is a postscript of sorts — for me, a very sad one. In the weeks during which this episode of "The Scales of Justice" was being prepared in September 1984, Arthur Maloney passed away. He was sixty-four. His death brought to a close one of the most brilliant and compassionate careers in the annals of Canadian criminal law. He always regarded the defence of Gary Staples as his greatest case. It is very hard to imagine anyone having done it better.***

# Producer's Notes

In 1970 a young Ontario man named Gary Staples was convicted of non-capital murder in connection with the death of a Hamilton taxi driver during a robbery. The bulk of the evidence against Staples consisted of the claim of his ex-girlfriend, a Mrs. Conklin, who testified that Staples had confessed the murder to her.

The dangers of convicting an accused wholly or largely on the unsupported testimony of any one witness are self-evident. These dangers only increase when the witness may be thought to have some personal animosity towards the accused, or may derive a benefit from testifying against him. Jilted spouses and lovers, people whose own reputations may be adversely affected, or those who hope to plea-bargain for a reduced charge in exchange for their testimony, are all examples of witnesses whose word should be received with special caution.

Recognizing this, courts used to warn juries about the dangers of convicting on the uncorroborated evidence of potentially biased or unreliable witnesses, such as accomplices, children too young to understand the nature of the oath, or complainants in certain types of sexual-assault cases. In the last few years the discretion of judges to deliver such warnings has largely been removed because of policy considerations. But much as we wish to facilitate the conviction of child abusers or those who commit crimes against women, the basic frailties of human nature are not likely to be affected by these admirable changes of emphasis in our social policies. People with a personal reason to lie will still give false evidence more frequently than unbiased witnesses.

Staples could not have availed himself of such a warning in connection with Mrs. Conklin's evidence in any case. All he could rely on was a jury's good judgement and common sense. Luckily, he got a second chance, an opportunity to be tested by another jury, when the late Arthur Maloney, one of the great criminal lawyers of the postwar period in Canada, successfully appealed his conviction and defended him at his second trial in 1972.

Maloney always regarded his defence of Staples as the most important case of his career, probably because securing an acquittal against considerable odds for an innocent client previously convicted of a grave charge is the most satisfying result for any conscientious lawyer. Certainly Maloney had many other cases that received far more media attention than the case of Gary Staples, but it was this case he commended to the attention of "The Scales of Justice" shortly before his death. Early in 1986 "Second Time Around" was one of the inaugural winners of an award jointly sponsored by the Canadian Bar Association and the Canadian Law Reform Commission to honour outstanding media treatment of legal issues. Enhancing our pleasure in this distinction was the name given to the prize: The Scales of Justice Award.

In this program, as in the Smithers case, Arthur Maloney's role was played by Michael Tait. His nomination for the 1985 ACTRA Award was no less than he deserved for his excellent performance. Similarly deserved was Jayne Eastwood's nomination for best actress in radio for her portrayal of the Crown witness Mrs. Conklin.

Chuck Shamata performed the role of Gary Staples with a fine combination of inventiveness and realism. In the other roles Lawrence Dane as the Crown counsel, Sean McCann as Sergeant Williams, Murray Westgate as Sergeant Thomson, and Nonnie Griffin as Gary Staples' mother merit special mention. As often, two of the best performances came in small roles: a garage mechanic played by the superb character actor Wayne Robson and a cashier played by the very talented young actress Dixie Seatle.

Though "The Scales of Justice" has always attempted to address a wide audience, there is a sense in which it is a lawyer's show. The meticulous assistance of the three lawyers who have vetted all our scripts — Dan Henry and Michael Hughes from the CBC's legal department in Toronto, and Edward L. Greenspan's law partner, Marc Rosenberg — is greatly appreciated.

G.J.